O—

I was captivated by the story. *Lessons* is fascinating reading. Dick's ability to interweave real life experiences with fiction made the story come to life. Anyone interested in achieving career independence and enjoying life more abundantly should read this book.
Boyd Baugh, Founder and Chairman, Pivot Interiors, San Jose, CA

Lessons provides great insight for enriching one's personal and professional life. I enhanced my knowledge and appreciation of life's leadership journey from my personal interviews with two of the Wise Men and by reading this great book. Dick Buxton has captured the lessons learned by eleven very successful leaders in the framework of a story that provides an excellent roadmap for anyone who wants to grow as a person and as a leader. Thanks, Dick, for improving my life.
Ralph Christie, Chairman, President and CEO, Merrick & Company, Denver, CO

It's really great reading for anyone who has the mildest interest in business…or just life in general.
Paul deVille, CEO, Pomare, Honolulu, HI

I enjoyed it enormously. The compelling point of the book is like all true wisdom…it's timeless. It worked for the eleven Wise Men and will work for me—as well as my children.
Bob Maricich, CEO, Century Furniture, Hickory, NC

I absolutely enjoyed the book! Well-written and wonderful content.
Mike May, President and CEO, Hawaiian Electric, Honolulu, HI

I very much enjoyed the book, and learned a lot along the way. Making tough decisions is something a CEO has to do all the time. Being able to separate your feelings/emotions from "doing the right thing" is why achieving Emotional Maturity is so important. Each chapter is a lesson. The book encourages, teaches, and challenges leaders to be better mentors. The Wise Men help us learn that our destination is ours alone, but feedback from a mentor helps us create our own vision of success.

Brian McShane, President and CEO, Advertising Checking Bureau, New York City

No one is successful unless both components of his/her life—business and personal—are intact. Many people experience crisis in both their professional and personal life and cannot solve one completely, without impacting the other. The sound, practical advice the book provides is a good road map for anyone experiencing change or challenge in their lives. The principles shared by the Wise Men are applicable to fixing either situation.

We have all experienced some defining moment in our lives where the guidance, organizational skills, networking and direction provided by the Wise Men would have been beneficial. Being grounded in who we are and where we came from is essential in maintaining balance and focus in our lives. The common elements of close family ties and strong outside influences (military, scouts, athletics, growing up during the Depression and the impact of World War II) shared by the Wise Men are not lost on this reader. Dick's book provides a good road map for challenges faced in the business world, but also touches on the personal and family battles we face during our journey.

David Nickell, President and CEO, AC Corporation, Greensboro, NC

Success is the result of a long journey that is paved with exploration, dedication, sacrifice, and sometimes criticism. Many have traveled this road before, and the trail is well documented. Why? Because one of the greatest traits of successful people seems to be their willingness to give. Study and apply the principles that these eleven men have agreed to share and you will find all of the markers that you will need on your quest. And, ironically, though this book contains the essentials to hasten the process, it also teaches that the journey never ends regardless of your speed.
Scott Sangalli, CEO, Morrison Supply, Fort Worth, TX

Comments from other present and former Senior Executives

It's full of profound insights and I got a lot out of reading it.
David Binns, Associate Director, Foundation for Enterprise Development, Washington, DC

Lessons proved what I have always known about Dick Buxton. The masters of super salesmen are the very best at selling products or services. This book is about the ultimate salesman and his unique ability to sell people on themselves. It is guaranteed to inspire and motivate at every level in all fields of endeavor.
Charles E. Bryan, Retired President, District 100, IAM, Miami, FL

An excellent view of the wealth of knowledge accumulated by eleven true leaders. Taking away a single idea from each would give one tremendous building blocks from which to build a successful business and personal life.
Bill Chetney, Co-Founder, Choice One, Capistrano Beach, CA

This is a readable novel with very important lessons to be learned—painlessly! *Lessons* is a real-life study of methods of becoming successful in life. The value of being a mentor and a mentee; having faith in yourself; getting trusted help in working out your problems—all wonderful advice for business and military professionals. This book definitely shows that there isn't a lot of difference in means to success in any profession.

William H. Ecker, Major General AUS (Ret), Greenbrae, CA

What a gripping tale! You got right into it! I've told my neighbor, John Grisham, that he'd better watch out! The story really does grab you right away, and the novel approach really does work.

Ron Gilbert, ESOP Services, co-author *Employee Stock Ownership Plans*, Charlottesville, VA

Knowing many of the Wise Men and then reading "Charlie Rowe's" sage counsel was like old times—reminiscent of many of the wonderful mentoring visits with Dick Buxton at various points of my career. One of the more significant mentoring events was his encouragement to write my first book. *Lessons* aptly portrays the process and benefits of mentoring. A fun and interesting read.

Hal Johnson, Founder, Leadership 20/20 and author of *MENTORING for Exceptional Performance*, Larkspur, CA

After reading *Lessons*, I was struck by the prescient timeliness of the book. Its message is a masterful story about how a professional crisis can, with the right mentoring, become a personal mandate to reconcile one's meaning and purpose in life. I strongly recommend *Lessons* to anyone seeking more career independence and peace of mind.

Keith Mericka, Senior Vice President, UBS PayneWebber, co-founder, The ESOP Advisory Group, Atlanta, GA

Dick Buxton's new book illustrates an important concept: A failure is as important as a success *if you learn how to fail successfully.*

Joseph Rafferty, Managing Director, Private Capital Corporation, Novato, CA (Former Commanding Officer, Presidio of San Francisco)

This book transcends the story of one man's plight to make a new career move and keep his family together. It is more than the individual biographies of eleven men who became very successful people. Dick's book embodies the adage that the whole is greater than the sum of its parts. It is a textbook for living life and a guide for becoming and being the best you can possibly be.
Mark Robbins, Search Solutions, Novato, CA

I found myself relating to the character in Dick's story and getting involved in comparing my own situation with his. *Lessons* is great because involvement creates interest and reflection. That is the significant value of the book. My first mentor used to say: dig a hole first, then throw someone in it; finally, offer them a ladder to get out. Don't try to sell the ladder before they are in the hole—they think they don't need it.
Michael J. Scherr, Managing Director, Private Capital—Hawaii (Former General Agent, Mass Mutual), Honolulu, HI

The book describes personal discipline and the kind of leader who develops successful businesses and people. It could lead to a workbook for a person who wanted a self-study guide using Dick's book.
John Thomas, Business Manager, Wheaton Academy, Chicago, IL

The content is rich with substance. There remains a wealth of information and inspiration that can serve anyone who is serious about life's secrets.
Dick Toomey, Co-Founder of TTW Agency and Viewpoint Studios, Greensboro, NC

Lessons in Leadership and Life

SECRETS of Eleven Wise Men

Lessons in Leadership and Life

SECRETS of Eleven Wise Men

Dickson C. Buxton

Director of Operations: Robin L. Howland
Project Manager: Bryan K. Howland
Book and Cover Design: First Publish

10 9 8 7 6 5 4 3 2 1

ISBN 1-58000-102-5

Griffin Publishing Group
18022 Cowan, Suite 202
Irvine, CA 32614
Phone: 949.263.3733
Fax: 949.263.3734

Manufactured in the United States of America
Printed by QUESTprint.

It is insight into human nature that is the key to the communicator's skill. For whereas the writer is concerned with what he puts into his writings, the communicator is concerned with what the reader gets out of it.

—William Bernbach

TABLE OF CONTENTS

SECTION II
Chapters

I had just completed my graduate degree at age 51, when my friend and mentor, Dick Buxton, asked me to read and critique a book he had written on mentoring. The last thing I wanted to do was read another theoretical "how to" or "what if" book on business and the economy. How could I say no? This person, who had helped me fulfill my dream of selling my company to my employees, is a close personal friend.

I read the book and called Dick, who asked me what I thought. My personality is to be brutally honest so I summed up my critique in one word: *"boring."* Like many business books today the content was excellent, but the story line put me to sleep. At first he was a little concerned —three years of work and he did not even get a decent review from a friend and colleague.

However, among his redeeming qualities are that he is resilient and he has one of the best minds that I have ever known. So together we came up with the idea of turning another boring business book into a business novel that people would not want to put down. In revising the book, *"Lessons in Leadership and Life,* Secrets of Eleven Wise Men,*"* Dick captures the essence of what is happening in the business world today.

In his book, he describes some of the problems and solutions that many successful and highly qualified men and women experience when losing their jobs to corporate downsizing and office politics. Not only is *"Lessons in Leadership and Life,* Secrets of Eleven Wise Men" informative, it is enjoyable to read. It is about a fictional character, Ken Wilson, who finds himself in non-fictional situations that could confront us all.

Also, the messages from "Eleven Wise Men" provide solid principles that can benefit anyone seeking success in both their personal and professional lives. Dick has written an interesting and informative book that will have a defining effect on the lives of many, while honoring some of the mentors who helped contribute to his life. I feel honored to have been asked to participate in this project.

Steve Love
Chairman, IdaPac
Boise, Idaho

Section 1

Chapter 1

Surfing the Corporate Wave

Monday

I'd never felt more isolated and insecure in my life—Ken Wilson, unemployed at age thirty-six! I sat at a corner table in the Bankers Club, in the financial district of one of the great cities in the world, San Francisco. I was trying to collect my thoughts and decide what to do, when an old friend of my Dad's, Charlie Rowe, stopped by and asked how I was doing. He was definitely of my father's generation in his formal speech and mannerisms, but his twinkling eyes hinted at a softer nature underneath. I asked him to join me before answering his question.

"Not well!" I said dejectedly. "I just did a very stupid thing and turned down a transfer. My boss just left after telling me I was to be terminated. My responsibilities are now being supervised out of Cleveland. If I don't want to live there, I'd better get my resume out to some search firms."

Charlie asked, "What's wrong with Cleveland? You're in a very large corporation with offices all over the world. Don't you know transfers are a way of life with most companies?"

"A man who used to work *for me* was transferred to Cleveland last year. He'd now be my boss. He's a conniving, political airhead! I'm sure he engineered this. Besides, I don't want to move out of the Bay Area. He knows that."

"Cool down, Ken. Try to look at this *problem* as an *opportunity* in working clothes. It is your chance to look at other situations that will meet your financial needs and also keep you here. By the way, didn't you see this coming?"

"No, I've been with this company for ten years, I've gone to night school to get my MBA. I had no indication from my boss that I wasn't one of his *team*."

"Do you have resources to allow you to properly investigate a new job? How much severance pay will they give you?"

"He said I should see Personnel. I can still go to Cleveland, otherwise, they'll accept my resignation. I have no idea how much termination pay I'll get."

Charlie said, "Try to keep an even keel, Ken, it's not as grim a picture as you think. Give me your e-mail address and I'll send you something tonight with a few thoughts for you to consider, as you make your future plans."

I wrote down the address, then Charlie shook my hand with his firm, reassuring grip.

I left the club and took the early Larkspur ferry. Fortunately, I didn't bump into any associates. I felt like I'd been kicked out of a fraternity and was now an outsider. How had I ever let myself get so dependent upon this company and their top people? My lawyer just left his firm, but I got a letter saying he'd take care of my legal needs through his new firm; my insurance agent represents many companies; my accountant got my account when he was with a firm he left several years ago. I stayed with *him*. My doctor sold his practice and joined a group. I still see *him*. I started to envy these business friends—they had portable expertise!

I then realized that I was a *dependent* of a corporation, just like my wife and kids were dependent upon me. I'd just been told I was dispensable! My insecurities were now raging so I went to the bar on the ferry and ordered a double martini, then a second one.

I looked at my reflection in the mirror behind the bar. My dark brown hair was beginning to show signs of gray around the edges. My brown eyes looked tired and dull. My once toned body, which I had always taken for granted, was slumped, my shoulders forward, head down. I needed to start running again—a relaxing time I'd enjoyed when I could let my mind run free as my feet traveled over the terrain. My mind wandered as a very attractive young woman walked up to the bar. She smiled and looked me over.

Fortunately, the ferry docked before I ordered another drink or did anything I would regret. I *carefully* drove to our new home in Mill Valley. We had traded up from our Petaluma home to save me commute time. Also, my talented wife, Pat, who wanted to take art classes now that the kids were in school, loved Mill Valley and its ambience…and I loved her—I still love her. So, we used most of our savings to buy the new place—a 3,000 square foot home on half an acre with beautiful views of the woods beyond. Pat called it our dream home, though the payments were double those of our Petaluma house, and Marin County taxes were astronomical!

I parked my company-leased Jaguar next to her SUV—also leased—and walked into the living room. Pat was in our spacious and bright kitchen working on an art project.

"Are you sick? What are you doing home so early?"

I walked past her and went to the family room bar and mixed another double.

"You'd better have one too, you'll need it."

"You've already had enough, it appears, for both of us. What's wrong?"

"I've been fired, so until I get another job, we're going to have to watch what we spend."

"You don't have anything else lined up? You didn't expect this? What in the world did you do to get fired?"

My response was to blame office politics while I drank my martini. I didn't get any sympathy from Pat so I went out on our patio to try to gather my thoughts and heard the front door slam and Pat's SUV start up the hill behind our home. Great!

Then, I started to think about her dependence on me. Many housewives in Mill Valley were like most others in a small town. They talked about their kids, their husband's last promotion, new furniture and their last or future vacations. Many also admired women who could balance a career, husband, kids and their homemaking responsibilities.

I had insisted that Pat quit her job when she got pregnant with our first child ten years ago. She was now totally dependent upon me and must really be upset about her future lifestyle and security.

What if we lost our home, had to pull the kids out of school and move back to an apartment in Petaluma? What would our friends think about that? No wonder she took off.

After a couple of hours, Pat had not returned, and the kids hadn't come home from school. So, I decided to drive out to the coast and see if I could clear my head. I had a strong cup of coffee to offset the effect of the martinis and drove to Point Reyes.

It was dusk by the time I completed my six-mile walk out to the ocean. I'd neglected to change shoes and my feet were sore, but I was, as always, calmed by the magnificence of the Point Reyes seashore, the surf crashing on the beach and the pristine green coastline stretching north and south for as far as the eye could see. I thought of the last time that I'd tried to surf during our vacation at our Hacienda del Mar condo in Cabo San Lucas. The undertow was so powerful it dragged me out to hit a big wave, which turned me upside down and around like a cartwheel until I was thrown onto the beach, only to be dragged back into the sea by the undertow. It took all of my strength to get out of *that* surf and my body ached for days from the pummeling I'd taken.

As I looked at the waves break on the beach, then saw the water recede for another wave build up, I visualized surfers I'd seen in Hawaii, who could ride big waves with great balance and timing. I'd clearly been caught in a *corporate* riptide and killer wave. My mind was spinning like my body had in Cabo. How could I learn to *surf the corporate wave?*

I limped back to the car on blistered feet and drove home. I'd just seen something more powerful than the *corporate* culture in which I'd been trying to live: the ocean, its currents, waves, undertow and riptides. I had to get some degree of control over my own life, just like a surfer must learn to ride the waves!

When I got back to the house, I found a note from Pat. She'd taken the kids and was going to have dinner with her Dad and Mom at their Marin Country Club home; I could join them if I got back early enough. I decided I didn't want to try to explain my situation to her Dad, who was very critical of me anyway.

I loved Pat for her zest for life, insights and the way she was raising our kids. So, since her folks raised her with these values, they weren't all bad. But her Dad, a workaholic and very independent businessman, made me feel like I was taking an exam during every conversation. He was definitely not laid back. I'd have to be *very* prepared to answer tough questions before I wanted to face him.

There was also an e-mail from Charlie Rowe. Charlie always seemed to be more of a listener than a talker. He was obviously intelligent, well connected and successful, but what did he do for a living? Charlie didn't have any advice for me. Instead, his message read:

> Ken:
> Please take the time to answer the following question. Try to keep it to one page. What is your greatest strength? In other words, what do you do best?

I started to list my strengths, and then prioritize them to get my *greatest*. Then, I realized I was too *close* to *me*. How can I determine my greatest strength? I do a lot of things *well*, but what do I do best? Another close friend, who had gotten into a losing battle with an ATM machine that ate his card said, when kidded about the incident, "It's tough to be me." That's how I felt now.

I fell asleep at my desk during this mental exercise. When I awoke, at 3:00 A.M., I was still alone in the house. When I realized Pat and the kids hadn't come home, I began to worry. What if Pat had been picked up by the Marin County highway patrol on the way home? Her Dad and Mom were serious drinkers and Pat was shook up when she left. She might have tried to drive back under the influence—well, I would have, but Pat had more sense than that. I called her folks' home to check on her, and their voicemail answered. I then got in my car and drove north to their home. Thank God, Pat's SUV was parked in the driveway. I drove back home and restlessly slept for a couple of hours.

Tuesday

I was awakened by Pat's SUV pulling in at 7:00 A.M. The kids came in and hugged me. My seven-year-old son, Michael, said he'd get yard work to help out and my nine-year-old little girl, Julie, said she'd get a job at her stable, cleaning out stalls. She was taking riding lessons and was crazy about horses!

Pat was busy in the kitchen, fixing lunches for the kids. When I came in, she said, "We missed you last night. Did you have a good time?"

When I said I'd stayed home she asked, "Why didn't you join us?"

Rather than telling her that her old man was not my favorite person, I said, "Charlie Rowe had me doing a project."

Pat seemed relieved. "Did you know our next door neighbors are friends of the Rowes? In fact, I think they're partners?"

"Dennis and Sharon? I didn't know that." Then, as I thought about it, Dennis was a financial consultant and I suspected that Charlie could be in that field. I called Charlie and got his voicemail, he was out of town.

I called Dennis to see if he knew where Charlie might be. I needed some elaboration on the reason for his question. Also,

Dennis had been a top executive in a major company and had resigned to build his own business. Maybe that's what I should do. The question was how to make the transition from *dependence* upon others to *independence* of others.

Sharon answered the phone. Dennis was on the golf course for a morning game with one of his clients. When I asked how he could play golf during the week, especially after he had just started with a new company, Sharon laughed. "He has a lot of partners. His role is to schmooze clients—others do the heavy analytical lifting." I told her I envied her husband and asked if he would call me when he returned.

I decided to find out how much severance pay I was going to get, so I drove into the City and went to my office. Ingrid, my great secretary, was cleaning out her desk when I arrived. She told me she'd been promoted to Fred's assistant. Another shot from that rascal. She asked how Pat was taking the news and I said, "Not well."

I went to my desk and found Fred's acceptance of my resignation and a memo from HR indicating I had ten weeks of pay coming. However, I should turn in my computer, car and my keys to the office that morning. They also gave me my 401(k) balance and said that 50 percent of any proceeds would be held for taxes and penalty for early withdrawal, unless I elected to roll my balance into an IRA. My group health insurance was good for three months, then, my premium under COBRA would be $600 per month. My group life insurance of $300,000 could be converted to whole life for $800 per month, but my long-term disability coverage of $7,000 per month was terminated immediately *and not convertible.*

I thought of another friend, who had been terminated with three years of severance income, plus benefits. He'd been smart enough to negotiate an employment *contract.* I joined this company right out of college and had never even *thought* of an employment contract. What a fool I'd been!

But even now, who could I get to represent me in any negotiation for a new contract if I could find a job paying me $150,000 yearly, plus benefits, to match what I'd given up? How would a new company respond to a request: "I'd like my lawyer to negotiate my agreement"?

I should have had my lines out long ago to investigate another position...but how could I have known? Then I thought about calling my lawyer about suing these bastards for wrongful termination.

I called him but he was in court. I also started to think about the fact that I'd been manipulated into *resigning* rather than accepting a transfer to Cleveland. I probably had no grounds for a suit; plus, I'd better conserve my funds for the readjustment period and not spend thousands of dollars in legal fees. Also, how would any potential new employer feel about hiring a man in the process of suing his previous employer?

I packed up my personal possessions and stopped in HR to fill out the paperwork so I could assume the lease on the company car. There was no way Pat and I could survive with one car right now. With the kids and all their activities and my looking for a job, I had to assume the lease even if we couldn't afford it. As I was leaving the building, Ingrid said, "Can I help out with Pat, we're good friends, maybe she'll understand things better if I call her." I said thanks and left, before my former associates could corner me to get the ugly details.

On the drive back, I started to think about finding another job, which would involve further dependency—unless I could find someone to negotiate an agreement for me. Then, I realized I couldn't really answer Charlie's question about my strengths. If I couldn't do that, how was I going to sell myself to others? I was reminded of a friend of mine who had broken up with his wife and had forgotten about how to go about asking a girl to go out with him. He was used to a wife who was just *there* for him.

I'd painted myself into that same corner! My company had been like my wife, or even more, like a country. It had just been there for me, until they lifted my passport. I was like a man without a corporate country! Now, how would I keep the other part of my security blanket—my wife?

When I got home, Pat was hopping mad. She'd gotten a call from Ingrid, who had not been too diplomatic when Pat had referred to that bastard *firing my husband.* Ingrid had explained that I had *resigned.*

Pat said, "What in the world were you thinking of? You could have gone to Cleveland for a short time, then put out your resume and negotiated a new position while still employed. Ingrid couldn't understand why you didn't do that. I *don't* understand either, unless you *wanted* to be fired so you could get out from under the pressure of supporting the kids and me. You've hinted about me getting a job, now I have no choice!"

Then she asked why I'd had Ingrid call, whether I'd shared martinis with *her* before coming home yesterday. Pat always saw Ingrid as a sexy and voluptuous woman who wasn't married or in a serious relationship. I think she felt ambivalent toward Ingrid—a little jealous of Ingrid's freedom, yet protective of her own family and lifestyle. Pat had always been a little envious of Ingrid with her independence, business education and the ease with which she dealt with powerful business executives. Pat was not in tune with business discussions. She was into kids, the house, her art and the activities other housewives share.

I'd always been careful to deal with Ingrid on a businesslike basis so Pat wouldn't get upset. Now, a friendly call from Ingrid had set Pat off—another challenge to handle while I tried to find a way to support my family. I had two and a half months before unemployment checks would start. Wow, how would I handle that humiliating situation—standing in line with unemployed down-and-outers, drunks, and malcontents and explaining to some civil servant why I wasn't looking for *any* work such as used car sales and the like. Also, what little we had in reserves would be used up soon with insurance premiums and car lease and computer payments. My $12,500 monthly salary was really worth a lot more than that when all my perks and benefits were included.

Maybe Cleveland was not such a bad idea. I called my former boss to see if that was still an option. He was on a field trip, but Ingrid said she'd heard the position had already been filled. I thought the Cleveland manager probably had the guy lined up and was waiting for me to try to throw my weight around by refusing the transfer, thinking I could write the rules and stay in San Francisco. He had orchestrated this little corporate coup!

I decided to drive out to the Meadow Club to see Dennis when he came off the course. I had to get away from the house, and Pat's very dark and disappointed attitude about the position I'd placed us in.

I sat outside and watched the golfers approach the 18th green. Most of them were older retirees. I'd have to ask Dennis how many of them had made it to retirement as executives of big companies. Many were younger, probably investment bankers, financial advisors, lawyers, CPA's, doctors. I started to think about how I could make the transition to a *professional* status, rather than a hired gun for a big company that could turn on me if I didn't do exactly what they wanted.

Face it, I had been a *corporate slave* but didn't know it. Not a good feeling.

Dennis' foursome was just coming off the 18th when I walked down to say hello. He introduced me to the other three people and asked me to join them for lunch. His guests were partners in an advertising agency. When, after a couple of drinks, I told Dennis and his friends that I'd resigned rather than transfer to Cleveland, one of them said, "Our partners are all from different large firms that like to move people around the world like chessmen. Even when you're a partner in your own agency, you have to please the client or be fired. Therefore, you'll always be working for someone else until you only have an investment portfolio to manage. Then, you have to work hard to anticipate inflation, recession, technological changes, management shifts. The only peace you'll ever get is when they plant you under a marker that says RIP!"

We all had a great laugh out of his unique, but compelling, description of the way we're all dependent on something or someone. His older partner had been listening carefully, not saying much, but when he spoke Dennis and the other two partners stopped all cross talk and listened carefully. I also found myself caught up in the way this man handled his words very carefully, measuring each to be sure it would send the right message.

Slowly and methodically he said the following which, when I left the group, I wrote down to contemplate: "The big difference between an independent person and a dependent one is that the former can fire his customers or clients and replace them rather easily. The latter only has one customer or client and it's sometimes tough to find one customer or client to replace them!"

The third partner agreed and added a succinct summary to his comments: "Be the boss, or be bossed. It's your choice." That said it all!

Dennis told me he'd meet me at his office at 5:00 P.M. He had some meetings after lunch that he couldn't break. So, I had over three hours to kill before I could get some advice from a contemporary—or was he a contemporary? I was starting to realize that, even though Dennis and I were about the same age, and both had MBA's, he seemed more mature than I felt, especially at this time in my life.

Dennis, as I reflected upon our discussions, seemed to *think* a little faster than most people. He also used humor a lot to make his point, never seemed stressed and was informed on almost every subject. Shortly after we had met and were getting acquainted, Sharon told us that each week Dennis read two or three books.

I thought about the long evenings that I spent making reports to my boss on every aspect of my life. I could have been reading serious literature to become as well read as Dennis. Also, I was a hacker and he had a four handicap. He was out practicing and playing golf, while I was on airplanes going or coming back from the fifteen or twenty field trips I took every year. He was with Sharon almost every evening. I was gone half the time. I began to feel like my resignation from *slave status* might be a good thing in the long run, but how to get established in a career like his?

Dennis was an *entrepreneur* and I'd been an *employee*. It was starting to dawn on me that I had to decide whether I was a leader, or a follower in a *leader's costume*.

I stopped by Borders bookstore and got a cup of coffee. I also borrowed a dictionary to see how Webster defined people like Dennis and his golfing friends: "An entrepreneur is a person who organizes and manages a business or industrial enterprise, taking the risk of loss and getting the profit when there is one."

Then I realized the difference between me and Dennis and his clients. They all reminded me of characters in movies where high stakes poker games were played. These were *players*.

Another of my Dad's friends, who heads a very large company, used a very good expression to describe the difference between people: "They're either *players* or *pretenders*. The key is to find out which, fast." I'd have to ask Dad if there might be a position open. The problem was his factories were all in the east. Also, what did I know about the furniture or fabric business?

Another observation from my lunch with Dennis and his clients was that they all had a different kind of charisma that made you *want* to listen to them. I looked it up to see if I had this quality. Webster defined charisma as: "Magnetic personality. The ability to inspire enthusiasm, interest, or affection in others by means of personal charm or influence."

Did I have this attribute? If not, what chance did I have of ever being an entrepreneur like Dennis and his friends? Then, I started to think about other entrepreneurs who were friends of my Dad's. Dennis and my insurance agent were the only two people I knew well enough to describe them that way. My Dad knew many entrepreneurs, but I didn't know most of them well. However, I made a list of those I'd met and was surprised to find different types of people who could inspire enthusiasm, interest or affection.

A very serious older man was sitting at a table next to me, reading a book. I decided to check on my feeling that charisma comes in different forms. "I'm sorry to interrupt you, but I'm having trouble defining a word."

He said, "Words are my business."

I asked what he did. "I'm a semi-retired PR man. What's the word?"

"Charisma," I responded.

He reflected on this, then said, "I'll give you a few examples of people with different flavors of charisma. George Marshall, the former Chief of Staff, had great charisma. He was quiet and unassuming, but a most thoughtful listener.

"Winston Churchill was a great talker, but his piercing intellect and insightful questions caused people to pay close attention to what he said.

"Some people walk in and *fill a room* with their colorful use of the English language; others get attention from everyone due to their high achievement. Others, through their quiet intelligence and use of white space in communication, give people an opportunity to think about everything the other person says.

"You could also say that truly great leaders have a *mystique* which attracts people like moths to a light."

I said, "How would you define mystique?"

"We don't have enough time for that discussion."

He then smiled and went back to his book—a gentle suggestion that the conversation was finished.

I had to decide *who I was* and determine my major strengths. Mostly, I had to see if I had the basic leadership *stuff*. If not, I'd better scale back my expectations, ask Pat to get *any* kind of job, then I would go back to school and learn a specialty so that I could eventually make a better than average living.

I left Borders and just drove around until 5:00, lost in thought, but starting to think of an alternative to getting another job. How could I become an entrepreneur without starting all over again at a small income? How could I maintain our present lifestyle and also get into a position of being able to fire my clients or customers rather than constantly being afraid of *being fired!* Once burned, you start to feel a little insecure about others having so much control over your life.

Dennis was just finishing his meeting, so I waited in his office, looking at his toy collection, golf trophies and several diplomas on his wall. I'd never heard him talk about his education much, just that he had an MBA. When I had a little party to celebrate getting my MBA, Sharon had casually told Pat, "Dennis has one of those too!"

I might go back to school to become an entrepreneur, but who teaches that?

Dennis came in and said he had just a few minutes before having to get ready for an important meeting that evening. So, there goes my impression of him as the happy-go-lucky, entertaining guy next door. He's a *serious* player.

We sat down in his office, Dennis behind the desk and I was in a chair opposite. I started out with my basic fear of running out of money before I found a job or career that would pay me enough to stay in our home. I also told him about Charlie's question and that I was having a tough time answering it.

He listened carefully, and then said, "You're *exuding* fear and insecurity, Ken. What's the big deal about a house? You've got your health, two great kids, and a talented woman who loves you. Don't be a slave to a house the way you sold yourself to a corporation."

When I started to justify my fears, he said, "Ken, you've got an attitude problem. Most people who rise fast in executive circles get too full of themselves and it sometimes takes an event like what you're experiencing to bring them back to earth. Let me give you an example: If you found out that your little Julie had inoperable cancer, would you feel worse than you do now?"

I said, "Of course."

"Put things into perspective, Ken, and work on your attitude. Then, you'll find your strengths and can answer Charlie Rowe's question. Until then, you're just going to mill around in your own self-pity. I'm not trying to hurt your feelings, but just as we both give our kids *tough* love, I'm giving you *tough* friendship."

As we got up to leave, he handed me a sheet of paper and said, "Why don't you occupy your mind with something that will help you whenever you feel down in the dumps. If you memorize it, you can retrieve it on any occasion." The paper read:

> The longer I live, the more I realize the impact of attitude on life. Attitude, to me, is more important than facts. It is more important than the past, than education, than money, than circumstances, than failures, than successes, than what other people think, say or do. It is more important than appearance, giftedness, or skill. It will make or break a company...a church...a home.

The remarkable thing is we have a choice everyday regarding the attitude we embrace for that day. We cannot change our past...we cannot change the fact that people will act in a certain way. We cannot change the inevitable. The only thing we can do is play on the one string we have, and that is our attitude.

I am convinced that life is 10 percent what happens to me and 90 percent how I react to it. So it is with you...we are in charge of our attitudes.

by Charles Swindoll

I read it several times sitting in the car and gradually got over the feeling of rejection from his *tough love* lecture.

Then I realized what Charlie was doing. His question about my greatest strength, which I couldn't answer, was causing me to go to a role model to try to find the answer. He and Dennis were in business together. I wondered if he talked to Dennis before our meeting. I guess I needed his woodshed treatment, as I was starting to feel sorry for myself. Not good!

When I considered how I'd feel if Pat or one of the kids were sick, there was no comparison!

How would I learn the rules for becoming an entrepreneur? They think, feel and act differently from an employee who is used to taking direction, doing their best, then waiting for approval, a raise or promotion. I used to think a good job was security! What an illusion.

On returning to the house, I found another note. Pat was going to spend a few days with her folks to let me sort things out. So, another lonely night.

I decided to walk downtown to a Mill Valley pub Pat and I used to enjoy. I was by myself at the bar for a while, nursing a glass of wine, when Ingrid came in with a friend. They invited me to join them for a drink, which I did. Ingrid was a strong person and a good friend.

After a couple of bottles of wine, all three of us were loosened up. Ingrid was in no condition to drive, so I insisted on driving her home. Then I drove her car back to my place and went inside.

Wednesday

Early the next morning I was awakened by a slap on my face. Pat was standing over our bed, shouting, "Where is that bitch?" I tried to tell her what had happened, but Pat got the clothes she'd come for, got in her car and left.

Ingrid drove up with a friend an hour later to get her car and thank me for being her chauffeur. When I told her about Pat's actions, she laughed. "This will be good for her, she takes you for granted." Then she left.

I started to wonder if Ingrid was glad that this had happened. Then, I realized that Ingrid had been married twice, had no kids and was in her 40's…and probably _looking_. This was not a good situation. I wanted _Pat_ back!

I remembered the expression from early times. "If a man knows he's to be hung in a fortnight, it concentrates his mind wonderfully." My mind was now focused on _two_ critical problems—keeping my wife _and_ finding a new way to support our family in the style to which they'd become accustomed.

I listed my options aloud to help me clarify them: "I have ten weeks of reserves and enough money to pay for my perks for about half that time. My 401(k) Plan will give me another six months, if I can't find the right position. But taxes will reduce that to three months. If I sell the house, the equity, after real estate fees, will carry us another three months. If I can find the right situation in two months, I won't have to sell the house or touch my 401(k)."

I e-mailed Charlie and said I couldn't answer his question yet. I didn't know what I did best! Could we meet?

A response came back within a few hours.

> Ken:
> Let me try to help you. What are your strong attributes? Which were you born with, which did you acquire? How did you acquire them? What is your most significant accomplishment? The second, third?

So, I e-mailed my attributes: high school honor roll, good grades in college and then I described some of my accomplishments in business. This was helping me start to feel better about myself.

An e-mail came back with another question:

> Who are your heroes? Whom do you most admire? In business and in life? Why?

When I answered those, more questions arrived:

> What about historical figures? Whom do you admire most? Why?

Then, Charlie threw me a curve ball with another question:

> What are your most critical improvement opportunities?

I responded that I had to think about historical figures. I had so many problems I'd have to think about the most critical.

Charlie's response was to the point:

> You have to narrow your focus; you're seeing life in a fuzzy, disorganized way. There are thousands of opportunities for you in the Bay Area, but you'll have to let go of your insecurities and start feeling better about yourself. You've been dealt a body blow and knocked down. Everyone goes through this experience. The real question is, can you get up? Why don't you try to identify your fears? Then, you'll have to overcome them. What is your greatest fear?

I couldn't answer that one either. I was really confused. So, I gave up on my self-examination and turned on the TV. A golf match was on and I tried to concentrate on the Pros and *their* ability to focus on the ball and the goal, ignoring the crowd and their competition and just having a total concentration on all the right moves to hit the ball.

That's what I needed, some exercise to clear my mind. I loved the game of golf but was not very good at it. I decided I might as well hit some balls, get some practice and then maybe pick up a game over the next day or two with some of my duffer friends—certainly not with Dennis, who intimidated me with his low scores.

I drove to a driving range in San Rafael, bought a bucket of balls and started to hit my midirons.

Another fellow was also working on his irons, but his shots went about twice as far as mine did. So after about five or ten minutes of his flawless execution and after I'd topped and shanked a number of shots, I stopped for a breather and asked him if he was a professional. He laughed and said,

"No, I just enjoy the game and like to go out and practice a lot. I could hit balls, all day long. It's a great way for me to relax."

I said that I was using this practice to get rid of some of my frustrations. He laughed and said that I would only increase my level of frustration by attacking the ball. "If you don't mind, I'll give you a few tips which will increase your enjoyment of this ancient and honorable game. First, your knuckles are white when you grab the club. You have a death grip. Relax. Let the club nestle in your hands. Then let the club do the work."

I couldn't help but think of the same advice I'd gotten from both Dennis and Charlie about my career worries. This fellow seemed to be very much at ease with himself and he appeared to have that intangible quality of *charisma*.

We chatted for a while, then I finished my bucket of balls and went into the bar and had a beer. He followed a few minutes later and sat down next to me.

I asked him, "What do you do?"

"Well, a lot of things."

"For example?"

"Well, I just finished a few days playing piano at the Club Mirage in Las Vegas."

"Are you a professional piano player?"

"No, I just enjoy that too."

"What is your day job?"

He laughed and said, "Well, I have several of those. I run a distribution company, but then I also have a construction company and a software company."

"You're an entrepreneur."

He laughed again and said he'd probably fit that description pretty well.

I asked him how long he had been an entrepreneur. He said, "Oh, about fifteen years. Ever since I got into a conflict with people in an organization and fell out of step with them. I was very unhappy for a period of time, then decided that I could only depend upon one person for my future—me. I joined a private company and then, with high interest rates, cutthroat competition and a few political problems, that company got into trouble and I became a *survivor*—rather than a *victim*. It took quite a few years to dig the company out of all of its trouble, but now it pretty much runs itself. With my partners watching every part of that company, I can spend time in other pursuits, like playing the piano, golfing and investing in a few *adventure capital* situations, a little more of a gamble than a straight investment—like my construction company."

While we were talking, another couple of fellows came off the driving range and joined us. We talked about the great game of golf. During a lull in the conversation, one of them asked me what I did, and I told them that I'd just resigned from my job and was trying to decide upon a new career.

At that point, they flashed broad smiles and almost simultaneously stuck out their hands and started congratulating me! I laughed and said I appreciated their thoughtfulness, but I didn't see that I had anything to celebrate.

The one with the New York accent disagreed. "You're at a defining event in your life. The best thing that ever happened to me was when my company faced some real problems. I decided to tackle them, even though it meant risking more money than I ever wanted to lose."

"That sounds like the common denominator for all three of us," another chimed in. "When you risk more than you want to lose, that's when you learn the game. All of us are entrepreneurs. We're no longer employees."

"That means you're just the guys that I want to ask this question. Can you tell me how I can make the transition from being an employee to being an entrepreneur?"

That stopped their good-hearted chatter. After thinking that one over for a minute, one of them said, "You're going to have to change a lot of habits, and that will be really hard. You're used to being part of a hierarchy, which doesn't sound good, but it's comfortable. I guess the toughest thing to change is thinking for yourself, making up your own mind."

"Plotting your own course," another fellow added.

They all nodded in agreement. They understood, but I didn't. I was even more confused. It sounded good, but what made them believe I wasn't already thinking for myself?

It was almost like someone telling me that I'd have to change the way I *looked,* which would be easier than changing the way I think. No wonder there are so few entrepreneurs and so many employees. I wondered if I could ever make this kind of transition in my thinking.

One of them said, "Ken, being an entrepreneur is not rocket science, it's just common sense. If you were to have to learn how to be a high wire acrobat, without a net, that would be a challenge. People who do that kind of thing start out at a very early age and work up to their high wire act. When you started out in life, you probably did a lot of independent thinking. However, with our parents telling us what we can and can't do, then teachers doing the same, then bosses, military superiors, wives, everyone telling us what we can and cannot do, we get defensive in our thinking.

"You have to get mad at yourself a little in order to change your behavior, and you also have to have a lot of desire and willingness to pay the price. All of us at this table have put in seventy and eighty hour weeks most of our lives to get to the point where we now put that many hours in because it's fun. You probably spent the same amount of time in actual work, in addition to worrying about how you were accepted by others in your company and how you were going to get promoted. Therefore, the mental exercise required to climb the executive ladder is about the same as becoming an entrepreneur. Only you have a little more control over the process when you're not taking exams every week or month to prove yourself to one or two people who have total control over your future.

"Keep your chin up. What may appear to you to be a disaster in your life is probably the best thing that's ever happened to you because it's happening when you're young enough to bounce back. You have many options. You just have to be sure that you keep a positive attitude. It's your attitude in life that will determine the *altitude* you reach in success."

There it was again, the *attitude* thing. I pulled out the piece of paper Dennis gave me and read it to them. They were impressed and I resolved to memorize it so that I could show off a little. I certainly didn't have great accomplishments to talk about, but at least I could show that I had a good mind.

I went home to another long evening of staring at the TV set, but at least I wasn't gulping down martinis and was starting to think.

Then, an e-mail came in from Charlie. Thank God, he was still thinking about me. It read:

Ken:
Go to the *San Francisco Business Times* tomorrow and ask them to loan you their *Book of Lists*. They list the top companies in almost every field in the Bay Area. Determine which of these fields has some appeal to you and make a list of fifty companies in these different fields. Then, compose a short, thought-provoking e-message for the CEO's asking for five minutes of their time; you'll only be there longer than that if they insist. Check with my partner, Dennis, and he'll help you with a message that will grab their attention. Then, occupy your time for the next four or five days with as many interviews as you can schedule. Your objective is to find out why the CEO selected that particular field and why they stay in it? Then let them talk.

I gave this advice to a young man many years ago. He wanted to find out if he could succeed in the sale of financial service products. He called on a number of the top business people in Portland, Oregon and merely asked them why they had decided on their career. He only asked for five minutes but spent hours, in some cases, listening to the story of their lives. He learned a lot and eventually decided on a career in my field.

His active listening skills helped him become one of my most successful associates.

Why don't you try to learn more about yourself and your natural aptitudes by getting acquainted with business leaders in different fields?

You'll be surprised how approachable they are, if you handle yourself well in your opening remarks. Remember don't say anything on the phone other than to get a personal meeting. If their secretaries try to screen you out, remember, that's their job. You may just have to drop in on some of them, if the secretary won't give you a five-minute slot on her boss's schedule.

Thursday

The next morning, with some direction in my life at last, I drove into San Francisco. The receptionist at the *Business Times* let me use their conference room to write down names from the *Book of Lists*. I finally had a concept or a plan and something to do. For the first time I started to relax. Charlie was right. There are thousands of jobs I might be able to get, but I was starting to think that maybe I didn't want a job. Maybe I wanted to be in business for myself. How would I do that?

I called Dennis' office and found that he was going to be out of town for a few days, so I had to be my own creative writer. Then I thought, rather than go to these fifty people as a stranger, why don't I try to find someone who knows them. Then I can at least use that person's name in the first sentence of my e-mail to assure that the balance of my message will at least be read. It might even give me that five minutes I now very definitely needed.

Dennis had introduced me to three fellows who were aware of my situation, I'd met three others on my own and Charlie knew a lot of people, so I decided to prepare a list of the fifty people. But how would I send this list to very busy people asking them which ones they knew and have them give me permission to use their name? That wouldn't work. I was already getting desperate.

But I did need help with that letter. So I composed an e-mail to each of the three people I met at the driving range and outlined Charlie's suggestion. I indicated I was in the process of drafting a short e-mail for busy executives that would allow me five minutes to talk with them. I said, "If you have any ideas, they'd sure be welcome."

Then I called Pat to see if we could have a truce; I really needed to talk with her. Her mother answered the phone and said that she'd tell Pat that I called. Pat was lying down for a nap; she hadn't slept much last night. Her mother sounded a little distant and annoyed, so I guessed Pat had told her about my evening with Ingrid—or Pat's version of it.

With the rest of the afternoon free, I headed for the driving range. This time I used some of the tips I'd been told and hit the balls a little straighter. I noticed another golfer, struggling with his club, attacking the ball as if it were a wild animal he wanted to tame. It felt good to be superior to anyone at that point and I walked over to tell him that I'd been in the same boat the day before and had received a great tip I'd be happy to pass on if he didn't mind.

His face lit up. "I'm an amateur with a capital A and need all the help I can get."

When I showed the way I'd been told to hold the club and let the club head do the work, he tried it, but it worked about as well for him the first time as it had for me.

After I'd hit my balls, I went up to the bar, ordered a beer and this fellow joined me.

Never before had I met someone who put me at ease so quickly. I also felt a sense of kinship since we were both erratic golfers. I asked if he'd like to play golf sometime.

He said, "Anytime. I'm retired."

"At your age? I can't believe it."

"Yes, I made a decision to retire at age fifty and when I hit it, that's what I did."

"You must have been very successful to be able to do that."

He responded, "I kept my goal in front of me every day, and I had a mentor, many years ago, who helped me find my way."

I told him about my great challenge in trying to find a new career and he thought Charlie's suggestion to meet with fifty different CEO's was a good idea.

"Why don't you just walk in and ask to see them? An e-mail can inform them you're going to be in their office at a particular time and you hope they have five minutes. Then, *they* have to make the move to tell you not to come and most successful people are very curious." Then he said, "Gotta go, here's my e-mail address. Let me know when you want to play some golf."

"I'll be in touch."

What an amazing guy! He really thought outside the box. I went home, fixed a TV dinner, had one glass of wine, watched a boring movie and called Pat's parents' home, but the voicemail answered. I hung up and went to bed. I had a good night's sleep, considering my wife had taken the kids and gone to her parents' and wouldn't talk with me. I had no job and no prospects. I was making progress, though, and was formulating a plan.

Friday

I got up early that morning and prepared e-mails to ten of the fifty people, setting up appointments on the hour, every hour, for the next day and the following day. After I sent them, I realized that the next day was Saturday, so I immediately had to e-mail to reschedule those meetings for next week.

Then, I sat back and waited for the responses. None came. Could it be that all of them were ignoring me? That when I arrived they'd tell their secretary to find out what my business was?

Now a new kind of insecurity started to settle in as I realized I could be walking into embarrassing situations on Monday and Tuesday. Nevertheless, at least I had a plan and was going to do something to get myself out of the rut.

I called the real estate agent who had sold us the house about the possibility of refinancing. She was surprised to find out that I'd resigned. In her gentle southern accent she gave me a little motherly advice, "Now, Ken, don't worry about *anything*, just let me pray for a great new opportunity for you...don't even think about selling the house right now."

"I don't *want* to sell, just refinance."

"But you don't have a job. The only way you'll get any money out of your equity is to sell! Then, you'll have to rent at a very high price if you want to stay in Marin County."

Our agent's husband had been a multimillionaire real estate broker and developer until a partner committed him to deals that didn't work out. They had to sell everything to pay creditors, and then start all over again as successful real estate agents. They'd also become very close to their family and friends, including my Dad and Mom and another couple they traveled with. They were among the most respected people of all my folks' friends. Yet, they weren't rich anymore.

Their example made me feel a little better. If I had to start over, I'd ask her husband to show me the ropes. I remembered his great spirit, his sense of fun, and his vivid imagination. His business reversal hadn't made him bitter. He just picked up and started over, lucky to have a wife as a solid partner.

By now I thought Pat had recovered from the little misunderstanding about my "accidental date" with Ingrid. I called her at her folks' place and got the recorder. A few hours later, her Dad called. Pat and the kids had left. He didn't know where they'd gone. "She's pretty unhappy with you, Ken," he said in a superior tone. His attitude ticked me off, but I bit my tongue and didn't try to explain my non-involvement with Ingrid.

Julie, my little girl, called later that evening. She was upbeat and said that Pat had taken them to the City for dinner and a show. They were going to stay with Myrna, a friend of Pat's. When I asked to talk to Pat, Julie said, "They went out with Myrna and her new boyfriend. We're here with Myrna's kids. I'm the assistant sitter, isn't that great!"

"Myrna's kids are only twelve and thirteen. Isn't there an adult there?"

"Dad, Myrna leaves them by themselves all the time, don't worry. Besides, we have her cell number if there's a problem."

I could hear lots of noise in the background—TV, kids laughing—and it all made me lonelier. I said, "I'll come over and see you in a while," and hung up.

Then, I started to do a slow burn. What in the hell did Pat think she was doing? I'd aged five years in five days trying to figure out how to maintain our lifestyle, and she was over at her folks' pouting, then out on the town with Myrna, who had two kids by two husbands and was looking for a third. She was a real party animal. What a great influence on Pat!

I decided to get the kids and bring them back to Mill Valley with me. That should bring Pat to her senses, I thought.

When I arrived at Myrna's apartment in the Marina, about 10 P.M., Michael was asleep and Julie was in her pajamas. Myrna's two kids were still wide-awake and objected to my insistence that Julie and Michael come home with me. I carried Mike to the car while Julie lectured me all the way, "Mom will really be mad, Dad."

After I tucked them into their own beds, I tried to concentrate on a late-night movie, but couldn't get over a feeling of emptiness. I was fighting this battle on my own. Pat was part of the problem, not my ally in trying to find a solution.

I'd drifted off to sleep in front of the TV when the phone rang. It was Myrna. She was very cool and asked why I'd taken my kids away from her place. I ignored her question and asked to talk to Pat. "She's not here."

"Where is she?"

"My boyfriend is driving her to your place, she's in no condition to drive."

Great! Myrna's boyfriends weren't too reliable and most of her dates were into heavy-duty partying.

At 3:00 A.M. I hadn't heard from Pat. I called Myrna's apartment; the machine answered.

Saturday

Early the next morning Pat drove up in her own car. She looked worn out and I hadn't slept at all. She didn't say anything to me, just walked into our room and packed some fresh clothes. Then as she left, said, "Myrna and I are going to Tahoe this weekend. You can take care of the kids." When I asked where Myrna's boyfriend was, she responded, "He was too drunk to drive. I went back to Myrna's and spent the night."

As she left, she didn't look at me, just quietly closed the door and left. I had that sinking feeling that she wasn't telling me the whole story.

When I called Myrna, I again got her voicemail. So, I was left with only a very active imagination of what had happened last night, and a quiet fury about what was going to happen in Tahoe with Myrna and Pat...and friends?

The kids got up after a while and I took them out to breakfast. I then dropped them off at my folks' for the day.

I decided that two could play at Pat's game. I was hurt, angry and after five days of total insecurity, I needed some R&R.

Ingrid was just getting up when I called to ask if she was up for a ride down the coast for lunch. She was and I picked her up about 10:30 A.M.

As we headed down Highway 1, I asked if she could hold off for a late lunch. She could, so we kept going until we reached Carmel and one of my favorite places—Highlands Inn.

We sat at a table overlooking the surf and I unloaded my problems on Ingrid: the whole five-day ordeal of betrayal by my boss, Pat's total lack of understanding, her attitude regarding Ingrid, Dennis and his self-confident friends, my financial problems, the other self-confident people I'd met at the driving range, Charlie's suggestions, then, just when I was feeling positive, Pat's actions had slapped me down.

Ingrid looked at me with her big blue eyes and said, "Ken, you are the most talented man I know. You can do anything you set your mind to do. Pat will come around, give her time. This has been a shock to her too."

Then, she looked down at her menu and I started to feel like a man again.

What a difference a woman like Ingrid could make in a man's life, I thought. I'm sure glad she's my friend! I don't feel alone when I'm with her.

Why did I feel alone when I was with Pat? It had been that way for some time. Our interests were so different. We only had the kids in common. I didn't get along with her folks. And she was a bit distant with mine.

I quickly dismissed this kind of thinking and ordered my second martini. Ingrid had white wine and said she'd drive back after lunch, to which I quickly agreed. In light of what happened a few hours later, that decision was not a wise one. I had a third martini, followed by some bar-hopping in downtown Carmel and dinner with Ingrid at the Mission Ranch.

Chapter 2

Surviving a Life Storm

<u>Sunday</u>

After I returned home Sunday morning, I e-mailed Charlie:

Charlie:
I've got to back away from any kind of job search for awhile. I had a nasty argument with Pat in Carmel last night. Yesterday afternoon at a bar in Carmel, I met a local personality, who says he knows you. I was with my former secretary, Ingrid, and he invited us to join him for dinner at Mission Ranch. He also offered to give me a golf lesson after I described my various handicaps.

We were having a great time and I was starting to really relax, when a few people at the piano bar started to sing with the piano player and we decided to join them. It was crowded, but this fellow got us a place at the bar and, to my surprise, I found that we were just across the bar from Pat, Myrna and two older fellows. They were having a great time until Pat saw me. She stared for a minute, then motioned for me to meet her outside. She gave me the third degree about what I was doing there with Ingrid. When I asked about her Tahoe trip, saying that Carmel was not on the way, she said they changed their minds. She told me the two older fellows were already at the bar when they had arrived and were strangers. She said a few other things about my being "in my cups" and that Ingrid could have me. She wanted out! That was a sobering thought and when I went back in to the bar, I got Ingrid and left.

We started to drive back to Marin, but I decided Ingrid had also had too much to drink, so we stopped at the La Playa and I got two rooms. After breakfast, we drove back and I picked up the kids from my folks'.

We're all at our home now, but I haven't heard from Pat yet. I frankly don't know what she's up to, but I'm in no shape emotionally to even think about a job. I want to hang on to my wife unless she's really involved with another guy. I'll be back in touch when I decide what to do about my very fragile relationship with Pat.

Charlie Rowe responded right away:

Ken:
You've been struggling for the past few days to get some direction in your life after being so focused on one career, with one company. Somewhere along the way you neglected to develop a strong relationship with a wife you love—but may have taken for granted. Now, you are all experiencing insecurities about how your lives will be affected due to your job loss and your turmoil. You have some important issues to work through with your family. That's your first priority, now. When you are ready to continue your job search, call or e-mail me and I'll be there to guide you.

I went into the living room to talk to Ingrid after I'd finished reading Charlie's e-mail. She was chatting with Julie and Michael, who left when I entered the room. I asked Ingrid how they were adapting to the present situation.

She said, "You'd better spend some quality time with both of them. They think *they* may be the cause of your problems with Pat. They think they are responsible for Pat being unhappy, because she's so tied down with them. And they think you're too busy with your own friends and ambition. They feel like afterthoughts. Incidentally, I'm a good *Aunt Ingrid*, not a good surrogate mother, so I really can't help you.

"I've got to get home, so please take me there as soon as possible. Your kids should go with us. After what happened last night with Pat, I'm very uncomfortable being alone with you...and you should feel the same way. If your kids think we're more than just good friends, you could alienate them like it appears we've alienated Pat."

On the drive back I tried to reach Pat at her folks' and at Myrna's on my cell phone and got a recording both places, so I spent the rest of the day with Julie and Michael and let both of them know they were loved by Pat and me. If anything happened to our marriage, it wouldn't change my love for them. They were too quiet for comfort, which indicated their disapproval about any talk regarding divorce. They both had friends who were from single-parent families and knew how lonely a little boy or girl could be when there weren't two parents to help kids come to grips with the trials of just growing up.

Pat came home after I'd gone to bed and said she was very tired; she'd sleep on the couch. I insisted on the couch and had a very bad night without much sleep.

Monday (second week)

I was not at my best that morning. I'd only gone through one week of insecurity, but it seemed much longer. My memory of the job satisfaction I'd had was fading and I could only think about how I'd been caught in a very bad life storm, without any real protection against the elements I was facing: no job, minimal reserves, angry wife, insecure kids.

However, I was coming to grips with what I had to do to gain control of my life. Thanks to Charlie Rowe's questions, I was starting to think about my *inner* resources rather than my precarious financial situation. I needed some peace of mind to focus on answering those questions, which I realized Charlie had posed to force me to focus on the *brute* issues. I needed to decide on the *important* issues to resolve, rather than the *urgent* ones—which might not be the most important.

I sent another e-mail to Charlie and said I had to get away, by myself, for a few days, to think things through and decide what I wanted to do with my life. I'd decided that since I hadn't received any replies from the CEO's I'd e-mailed, I wouldn't risk more humiliation by showing up at their offices without appointments. I told Charlie I'd be in contact soon.

I got on the phone and called for reservations at an inexpensive out-of-the-way motel or hotel where I could hole up. I found one at Half Moon Bay, so I took my computer, small suitcase and left. I told Pat I'd call her when I settled in; I had to be by myself for a while and sort some things out. She did not seem to care one way or the other. I realized my marriage was definitely in trouble when she didn't even ask if Ingrid was going with me. I guessed Pat, at that point, had given up on us.

When I checked in at the motel, I hooked up my computer and found a lengthy message from Charlie:

> You're doing the right thing, Ken, to back away from your current troubles and get some perspective. Little things bother little people and I don't think you perceive yourself as a *little man*. You're as big as the things that bother you, and if you think about it, you'll realize you are a *big* man. Those with mediocre talent don't get an MBA, while working full time, or reach the level of responsibility you attained with your company. Your mistake was in not understanding the kind of networking that was necessary for you to survive in a big company as a senior executive.
>
> Some people call it politics, but that is not true. Politicians have to be elected periodically by lots of people, so they try hard not to alienate anyone. As a result, most of them are not real leaders, they merely discern where the crowd is going, then get in front and pretend they're leading. There are some exceptions, but just a few.
>
> Business executives have to achieve bottom-line profits, or they're replaced. They make hard decisions affecting the lives of many people. However, they have to cultivate a number of colleagues, both those with whom they work, and those to whom they report, so that their actions are understood at all times.
>
> Your former boss probably had no control over your transfer. You should have accepted it, then decided whether you really wanted to stay with that company. You'd have bought more time to choose what kind of career change was the best for you, considering your background and training. However, that's water over the dam. We play the cards dealt us in life. Your cards

would indicate that trying to join a company at an executive level would only be possible through a good executive search firm. I know several good ones and, after you've made the decision that a salaried position is what you want, I'll introduce you.

However, there are a lot of entrepreneurial opportunities in the Bay Area as well. Many venture capital (VC) firms are looking for CEO's to take over smaller firms that have a good product or service, solid employees and mid-managers, but lack a professional business management team. Many entrepreneurs build fine companies, but fail to groom their successors. When they sell to a financial buyer, a new CEO must be brought in. So, you'll have to prepare yourself for a different kind of interview with the senior partners in these VC firms. They're looking for a different type of person than a large company with a very structured environment would need. If I were interviewing you for a CEO slot in one of our portfolio companies, here's what I'd focus on, in order of priority:

•   Your *character*. Who are you in the dark? Will you sacrifice the truth to get your way or make money? Would I give you my power of attorney to make decisions with possible financial or legal implications, in other words, could I trust you totally to do what's right for all concerned.

•   *Commitment*. Are you a finisher or just the type of person that talks a good game? Do you walk the talk? If you set a goal that is realizable, will you let nothing get in your way to achieve what you plan?

•   *Empathy*. Do you feel another person's pain or loneliness and try to help them feel better about themselves, or is it "every man for himself"?

• *Imagination*. Do you think independently and outside the box, or do you need direction in achieving your part of an over-all plan? Also, are you imaginative or are you a dreamer, coming up with all sorts of ideas, but not thinking them through carefully.

What you say in the first five to ten minutes of a conversation with a trained observer of human nature, which a good VC must be in order to succeed, will either buy you more time with them or you'll be told to "stay in touch."

That's just another way a VC can tell you that you're not a horse they want to bet on! It's not like the interviews a search firm will have with you to place you in a company with a structure, where others will supervise you. So, let's see if financial backing from a VC is the path you should take, or that a position offering more structure would be better.

Try to think through your answers to the four questions that I asked you last week—the first four listed here. Then, try to answer the additional questions:

1. What is your greatest strength?

2. Who are your heroes?

3. What are your most critical improvement opportunities?

4. What is your greatest fear?

5. What is the biggest challenge you've faced in life? How did you meet it?

6. What do you want the most out of life? Your ultimate goal? Do you have a personal mission statement to assure that you attain your ultimate goal?

7. Do you lead a balanced life? How do you balance your commitment to your career, your family and yourself? Do you have a few close friends or many acquaintances?

8. Describe your physical and mental health. What do you do for fun? What are your hobbies? What sports do you play or watch? What kind of exercise program do you have?

9. Do you consider yourself well read? Name the last five books you've read. What are you reading now?

Ken, if you can answer the first nine questions, you'll be able to answer the following question and, what is more important, you'll be able to follow up with an action plan:

10. What action could you take that would have the most positive impact on your life? What is your plan to achieve this? Put it in writing, with deadline dates to assure achievement. What are the consequences of not attaining your plan?

When I finished reading the e-mail, I tried to answer the first question by listing my educational achievements and career advancement, but was too upset to think about my greatest strengths, heroes, improvement opportunities and fears. I only knew I was in a *life storm* and wanted to find a safe harbor, but didn't know how to find one.

I went out for a walk around the Half Moon Bay golf course to clear my head. It was late and I almost had the course to myself so I walked out to the hole that runs along the ocean and watched a golfer drive the ball across an inlet and onto the green. He then started toward the green and I caught up with him and commented about his great shot. "I'd have put three or four shots in the ocean if I'd been trying to carry that much distance. How do you keep your mind off the water and on hitting the ball?"

He smiled. "All of us twenty-two handicaps have our little secrets." He then walked up and holed out a ten-foot putt.

I thought to myself, twenty-two, boy, what a sandbagger! However, he was an easy guy to talk to and I was lonely, so I asked if I could be his gallery as he finished the last few holes. "Sure, I'll even buy you a drink if I par the last three holes." That confirmed it—he sure wasn't a twenty-two!

He had par on two holes and a bogey on the last one. But he seemed happy with his game. We went into the clubhouse bar and we introduced ourselves.

Frank said, "What are you doing out on a course without clubs? Looking for a job as a caddy?"

"I'm open for anything right now—I'm unemployed." I then told him what had happened to me a week earlier.

He softened a bit and said, "That calls for a drink to celebrate your freedom from a company that deals with people that way."

When the drinks arrived and we'd toasted my freedom, he asked me a few questions about my plans. He then stopped, and with a twinkle in his eye, said, "You're going to find out what kind of stuff you're made of, Ken. Take plenty of time to decide what you're going to do; talk to lots of people— you'll be surprised how easy it is to get some good sound advice. The bigger the person you ask, the easier it will be to get quality time with them, if they think you've got the *right stuff*."

"What is the right stuff?"

"That depends upon what you decide to do."

"How do I finance myself while I'm taking plenty of time to decide? That's my problem."

"Sell the house, put your old lady back to work, get a job tending bar, selling cars, *anything*, but don't get back into the rat race until you can compete with the larger rats!"

We both had a good laugh as I described my rat, who I believed had engineered my dismissal, and he described his rat, the man who had taken over as CEO of his former company. He had been CFO and took early retirement rather that "work for that scumbag," as he described his former boss.

It seemed that he had not fired his secretary, as his boss had demanded. She was accused of insulting the CEO's wife, a former co-worker of hers. Frank said, "His new wife should not have lorded it over a former co-worker. He and I didn't see eye to eye after that."

I was really enjoying this conversation with him. He had no pretensions and was a direct, no nonsense guy. You'd want to be in a foxhole with a guy like him. We discovered we were both Cal graduates and both had MBA's. Still, he said, "You can make a good living driving a truck. So don't let your MBA get in your way. The most important thing is to be sure those kids have a full-time Dad. Your old lady will respect you for that and come around. If she doesn't, throw her out—she isn't worth it."

When I got defensive about the way he was talking about Pat, he laughed. "So, maybe you're not ready to call it quits with her. Let her know how you think—after you know what you're going to do. Don't expect her to help you other than to encourage you in whatever decision you make."

What a breath of fresh air. He had made it seem like this life storm was just a breeze. I wanted to get to know him better.

After I left him and returned to my room, I had an e-mail from Charlie:

> Ken:
> I've been giving you advice on how to turn your career adversity into an opportunity. However, you don't need advice, you need a mentor.
>
> I'm writing a book on how to *become* a mentor and I've interviewed eleven men who have become Leader/Mentors. They've shared the *secrets* to their own success. I've also identified some *Guiding Principles* they all adopted in their early development.
>
> Also, they all had mentors, who helped them understand themselves while overcoming many kinds of adversity. I'll put you in touch with one of them. He may be able to help you discover yourself.
>
> Bill Dauer is an old friend of mine and he can see you tomorrow. He lives in Lodi, and will meet you for lunch at his club. I've shared your situation with him. He knows a lot of people and may be able to help you with some contacts.

I ordered room service, watched a TV movie, and called home to check in. There was no answer, so I left a brief message on the machine before going to sleep. Charlie was help-

ing me create a support group. I'd have to introduce him to
Frank, the man I'd just met. They'd get along well and he'd
keep Charlie laughing. Charlie tended to be a bit serious, but
boy did he have empathy for my situation. Now, it was up to
me to take advantage of his connections.

Chapter 3

Focus and Drive

I drove over to Lodi and met Bill Dauer at Woodbridge Country Club. He listened as I described my situation, then said, "You've just experienced a _defining event_ in your life. You're lucky it happened at a young age when you are in good health and have marketable skills. I guess Charlie wanted me to be the first person you see, because I spent most of my life in Chamber of Commerce work where I met and did business with hundreds of different types of people each year. I also made many good friends over the years, including our mutual friend Charlie. So, I'll help you out, because of that friendship…and, who knows, we may become friends too. Let me tell you about _my defining event_ and how it shaped my life.

"During my first job with a Chamber of Commerce, the President of the largest bank in our small town telephoned and proceeded to unfairly criticize a friend of mine. I softly put the phone down on my desk, walked out the back door of my office, went across the street, around the corner, and entered the bank. I went past the receptionist guarding the President's door, opened the door and grabbed him. He was still shouting into the telephone, thinking there was someone listening to him at the other end. I shook him, told him to shut up and to never badmouth a friend of mine to me again. I then slammed him back into his chair, turned and walked out.

"I was in my office cleaning out my desk, thinking about the job offer I'd just turned down with an advertising agency, when my boss, a gruff, tough, old pro, came in to ask if I'd please join him in his office. There was a rather grim look on his face and I got prepared for the consequences of confronting a loudmouth, power-freak, bank President.

"However, when I walked into his office, the local Ford dealer and President of the Grand Island, Nebraska Chamber of Commerce, got up, stuck out his hand and said, 'Congratulations, someone finally told our banker friend that he has to stop talking about people that way.'

"Then my boss said, 'Bill, tell us your side of the story. We've gotten an earful from our banker.'

"After I described the intemperate language he used, our President said to my boss, 'You've got a great guy here. Don't let him get away.' At that point, I knew what it was like to have solid backup in a job and decided Chamber work was not all that bad!

"A little while later, returning from lunch, my boss told me, 'The Chamber board has offered to pay my initiation fee for a country club. Do you mind if we stop by and I fill out an application on the way back to the office?' I indicated that I had no pressing business that afternoon and had always wanted to see the country club that he was going to join.

"I walked around the clubhouse while he was busy with the manager, and then went out on the practice green and watched the members get ready to tee off. At my pay level, with my family responsibilities, there was no way I'd be able to enjoy this kind of life in the near future. However, I could dream, couldn't I?

"On the drive back to the office, my boss asked, 'Bill, would you like to join the club? I've asked the manager and he's indicated that there'd be no difficulty in getting you sponsors. I know we're not paying you enough to afford the full initiation fee and dues, but if you're willing, we'll split the cost of the initiation fee and monthly dues. You and I will each pay fifty percent and the Chamber will pay the balance. You'll need to start getting better acquainted with some of the country club members who belong to the Chamber, and this is a good way to do it.' I quickly accepted and when I told my friends about it later they all agreed that my boss was a very unselfish mentor and I was one lucky guy.

"This all occurred when I was twenty-five years old and for over five decades, in all of my business and personal relationships, I think about how my first boss treated me. Those two events, backing me up against a powerful person, and then unselfishly sharing a great corporate perk made him my lifetime role model. Many other mentors had an impact on my life, both before that event and afterward. However, he stands out as the single most important mentor in my life.

"By the way, the banker, after he got over the shock of having been put in his place, reassessed his attitude, then tried to recruit me for the bank. We eventually became friends. Therefore, I might have had some small influence in his life."

Bill then said, "I'll ask Charlie to introduce you to some of the other people he's interviewing for his new book. They're in different fields and can give you some perspective regarding their businesses. However, they can all give you a slant on how to transition to independence and how to build effective teams, no matter what executive or entrepreneur position you take. They're all *Leader/Mentors*."

When I asked Bill to describe a Leader/Mentor he laughed. "Let Charlie tell you about that. Everything I know about the subject is now on record."

He then got up, we shook hands, and he joined a threesome waiting on the first tee.

I called Charlie on my drive back to Half Moon Bay and thanked him. When I asked him to describe a *Leader/Mentor*, he said, "I'll e-mail you a short story on Bill. He's a world-class leader and mentor of many other leaders. I'm glad you could meet him personally. Incidentally, try to think of yourself as a b*uyer*, not a *seller*. You want to buy an opportunity, not sell yourself. There is a subtle difference when you are talking to people. Don't be too hungry. There are thousands of opportunities in the Bay Area and *very* few people with your natural gifts. Let's try to define what they are."

When I got to the room, I read Bill's story and was impressed by the way Bill reacted to a challenge. He had been very poor as a boy, but loved by his parents. I thought about the *material* things I did for Michael and Julie. However, they didn't get much of my time. Bill became tough because he had a lot of self-confidence. This was established, early on, when he had *no doubt* about how much his father and mother loved him. My life priorities had to change and I thought about Frank's suggestion that I drive a truck if necessary, as long as I could stay close to my kids.

Bill's list of qualities of a *Leader/Mentor* was on target. I'd never worked for a person who had all of them…I wondered if I could develop them? Being with him gave me an appetite for an opportunity. Bill's comment that he was hungry and could outrun his competitors was a compelling message. I liked the way he described the most important attribute for success: "Respect for other people and loyalty to those you work with."

He also said a person had to have *long-term focus* and *persistent drive*. I guess that was one of the secrets to his success.

I e-mailed Charlie and described our meeting. I also asked if he'd introduce me to the other people he interviewed for the new book. Charlie responded that he would tell me about his *Wise Men*, if I would help him with his book. After I had read their short stories and met some of the men—I'd already met the first—I was to give Charlie some feedback on my reactions to the *Wise Men*. I agreed, and Charlie said he'd contact Bodie Bodenheimer, who taught at Appalachia State, after leaving his position as President of the fourth largest bank in North Carolina and before buying his company.

He also wrote:

> You'll have to concentrate on acquiring new *knowledge,* no matter what opportunity you select. Bodie can give you some rather unique insights into how to do that.

Chapter 4

Knowledge and Lifelong Learning

Wednesday (second week)

I had a good night's sleep after my meeting with Bill Dauer and in the morning read his story again. What a motivator. Meeting him and reading about his life made me feel stronger because of the aura of strength he generated. He'd told me during our visit that he'd had open-heart surgery and cancer of the prostate. It didn't seem to faze him. He was just grateful the operation was a success and that the treatment for cancer was over—that *it* had been killed, not him! His problems made me realize how minor mine were.

I got an e-mail from Charlie about Bodie Bodenheimer. He said that Bodie was a very successful Leader/Mentor, who had been successful in business, rising to President of a large bank, and in the military, retiring from the North Carolina National Guard as a Brigadier General. Now he was a CEO in a totally different business. In his e-mail, Charlie said:

> A major secret to Bodie's success is that he is a lifelong learner. He's curious and interested in almost everything. Another great southerner, Thomas Jefferson, said, "Genius is ninety percent interest."

One of Bodie's *defining events* occurred when his physics teacher told him he was going to fail unless he had a learning breakthrough. Bodie made physics one of his best classes and said it taught him to *believe in laws and examine results.* Ken, if you're unhappy, go and learn something—you can't be taking in new knowledge and be unhappy at the same time.

What great advice. I was really looking forward to learning about how Bodie had met his challenges.

A few minutes later, I got a call from Pat that brought me back to the cold, hard reality that I hadn't spent enough time with Michael.

"Ken, come home now. Michael is in deep trouble. He stole a stereo unit from our neighbor's car. I don't know him well, but he's the Assistant District Attorney of Marin County, so I can't imagine a worse situation. I've got to call him and hope the return of the stereo by Michael and an apology, will be enough. His friends say our neighbor is really tough, so *you'd* better go see him first."

I told Pat I'd be home in a few hours, then, during the drive back, tried to decide how to teach Michael a real lesson. I wanted him to face the music so he wouldn't steal again. Lots of his friends had been in trouble with petty theft. I didn't want Michael to think it was *cool* to show his friends how brave he was by this kind of act.

When I arrived, I took Michael out for a walk and asked how he'd stolen the stereo unit and why he did such a stupid thing.

"I climbed out of my bedroom window last night, went across the street and opened a car door, then slipped the stereo out. It was easy, but I know it was wrong, so I'll never do it again."

He appeared serious, but I decided to let him put it back the same way he stole it, without directly confessing to our neighbor. I said, "Michael, tonight, after we're all in bed, you can climb out your window and replace the stereo."

"What if the car door is locked?"

"Then you've really got trouble. I don't think you know how to jimmy a lock—do you?"

"No—and I really don't want to learn while I'm in front of our neighbor's house."

I insisted he take his medicine and returned to my motel where I had an e-mail with Bodie's story and a cover note from Charlie:

> Contact Bodie later, after you've decided what kind of career you want. He's very well connected in banking and other business circles. He was also one of our partners for a couple of years until he bought Zickgraf, one of our client companies.

After reading Bodie's story, I was really impressed with his self-discipline and the way he'd taken control of a failing business he knew nothing about, so I sent a note to Charlie:

> I really like Bodie's philosophy. He said, "One of the things absolutely necessary is making sure people feel good about themselves. I think all of us have to know we can do about anything that we want to do, even with just a normal kind of intelligence." A concept we hear a lot in these stories is you must have DRIVE! Another interesting quote: "I have always felt very

strongly that the most important thing that you have in your life, and in the life of a company, is a plan and the next most important thing is the implementation."

He says that discipline opens up all the opportunities. You need discipline in everything you do, and then you will do it right. Discipline is the beginning of all good things; until somebody starts worrying about something, nothing good happens. Discipline forces you to be concerned. Bodie says, "Discipline is the greatest direction in a person's life."

Another great quote is, "Don't run out of money and don't try to do it by yourself." He says you have to believe in yourself, you have to believe in God and you have to believe in your people.

Charlie, those are very profound thoughts, but how do I get backers if I find a business opportunity and am willing to learn how to make the business more profitable?

Charlie replied:

There's a lot of investment money available for the right person who has found the right opportunity. First, you'll have to find the opportunity. Then, you'll have to make your case with the investment groups we can introduce to you. Your *attitude* will be the most important factor in getting people to invest in you.

I'll put you in touch with Joe Dacey. He's another self-made man who has overcome many obstacles to become one of the most respected men in Hawaii.

Chapter 5

Attitude Determines Altitude

Thursday (Second Week)

I slept fitfully thinking about Michael. What if he'd been caught? Where had I gone wrong in raising him? Lots of questions without answers. I knew that Michael and Julie had to be higher priorities than they had been.

The phone rang as I was getting dressed. A very serious Michael told me how he'd been scared to death that he'd be caught _returning_ the stereo and then accused of _stealing_ it. He promised he'd _never_ do that kind of thing again. When I talked to Pat, she was relieved and so was I. Maybe we could find other common ground besides the kids and work through this difficult time. But now wasn't the time to talk. She'd hung up so I returned to my studies of the _Wise Men_.

Dauer _and_ Bodie were both self-made men, born in small towns with parents of modest means, and both had very strong positive mental attitudes. Even though I'd spent only two hours with Dauer, after reading his biography, I felt that I'd known him for years.

I'd never met or talked with Bodie, but his bio made me feel that I almost knew him. These men were high achievers, but were modest about what they'd done. I'd met very few people in big corporations like them. I guess it's because of the corporate culture in my company and other companies I'd dealt with: promotion, prestige, a bigger office, and more expensive car. Those reporting to you butter you up; those to whom you report leave you wondering about how *they* feel about you. Some play you off against others trying to get promoted. I was glad to be out of that kind of rat race.

Now I was attracted to a career with a smaller company, like Bodie's Zickgraf Industries. But I couldn't finance myself as Bodie did. So, how do I convince others to back me? How do I develop the kind of positive attitude Charlie said is so vital? If I find the right opportunity, how do I come up with an investment so others will also be interested in investing? I'd have to sell the house. How would Pat react to that?

Pat called to tell me she and Ingrid had spoken. Ingrid assured her that she and I were not having an affair. Pat told Ingrid that she wasn't either—the two fellows at the bar in Carmel were just nice guys having a good time. Myrna and Pat had left the bar alone! Pat's voice was still chilly and distant and I responded with short clipped questions about the kids. When I hung up, I was relieved that Pat hadn't been out for a one-night stand, but angry that the possibility had come up at all.

As I was stewing about the phone call, I got an e-mail from Charlie:

> I'll try to share my philosophy with you on *attitude*, which is your next challenge. (Perfect timing, I thought.)

> First, our emotional state determines our reaction to every situation. If you're a *hot reactor*, you're impatient, too competitive and hostile to what you don't fully understand. If you don't curb this hostility, some

experts in the field feel that type of thinking can attack your immune system resulting in ulcers, hypertension, even cancer and other serious health problems.

At the other extreme, a *cold reactor* feels inadequate, defeated and becomes too passive. These same experts believe this type of thinking also weakens the immune system and results in diabetes, rheumatoid arthritis and other types of illness. So, your attitude is just about the most important factor in maintaining good health *and* in achieving financial success, while enjoying *happiness*. Don't even think about a career that isn't fun for you. It's all a matter of selection, with *you* doing the selecting.

One of my good friends recently sold his very large home and bought a smaller one to assure he had the reserves to make the right career decision, after the family that owned his company decided to downsize and become an investment company. He's now repotted and is CEO of another fine company. He had the resources to make the *right* career decision. You should be prepared to do *anything* to buy you time to make the right career change.

Henry Ford is quoted as saying: "Failure is not failure but the opportunity to begin again—more intelligently."

Joe Dacey's short story was attached. Charlie indicated he had briefed Joe on my situation, and Joe was waiting for my call.

I made a lot of notes as I read a most interesting story about how *love*, or a sense of *aloha*, had built a company and, from what Charlie said, a very large circle of people who not only respected this man, but actually had loved him. I'd never met anyone like that, so I was a little excited when I called to talk to him.

"Mr. Dacey, I can only say that your life story was really inspiring. Did you actually help support your family at age twelve?"

"Yes, but that was not unusual in those days. Families pulled together. It made me feel good about myself that I could help out. It also gave me an appreciation of money. When you have to earn it, you're careful how you spend or save it. But that's enough about me. Tell me about you. Where were you born? Tell me about your early life."

I started to talk and Joe listened very carefully, merely saying, "I see," or chuckling if I said something humorous. I was really starting to relax. In telling my story to Joe, I understood what Charlie had told me about *active listening*—Joe was one great listener. No wonder he was so popular!

After about an hour, I said, "You've been great to take this much time with me."

"Ken, if I hadn't had many fine people listen to me all of my life, I wouldn't have had the great life I enjoy now. But tell me about your marriage. Can you salvage it? I had to go through a divorce many years ago. Since I had small children, I decided to stay single so I could devote more time to them. They turned out very well and I have no regrets. I dated a lovely woman, who was raising her kids by herself. We eventually married and all our kids get along wonderfully. So, divorce isn't the worst thing in the world, but try to make your marriage work—it's a lot easier for all concerned."

He closed with an invitation for me to visit the islands. He knew a lot of people who could help in my search for a new career. I e-mailed my thanks for his time and sent a copy to Charlie.

I also sent Charlie a summary of my review of Joe's story and added:

> Joe believes that you must be focused on what you want to do, and have a certain amount of persistence in doing it. Without focus, you're not going to be effective. Joe also said, "Whenever you deal with your customers, if you are not honest with them, you're going to lose business." He also noted that honesty is a good pattern for your life; always try to do the right thing. He made the statement, "Money is not necessarily the objective...living your life properly is." Just like Bodie, he says, "No one person can do it all by themselves." Charlie, I'd really like to meet Joe. He has a contagious positive mental attitude.

Charlie responded:

> You should have a visit with Joe. Some personal time with him would be a real tonic for you. He has the Aloha Spirit in spades and, in Hawaii, you're a stranger there just once.

> Joe is also a *star* and helps everyone he knows try to become one. Joe and I attend the Hawaii Executives Conferences. Last year, the Worldwide Managing Director of Bain Consulting, Tom Tierney, addressed our group. I made a few notes and will pass them on to you.

> When you interview a company CEO, try to determine whether they have a *star* system in place. If they don't, go on to another company, as you'll just get frustrated with any other system. Bain Consulting

helps their client corporation develop this type of environment. Here are some of the *star concepts* Tom described:

• A relaxed CEO who stays rested, alert and focused will attract and retain *star quality* leadership who will, in turn, attract other talented people. These CEO's carefully select their stars, compensate them well, and then share ownership with them and *their* protégés. However, they demand high achievement and have a culture that assures there is no place for low performers to hide.

• Turmoil creates opportunities for stars who develop a thoughtful strategy. *Star builder* CEO's give their stars room to re-pot from time to time. The stars are treated like customers and they have lots of options. These CEO's see everything, overlook a great deal and correct a little. They have no time to be in a hurry. They believe that what you have in your gut is more important than what is in your brain.

• The *star builder* CEO is also results-oriented. Bain's first commandment is, "It's all academic unless you get results" and "what you measure, you get."

Ken, look for an organization of zealots in the right positions. The positive atmosphere this creates is contagious. However, zealots in the wrong position can be disastrous.

Try to determine the mission-critical roles in any organization you contemplate joining. Find out how many stars they've lost and why? It's important that all of a management team agree on the priority of problems to solve, so talk to several key people in a company before you make up your mind on an offer.

Tom described other Bain concepts:

• Don't be too concerned about organizational charts. They don't matter very much. It's not the boxes that count; it's the capability of the people who have the *responsibility* and *authority*. The stars should be in key positions. The forces of gravity will bind them together and increase their collective energy. If a *loser* is included with a *crusader* on a team, the company may lose stars.

• Most people will give up before they'll change— even when the status quo is life threatening. Many CEO's don't realize this concept and their companies fail because they don't have their stars in the right position.

He also described *Crusaders,* who feel they have a God-given mission to achieve high goals; *Cruisers,* who, unless they are mentored by Crusaders, will not attempt to achieve higher levels of performance; and *Losers* who tend to blame others for almost every problem that occurs. The management team that builds a company that can be perpetuated must recruit and retain *crusaders* and assure that each crusader assumes the responsibility to motivate a few *cruisers* to seek a higher altitude at which to cruise. These crusaders and motivated cruisers can help the CEO identify, early on, the *losers* who can destroy an organization. *Losers* in one organization might be able to adequately *cruise* in another firm where they might fit in better.

Tom closed his talk with a very profound statement, "Bain is always going out of business, reinventing themselves. A CEO is accountable for recruiting *stars,* who sell and service the accounts." Ken, look for that kind of CEO!

What wisdom! Tierney must be a *super star*! Charlie's overview of his talk just reinforced my conviction that I was going to do the selecting, not a prospective employer, and this thought gave me even more enthusiasm to get on with the process.

Later I got another e-mail from Charlie:

> We have focused on the importance of *knowledge* in selecting a new career. Your *attitude* appears to be improving and you are looking upon your situation as a *defining event*, rather than a problem. Now, you need to match your inherent *human relations* skills with the right opportunity.

> I'm going to put you in touch with Bob McKinnon, who has been a CEO or COO for the past twenty years and currently runs a very large company. Bob is a *people person*, like all of the other *Wise Men*. But, one of his strengths is in his great *networking* ability and *team building* expertise. He may be able to help you focus on the right field of endeavor. His story will also be inspiring and full of great concepts for you to learn *and* understand.

> Incidentally, the real secret to Joe Dacey's financial and personal success, in addition to his *positive mental attitude* and love for most people he meets, is that he is also a *lifelong learner*, like all of the eleven *Wise Men* I interviewed for my new book. At age seventy-six, Joe is still going to conferences, reading the latest books on a wide variety of subjects and talking to experts in every field. A visit with Joe always leaves me

energized. Take him up on his offer to visit him in the islands after things are squared away at home.

A few years ago, on a trip to Ireland in connection with a conference hosted by one of my good friends, we had dinner in a little Irish pub. A small sign above the table reminded me of Joe. It read:

> *We can make our minds so like still water that beings gather about us that they may see, it may be, their own images, and so live for a moment with a clearer, perhaps even with a fiercer life because of our quiet.*
>
> W. B. Yeats

I made a visit with Joe a priority!

Chapter 6

Human Relations Skills

<u>*Friday (second week)*</u>

I read myself to sleep last night by reviewing the printouts of all of Charlie's e-mails, rather than by watching TV. The stories of Dauer, Bodenheimer and Dacey were examples of how three men all became successful in life and in business by overcoming great obstacles that caused most people to fail. All started out poor but proud and had to work their way through school. All were lifelong learners, had very positive attitudes and great skill in dealing with people.

When I awoke, there was another e-mail from Charlie:

> You are at a crossroads, Ken. I've known many brilliant people, who are experienced, have great ideas and impeccable character. Their one and often fatal flaw in attaining their goals is with their temperament. Ken, you're as big as the things that bother you. Anyone can solve the problems of today. It's reliving the problems of yesterday, or anticipating the problems or promises of tomorrow that can bring the strongest person to their knees.
>
> What you are speaks so loud that most people don't hear what you say. Every action or interaction with

another person results in either a positive or negative impression on that person and others who hear about that action. "Actions speak louder than words."

It appears you may have lost the trust you had in your former boss. Trust is very difficult to build and, once broken, is very difficult to rebuild. Personal or business divorce is the result of many factors, but being temperamentally incompatible is one of the most common reasons. You should try to be patient with him, and with Pat. *You* may be partially responsible for the separation from your company, and Pat was, and is, financially insecure. Try to repair the relationship with both of them.

I'm sending you Bob McKinnon's short story, which illustrates his uncommon skill in *human relations*. I'll alert him to your call. He's a close friend and well connected with a big network in the furniture and textile business, so he can help you in that and related fields. You'll also find his life story motivating and instructive.

The story on McKinnon arrived a short time later and I read it with great interest. I realized I had a serious *human relations* issue to resolve.

McKinnon was successful because he listened to mentors. I thought about my early mentors: my Dad, Mother and a third grade teacher who really listened to me. Bob McKinnon now had a lot of *protégés*. You could tell that he really cared about people, another common denominator in the people I had read about and talked with.

I called him and got his secretary, who said he was expecting my call. He'd return it after lunch, which he did.

"Ken, Charlie tells me you're taking a little time out to look for an opportunity to take a new direction in your life. That's just great. Tell me about yourself."

His slow, distinct, southern manner was very calming and I found I could talk to him as if I'd always known him. He was a world-class business leader, but his manner was such that he could have been my next-door neighbor. How do you develop this style of communication?

As I told him how I was manipulated into resigning to reduce my severance pay, he laughed and said, "Well, you walked into that one. Bet you won't lose your temper so easily in the future when provoked.

"Hey Ken, business is a game—just like golf, which I love. Don't nurse a grudge, it only hurts you. They did you a favor. Look at the new friends you've made. Charlie has given me a run down on the people you've met, or read about, and I'll be looking forward to a visit when you decide what you're going to do. Just remember that the only thing in life that you can control is who you are. When you know that, you can select from among thousands of opportunities.

"However, don't limit yourself by trying to find your future in California…North Carolina, and the South in general, are great areas for an entrepreneur. In my own state, we have many company founders in their seventies and eighties who started their businesses after they got out of the army and graduated from college on the GI bill. Many of them have groomed successors, but many haven't.

"Bodie and I can put you in touch with bankers, who can introduce you to those who want to sell out, and Charlie has lots of venture capital connections. We have a strong work ethic in our state and an independent nature. Take our state flag, for example, a coiled rattlesnake with the motto 'Don't

tread on me.' We also have a free enterprise/worker mental-
ity in our state. Incidentally, has Charlie told you about his
longtime study of another independent thinker, Winston
Churchill?"

"No, he hasn't."

"Well, do yourself a favor and go pick up his biography.
Churchill overcame more obstacles than most people have
ever faced to become the most important leader of the twen-
tieth century. Incidentally, adopt some mentors—they are the
roots of our value system. Count on me to help out."

I told him about Charlie's questions and how I was trying to
answer them. He responded: "I was asked that question by
my most important mentor. My answer was 'I know how to
make money,' which got me the job. Try that!"

It was very obvious that one of Bob's secrets was his kind of
human relationship skills—he was a natural.

After my phone conversation with Bob, I sent an e-mail to
Charlie to thank him again and ask which Churchill biography he'd suggest. He responded by e-mail later that day:

> Martin Gilbert's latest biography is the best. Then,
> you'll want to read Churchill's *History of the English
> Speaking People*. You'll be interested in his succinct way
> of illustrating how our world has evolved over the
> past two thousand years. Incidentally, Bob McKinnon
> is reading that series and I've gone through it twice.

I decided I had to really focus on *understanding myself*. I also
liked the way Bob McKinnon talked about his ESOP partners. His Employee Stock Ownership Plan provided *broadened ownership*. I could get excited about being an
entrepreneur in a company where I had some ownership, so

that there was a reward for taking a risk by investing. I also decided to learn more about North Carolina!

Bob had the same kind of early background as Bill, Bodie, and Joe Dacey. I started to wonder if I was at a disadvantage because my Dad had made my early life so easy. I had gone from dependence upon him to dependence on my employer. "Well," I thought. "I'm still young enough to learn how to walk without the crutch of a steady paycheck and am now almost convinced I want to become an independent entrepreneur even if I have to take some interim job until I find a field of endeavor that is fun *and* rewarding."

At the end of the day I decided to drive back home Saturday and try to patch things up with Pat. I called and she agreed to have dinner with me. She still seemed cool, however.

Chapter 7

Habits for Superior Performance

Saturday (second week)

After a refreshing night's sleep, I awakened more positive about my future and ready to start thinking about repairing my relationship with Pat. Then, I needed to look for any kind of work so I could buy time to find an entrepreneurial opportunity.

Before I left for Marin County, I got another e-mail from Charlie:

> Can we meet for lunch in the city? I've tracked down Curt Ford and he's available. I've told Curt about your situation. He suggested we get together and chat. I'm enclosing his story. Can you look at it before lunch?

I did and reflected on some real nuggets from his oral history: "Intellectual stimulation requires re-potting from time to time"; "Invest time like money"; "Certain questions are best answered by other questions." What a great way to get to know someone! "Don't take yourself too seriously; look afar and see the end from the beginning because the bumps in the road smooth out as you look further down it."

Ford had a reporter's way of netting things out, an attorney's way of organizing his thoughts and a great human touch.

As I drove toward San Francisco for my luncheon, I thought about his *habit* of meeting every goal he set. That was Curt's secret. He also learned from everyone and adopted or adapted the qualities he admired in his mentors.

I could never be a CEO unless I had Curt's flexibility. Then, I thought about the qualities of the other *Wise Men* I'd read about. They were all very flexible in their thinking yet were very disciplined. So, I'd have to develop *habits for success.*

When we met for lunch, Curt asked me to describe my situation. I started to talk and they both listened.

After I had finished my story and described some of the people I had met through Charlie, Curt asked what I had learned so far from reading the short biographies of different people, with different backgrounds and in different fields. I responded that Charlie's emphasis on knowledge, attitude, human relations skills and sound work and study habits made sense.

Curt responded, "Ken, there is a price tag on everything. One price is when you do something. However, there is a higher price when you do nothing."

I mentioned that my neighbor, Dennis, had been a little critical of my preoccupation with myself. Charlie commented, "Dennis is a gifted coach and built a great organization of financial planners, just like Curt Ford. They both come out of the same General Agent school of selection and self-development of independent entrepreneurs. You can drop Dennis or Curt into any town in America with enough money to last for a week and within a month they'd be established and would have gained the trust of five or six people who want them to handle their financial affairs. They have each trained many people to be able to do that. You are lucky to have Dennis as a friend because he will always give you the straight scoop."

Curt laughed. "Things aren't as simple as they sound, Ken, sometimes they are even simpler! All you have to do is, with every encounter you have, know that whoever you are talking with is saying WIFM." When I asked what that meant, he said, "What's In It For Me."

Curt continued, "You are at a great crossroads where you can decide to take one path and become an executive with a large company, or take another path and eventually become independent of any one company by becoming a consultant, financial planner or owner of your own small business. There is plenty of backing for people with your background and experience. The sky is the limit if you are able to develop the kind of *plan* that works for you. Therefore, your next challenge is going to be in developing a feasible plan. Charlie will have some ideas for you on that, but I recently read something by A. E. Hotchner that applies to your situation:

> Of course we all have our limits, but how can you possibly find your boundaries unless you explore as far and as wide as you possibly can? I would rather fail in an attempt at something new and uncharted than safely succeed in a repeat of something I have done.

"I only have a tolerance for doing the same thing for a limited period of time," Curt continued, "and then I have to move on to something else. Some people call it getting repotted in a larger pot where our roots can grow a little deeper. I call it re-tired. My chassis has worn out several sets of tires in different careers and that keeps me stimulated.

"I'm taking courses at a Junior College that interest me, not to get a degree, I already have several of those. I'm doing it to learn something new so that I can stay happy.

"Also, don't be too worried about your relationship with your wife. I went through a divorce with my wife and best friend many years ago. That didn't change our relationship and we were still best friends, raised our kids together and celebrated anniversaries, but lived apart. She is now deceased, but my memories of her are warm and enriching. It's tough to stay under the same roof with someone with whom you are incompatible.

"You ought to have a good talk with Pat to see where she really wants to go. If she is not one hundred percent in your corner, she deserves the chance to go out and find someone else, or make her own way. You've protected her for some time, so maybe she does need a little breathing room."

Charlie said, "Ken, try to patch it up. There's nothing like a great marriage and your kids are young. Betty and I have four children and I'm just delighted that she puts up with me. So try hard to make it work.

"Also, there is another common denominator with all the people you've met, talked to and read about—they all care about other people. When you talk to them, it comes through. We are all mentors. I had something to do with the self-development of my associates and that is something that can never be taken away from me.

"I don't intend to lose the investments I've accumulated over the years, but if I did, I'd go out and try to make it back. But what I couldn't ever buy, inherit or steal is the respect some of my associates have for me because of what I was able to help them do for themselves. Curt has mentored a large number of people, which is what makes his life so full. In addition, he made money along the way, much of which has been deferred, to give him a lifetime income and to allow him to do whatever he wants to do when he wants to do it."

Charlie had to go to another meeting, so I drove Curt back to his beautiful home in Mill Valley—he had taken the ferry to the World Trade Club. During the drive Curt asked how long I had to find a new career and when I told him three or four months, he asked, "How long have you been making good money? By that I mean, more than enough to make the mortgage payment and feed your family?"

I responded that I had been making an above average income for over ten years and he said, "You've made well over one million dollars in that period of time, haven't you?" I indicated that I had, so he continued, "Are you happy with what you have set aside for emergencies like this?"

Before I could answer he responded, "Don't get defensive, because you are in the same boat as most other executives who depend upon a corporation for their future security. I have trained a lot of people to help their clients learn to live on eighty cents out of every dollar and put aside twenty cents for the future. If one of my associates had worked with you ten years ago, you could afford to take off a few years, get a law degree and practice law if that's what you wanted to do. Or you could get a degree in accounting and become a CPA, or buy an interest in a company, as you would have $300,000 to $400,000 in liquid reserves. Charlie calls it creating your own 'go to hell fund' and I agree with him.

"No banker has ever been able to dominate me; no employer has been able to do it; if I don't feel good about another person, I move away from them no matter who they are. That's true happiness and that's also *freedom of action*. Until you have independent financial security, you are going to be a slave to something or someone.

"Those fellows in the advertising agency that you talked about will build a great company. But I'll bet Dennis is talking to them about getting liquidity. He specializes in that field.

"Charlie's company has put in over a thousand employee stock ownership plans—ESOP's—over the past twenty-five years, but I remember when he had the same kind of organization that Dennis and I built. It was one of the biggest in the country for his company. Then he decided he was too dependent upon the financial institution that he represented, so he went independent. He's now developed client relationships with CEO's of companies all over America. You are now meeting or reading about some of these people.

"However, don't even think about entering the field of financial or investment planning until you have plenty of reserves. Someone who isn't successful in their own financial planning will have a difficult time helping others do it. Therefore, I'd suggest you find some kind of work that pays a steady income for a while so that you can maintain a good lifestyle for your family. Then take some courses on financial planning in school, if only to help yourself become independent. After you have some reserves, if you want to investigate my field, get back in touch with me and I'll introduce you to the person who took over my organization. They have a great training program, but they only contract with entrepreneurs who are independently self-sufficient."

I got home around 4:30 P.M. and told Pat that I was going to take a little nap before we went out. She didn't seem to mind that I took my bag into our bedroom and unpacked, so I guessed I was out of the doghouse.

I stretched out on the bed and tried to relax but kept pondering Curt's comments about my financial irresponsibility. If I had only saved half of what he suggested should be put aside, I'd be in a more comfortable situation. As it was, I needed to scramble to be sure I didn't go through everything I had spent my life trying to accumulate. Also, I had been pretty desperate before Charlie started introducing me to his friends. I now realized that I was better than I had given myself credit for. I must be or these people wouldn't be bothering with me—nor would Charlie.

I resolved that, no matter how much I made in the future, I'd set aside 20 percent of my income for a rainy day, and also eventually have the great lifestyle that Curt and Charlie had. They had paid the price, received a good education, and had positive attitudes. They were skilled in dealing with people and had very disciplined habits. Curt had also developed the habit of "doing it now." I'd only known him for one day and he had already had an impact on my life.

In the evening, Pat and I went to El Paseo in Mill Valley where one of the co-owners Mark gave us a table right by the front window—our favorite. He and Gunther had started out working for Ernie's in the city. Mark brought over two Kir Royals and made a big fuss over us, which these fellows always did. They made you feel as if you were the most important people in the world, which was a major reason for how they'd built a world-class restaurant.

We talked about the people I'd met and my plans to take any kind of job now to buy time until I found the right kind of career—where I would not be dependent upon any one boss in the future. She said she would try to get a part-time job and it was starting to feel like old times. I started to relax and, unfortunately, drank most of our bottle of wine, gulping instead of sipping. Pat was reasonably sober, but before we left, Mark sent over a couple of glasses of champagne, which we didn't need!

As we drove out of Mill Valley, Pat noticed that I was a little unsteady and suggested that she drive. As she was pulling out from the side of the road, she almost broadsided a car, which she had not seen coming up behind her in the dark. We stopped and were examining the slight damage we'd done to the other car when a Mill Valley police car pulled up behind us with the lights flashing. We were blocking the road. I started to explain to the officer that everything was all right, which was the worst thing that I could do. He asked me to relax; he wanted to take Pat through a little test. When I protested that Pat had just gotten behind the wheel and shouldn't be held accountable, he asked me to please be quiet. It was his duty to check her out.

Fortunately, Pat passed the sobriety test. However, I caught a lot of flack from her on my drinking habits.

Sunday Morning

I had a terrible hangover and Pat was still angry about her close call. I decided then to stop drinking altogether until I got my life back together. This pressure cooker that I was living in had caused me to drink too much and almost get Pat into serious trouble.

I got an e-mail from Charlie on Sunday afternoon:

> You've just spent time with a living legend in the life insurance business. Listen to him carefully when you ask for advice. He's a great coach for someone wanting to learn how to deal with people in any kind of sales field.

> If you decide to investigate the financial planning world, I'll put you in touch with my friends at the American College. Take plenty of time to prepare yourself—only the best succeed! You'll need good

cash reserves, must be a quick study and have well developed human relations skills. You might first consider becoming a manufacturer's representative in your own field. Then, when you're successful in selling a tangible product, you may be able to make the transition to the persuasive human relations skills needed to negotiate financial contracts that satisfy future *needs*, which you'll have to help a person *want* to satisfy, *today*!

Stay in touch with Dennis and Curt Ford—they've both been General Agents of successful agencies. Curt is retired and dedicated to giving away what he accumulated; Dennis has added a new dimension to an already sophisticated practice, investment banking for private companies, working with us.

A second e-mail from Charlie arrived later Sunday afternoon, which read:

One of the greatest planners I know, Thurston Twigg-Smith, agreed to an interview for the new book. I am attaching his short story/biography.

Chapter 8

Prior Planning For Performance

Pat told me, "You have to get a grip on your life, Ken. Your drinking almost sent me to jail!"

I quietly told her that I had quit drinking until I was settled in a new job or career. She looked at me thoughtfully and seriously as if weighing my statement, but she didn't reply. She just left for a walk.

At least I didn't have to worry about her taking the car and disappearing with Myrna! I supposed we both needed time to think. The kids were at a neighbor's playing and I took the opportunity to review the life of Thurston Twigg-Smith.

What a Renaissance man! A graduate engineer, who had a scholarship to Yale, worked in sales, business management and editorial departments before, as a dealmaker, he acquired control of the *Honolulu Advertiser*. Then, he built one of the largest private companies in Hawaii and shared ownership with his employees. What a *planner* and what *performance*.

Twigg was just considering retirement at age eighty-one! I had a long way to go to that age, but his was an inspirational story.

I called Dennis and found him home. He asked me over for a drink and I said I'd have a Coke. I went next door where he listened to my story of the previous night.

Laughing, he said, "That's the best thing that could have happened to you. Right now you should be focusing on your future, not partying. Pat's probably very upset with herself too and scared about what might have happened. Give her some time. *Show* her that you are the responsible man she married.

"Incidentally, I know Twigg. Talk about Jonathan Livingston Seagull! Man is he a motivator for me. I feel like I'm marking time in my career compared to what he's done. I like his motto: Be in business with people whom you trust, and who have fun at what they do. Try to visit with him if you go to Hawaii. It will be a rare treat.

"Planning is a state of mind, Ken. After you finish your Coke, you should sit down and write down everything that is significant that you've learned over the past week of soul searching. The solutions will start to become apparent as you write out the problems. Give me a call later, I've got to work on a project for a client this afternoon."

I spent a few hours collecting my thoughts and envied Dennis for being able to talk with a man who had done so much with his life. I called him later as he requested. He started the conversation by saying, "Washington Irving said, 'Great minds have purposes, others have wishes.' Where do you fit, Ken?"

"Somewhere in between. I'm no mental giant, but I'm not a dummy." I was a little irked by his question. Was he trying to put me down just because I was unemployed?

He sensed my mood and said, "Don't get defensive. I'm trying to help you put your situation into perspective so you can develop a long-term focus. You can't plan anything until you know where you are now and where you want to be. So, let's discuss where you are now. Did you ever answer Charlie's questions?"

"I'm starting to understand myself better, Dennis. Until I feel better about myself and can stand tall with my family and friends, it's hard to even think about the future."

"This is getting us nowhere fast, Ken. Do yourself a favor and stop thinking about how *others* take to you. Think about how *you* take to *them*! What if you had a net worth of one million dollars and had just resigned. Would you feel good and stand tall? Of course you would. You'd be financially independent.

"So, who knows what you're worth? And the people who matter don't care. Do you think Charlie's *Wise Men* are highly respected because they're rich? No way. They all happen to be affluent and serve as role models for those who want to become financially independent. But it's not their net worth that makes their lives fun and interesting. *They* are fun and interesting; they're also not preoccupied with themselves.

"There are a lot of people in our country who are worth one million or more. I'll send you an e-mail in awhile on the number of affluent people in our country. That should send two signals to you. First, you too can become affluent, if you plan to do it and then follow through. Second, even if you don't achieve some wealth, is everyone who is not wealthy in America considered a failure? Of course not! Educators, the military, gifted civil servants, doctors, nurses, social workers, skilled workers and many others find pleasure in their work, friends and family. Money is not the way to gain respect for yourself, or for others to respect you. *Caring about others* is the road to inner serenity and peace of mind.

"Go into the city and talk to a few homeless people. Then, come back and start to write down all the good things you've accomplished. Your *greatest* strengths will emerge, put it in writing."

I sat for a moment holding the telephone and letting his words sink in. Then he continued, "Ken, you're more relaxed now than you were a couple of weeks ago. That's great. We must rest our minds from time to time for the cream of our ideas to rise to the top. Charlie has been keeping me posted on your contacts with the *Wise Men*. Their stories are motivating, aren't they?"

"I'm motivated, but to do what? I know I have to have a plan, but how in the world do I formulate a plan. I have a lot of options, but not much time to examine them and now I'm having to deal with a very upset wife."

"Don't stay so busy chasing ants that the elephants get away. Pat doesn't want you to continue to mill around in a quandary about your future. Put everything into perspective. Talk straight to her! She deserves honesty, don't you think?"

After I hung up from a very serious conversation with a guy I'd considered happy-go-lucky, I reviewed his e-mail about wealth accumulation and printed it out. I then went in to the kitchen to talk with Pat.

"How would you define *perspective*?"

"Why are you playing word games? Go look it up!"

So I did and found it meant, "A view of *things* or *facts* in which they are in the right relations to one another."

I went back in to see Pat and said, "We need to discuss some *things* and some *facts*. I need help to put this situation into perspective. I don't have a job and we don't have a lot of money saved to continue our present lifestyle.

"Facts: If we sell our home and move to a community where we can stretch out our funds until I can find and get established in another job or business, we'll both be unhappy in the short run; but happy in the long run. If we use up our reserves too soon, and don't sell the house until then, there will be a forced sale and we'll lose most of our equity.

"A lot of people are helping me get my head clear so I can develop a plan. I have a good basic education and broad knowledge about business. I'm improving my attitude toward life in general, through all of the exposure I've had with a group of younger highly successful people as well as the oral histories of some very successful older people.

"I'm motivated to develop a good plan and then work it, because the people I've read about are all planners and have the habit of finishing what they start. I think I have the right stuff to eventually become financially independent. But you don't seem to believe in me, or, if you do, you're doing a good job of sending the opposite signal.

"I just got an e-mail from Dennis, who told me that most of my problems would go away, if I were rich! He said that next year over sixteen million households in America would earn over $100,000 annually and have a net worth excluding their residence of $500,000; that there would be 3.6 million people worth over one million dollars plus their home equity.

"We live in the most affluent county in our state; the second most affluent in America. It's not an easy place to live if you try to keep up with the Joneses. I have no job and you haven't worked in ten years because you've been raising our kids. We also have little in the way of savings."

Pat sat impassively trying to take all this information in.

"Now," I continued, "here are some *things* we have to talk about. When I get a focus on how we can resolve these *things*, I can face facts and we can make a decision.

"First Thing: I love you and the kids very much. I'm not going to take a job that will keep me away from you or them all the time.

"Second: Friends of my folks moved to a new town to start a new career. They still have all their old friends; their kids are successful; and they have the respect of their associates. Money is secondary to them now, but they still earn a good living. I'm ready to sacrifice high income now, for a long-term career like they have. Are you?"

Pat was very quiet. Then she got up and left the room. *Great communication*, I thought.

I decided to call Dennis again. I was really starting to depend upon him for counsel regarding my conflict with Pat. When I told him about Pat's reaction to my straight talk, he said, "Of course she's unhappy, her economic world just collapsed. Life as she knew it doesn't exist anymore. Look, she's had a tremendous shock. Pat's a good person, Ken, and I think she loves you. Eventually she'll come around. Just keep your eye on the ball. She'll think about what you said, and if you have to sell the house, she'll adapt.

"You can't solve all your problems at one time. Determine the most important and solve that one. Then the next one, and so on. You just have to prioritize your problems. You've accomplished one thing: Pat now knows how serious you are about looking at the facts. You have her attention.

"Ken, I read a lot of military history. I just read about a CIA agent who was in charge of things for America in Laos during the Vietnam War. Marlon Brando played the guy in the movie *Apocalypse Now*. This former CIA man is now in his late seventies and lives in the Bay Area and was interviewed by the *Wall Street Journal* last year.

"He once got the attention of villagers in Laos, who were flirting with Communism, by dropping human heads on their villages. Those villagers who were wavering, quickly lost their enthusiasm for Communism. He was reprimanded, but the message was clear. Consider that man's methods for attaining his goal when you consider how to persuade Pat to understand your situation."

We both laughed at his outrageous story. He could be very entertaining and was never uptight. So I asked him, "How do you stay so laid back? Nothing seems to faze you. Don't you ever get stressed?"

"Sure. That's why I take so many vacations and get away from my business. It drives Charlie nuts because he has to cover for me. But we're all independent; we eat what we kill. So, Charlie and my partners all cut each other lots of slack. We all pay our own expenses, have no salary and contribute part of our gross income to the partnership to keep operating.

"Don't even think of doing what I do until you've got plenty of reserves and have taken some specialized courses. You're a few years away from that. However, I envy no man in what

I do, Ken. Eventually, you should try to enter this kind of career. Talk to you soon."

I called Charlie and luckily caught him in. I described my conversations with Dennis and Pat. He said, "Don't jump to any conclusions about how long it takes to find the right niche. Creative thinking and stability come from a system that you can create all by yourself. That takes time. Also, try to stay objective about the synchronicity of your situation."

"Synchronicity? What's that?"

"It is a synchronization of events which were preordained and which results in behavioral change."

"My behavior has certainly changed and so has Pat's. Why was this preordained?"

"You made the decision to decline the transfer. You had to have some reason to bring things to a head—even if it was a sub-conscious thought.

"You and Pat are now facing a mini-crisis that can be solved easily. If your marriage can't survive this, how would it survive a more serious challenge? Best to find out while you're both young and can find another life partner, than to have it happen later in life. This situation is a blessing for you both!

"Get creative, Ken. This doesn't come from intelligence. It comes from the capacity to see what is already there.

"Why don't you consider a meeting in North Carolina with Grason Nickell. Now there is a piece of creative work, he always thinks outside the box. Use some of your airline miles and I'll put you up at Sedgefield Country Club in Greensboro."

I said I'd get back to him, then called my Dad to bring him up to speed and share the notes I'd taken after reading the life stories of five very experienced business leaders. "Dad, I have a lot of knowledge, but it's not very well organized to help me now. My undergraduate and graduate studies were so general in nature that I'd have to go back to school to refresh my knowledge of what I learned."

"Son, what you don't *use*, you lose. All college does is help you learn how to study problems. It doesn't give you wisdom. You've studied problems for over ten years to become an executive with your former company, don't sell yourself short. What you need to do is decide on the field you want to re-tire to. I like Ford's description of re-potting by changing career fields. Charlie Rowe has done that a few times in the almost forty years I've known him since he moved to Marin.

"After you know what you want to do, you can get specialized knowledge in that field. Your friend Dennis seems to be in school all the time. You should ask him why he continues to study. He joined Charlie in a new career a few years ago."

"I'm in frequent contact with Dennis, as it happens. Dad, would you and Mom want to come over tonight? It might help to have other people around."

"No, Son. You and Pat need to learn to communicate again. It will happen more quickly if there are fewer interruptions. We'll talk soon."

That night was a quiet night in our home. Even Michael and Julie sensed the distance and chose not to talk much at dinner except for the necessities like, "Pass the bread, please."

How do you re-learn communication skills?

Monday (third week)

The next morning, I met Dennis for coffee at his office. He started our conversation with: "Have you been to the San Francisco skid row area lately?"

When I responded that I hadn't, he said, "Well you can probably imagine how people end up down and out. They let their emotions cloud their judgment and don't face facts. Then, they give up and become beggars. Or they go a little crazy. Both types end up on the street. So, remember the expression: 'I cried because I had no shoes, until I met the man who had no feet.'"

I asked him about his continuing education program.

"Even before I joined Charlie's firm as a partner, I was in a field that required that I be able to deal with lawyers, accountants, bankers, CEO's, CFO's, plant managers, investment advisors and many others. I was paid in commissions on financial products for my advice and counsel. If I gave the wrong advice, I could be wiped out in a lawsuit. So, people in my game stay up to speed in a number of disciplines. We don't have to have advanced degrees in all the fields in which we're involved, but we have to know enough to communicate with those that do. We also have to speak their language, interpret their conclusions and, for our senior executive clients, the rationale.

"Charlie has the same background and academic credits as I do. However, twenty five years ago he created a business that incorporates what I do, plus a number of other disciplines, and we charge a fee for our consulting expertise. So, it's back to school for me, just as it was for Charlie, to be able to advise my clients on all the new issues we can help them resolve.

"In fact, Charlie helped Twigg *go public internally* with an ESOP and build his company through assisting them with acquisitions. Then he helped Twigg and his financial guru, Paul deVille, start to diversify the company by helping them sell the *Honolulu Advertiser*.

"I'm now involved in that kind of corporate financial consulting. The American College has courses I can take locally to get the formal knowledge. Working with Charlie and our other partners gives me experience. Put those together, *knowledge* and *experience*, and you eventually develop *good judgment* concerning the issues you study. Then, people retain you to be their business advisor."

I decided to go home and have another talk with Pat. I was starting to develop a tentative plan, in concept, now I had to put it in writing. But Pat's folks dropped by to take her and the kids over to their house. Her Dad was very frosty and asked if I had filed for unemployment. I told him to mind his own business.

In fact, I had no plans for doing that. I was thinking about becoming a consultant in my own field, so by the time I got my first unemployment check, I'd have income. I surprised myself and didn't get mad at Pat's father. He was reacting like almost any father faced with a daughter's potential marital break-up. Pat was evidently going to go her separate way. So be it. I resisted the urge to fix a martini and instead went for a long run. I picked up a TV dinner, stayed at the house and wrote out every task I had completed successfully for my company to try to answer Charlie's first question: "What are my strengths?"

Chapter 9

Organizing for Success

First thing in the morning, I called my former boss and he confirmed I did not have a non-compete agreement. He then called back to ask if I'd consider a contract to be a Manufacturer's Rep, as they'd pay a good commission on what I sold, but that I couldn't call on certain house accounts. I told him I'd think about it.

He had _competitors_ who would like those _house accounts_ and I knew the key people in those companies. It might be fun to try to take some business away from my former company!

Charlie's e-mail came in with the Grason Nickell story, which I read immediately.

Nick's experience in college and with the University of Virginia honor system was refreshing. Also, he had a good outlook on money. His company would do anything that was honorable and profitable—in that order. He was certainly short on greed which made me think about my goals. Did I want to get rich (a pipe dream at this point) or did I want a secure career that would provide a good income. I'd settle for that!

I wanted to meet this man, even though it would use up a few days of my time on my *own* meter. I was already starting to think like Dennis. I was only going to make money if I created the method for doing it. I was excited, and a little scared. Maybe Nick could steer me to some other East Coast companies I could represent. So, this was going to be a sales call. Great, I was starting to think like an entrepreneur!

Pat came home around noon and said she'd had her folks drop the kids off at school. I asked if she'd like to have lunch. She said she'd fix it, as we couldn't afford to go out. Since she seemed reconciled to a more modest lifestyle, I said, "I'm going to make arrangements to fly to North Carolina for a possible business opportunity while you're fixing lunch."

This cheered her up, which surprised me. She was open to a move!

After I arranged a red-eye flight for that night and reserved a rental car, I called Charlie. He said he'd already alerted Nick about the visit. I should call Nick's longtime assistant, Eloise, to make reservations for the apartment at Sedgefield Country Club. Eloise had a soft, gentle, ladylike southern accent and took care of all the arrangements. I was looking forward to meeting Nick and tried to learn more about his assistant during the phone call. She'd worked for Nick for many years and obviously had a great admiration for him. When I asked if she lived in Greensboro, she responded that she lived in Climax!

When I told Pat about this conversation over lunch, we both started laughing about a possible move to North Carolina where I'd become an independent sales agent, with my home office in "Climax, North Carolina," as Pat said it with a southern drawl. My mail would sure be opened! Thank God, Pat was getting her sense of humor back.

I took the airporter to San Francisco International and slept soundly on the flight to Charlotte. After a change of planes, I landed in Greensboro about 9:30 A.M. on Wednesday and was in Nick's office an hour later. He'd just arrived.

"How's that turkey, Charlie? My radar system normally alerts me to his visits, but he's staying home more now that he's slowing down."

Nick's big smile and the warmth he exuded put me at ease right away. He then spent about an hour talking about some of his and Charlie's adventures together. His stories were really funny. This guy could be a talk show comedian. Yet, he was an academic, engineer, super salesman and had built a fine private company.

I asked how many of his 700 plus employees he knew. He said, "All of them—and by name. Come on, I'll show you." He then started to wheel his chair out the door. I hadn't realized he was in a wheelchair when he was behind his desk. As we proceeded down the hallway, I asked if I could help him, but he said he was just fine scooting along. We got to the first office and he said, "Hi, Sporty." Then another, and he said, "How are you doing Lockheed?" He continued this for five or six offices until he called an engineer "Sporty" and the fellow said, "Mr. Nick, I'm Lockheed!" We laughed at his system of calling someone by one of two names. Nick could sense whether a person was on the carefree side (Sporty) or a bit more serious (Lockheed). What a personality!

Nick and his son David joined me for lunch at Sedgefield Country Club and got me settled in the cottage—The Cobweb Corner—as the apartment was taken.

Over lunch, David explained why he'd decided to give up a career in the ministry to join ACC and Nick described how he'd done a blind survey to find out who the top sixty of his colleagues (great term—much better than employees) would prefer to be their leader. They *elected* David. When I commented that the Viet Cong selected their leaders the same way, Nick got serious and said, "That was a war we should not have gotten into. A lot of good boys got killed or addicted. I'm just thankful my two boys didn't have to go." Then he said, "Look, I have to go home for my nap. So tell me how we can help you."

I described my goal of becoming a Manufacturer's Rep and David said he'd make a few calls for me while I was there. He invited me to use one of their vendor's offices that afternoon to set up meetings.

After Nick left, David told me more about Nick's organizational system. He had created *Teams* to meet every need that was within their ability to satisfy. He also told a story to describe his Dad's independent character. The Men's Grill bartender, Buford, was trying to tell an ACC customer why Nick was late for a meeting at the club. After this customer kept asking why Nick was late, Buford finally said, "Mr. Nick is gonna do what Mr. Nick is gonna do!" That said it all. Nick marched to his own drumbeat.

That afternoon I called several company executives and was invited to submit my resume and potential accounts. The fact that my return number was answered "AC Corporation" helped me establish immediate credibility. It made me think about the value of a company's—and a person's—reputation.

One executive, who played golf with Nick, said, "What else is that rascal going to do. First, air conditioning, then electrical, plumbing, fabrication, instrument panels, personal response systems for the elderly and disabled—now a Manufacturer's Rep Business?"

I assured him that AC was not in that business; Nick was just helping me as a favor to a mutual friend, Charlie Rowe.

He said, "What in hell does Charlie do? I always see him at the Blast. When I asked Nick what he does, Nick said he's in the protection racket. It that true?"

I responded that as far as I knew, Charlie was not involved in any scheme for protecting a business.

When I saw Nick that afternoon to report on my progress, he asked the name of the man who had asked about Charlie. When I told him, he laughed and said, "Good. I like to keep him guessing. Charlie is in the *financial* protection business. He helped us protect against bankers trying to take advantage of us by designing a program that creates investment reserves for our company. We've used these reserves to finance the repurchase of our stock and, when necessary, to get better interest rates on our bank loans because of our access to low interest loans on our corporate life insurance cash values. The insurance company has also paid a few claims over the past twenty-five years when a key person died.

"Our bank wanted us to assign our cash values some time ago and we refused. Charlie calls what we created a 'go to hell fund.' He used his own personal investment reserves to finance his company when he founded it. I didn't tell our banker to go to hell; he's a nice guy. I did say, 'Fooling with our cash values is like fooling around with my wife!' He got the point. If he hadn't, we'd have just used our reserves as an interim loan while we got a new banker. So, that's the kind of protection Charlie provides. We're protected from dependence upon a bank and from having to borrow money at high interest rates to buy our shares back from our employees when they die or retire."

Nick looked at me for a moment, then said, "Ken, you're at a defining event in your life. We all have them. You'll remember this experience the rest of your life. I went through the same kind of agony over fifty years ago. Thank the Lord I had a good wife who helped out and encouraged me, and a man who gave me the chance to eventually own a good piece of this company. Now we have a lot of partners and our employees share ownership through the ESOP Charlie and his former partner installed.

"I was so impressed with what Charlie and his partner did for us that I contributed a son to their business. He invested and, when Charlie sold his interest in that company to build his present company, Nicky and Charlie's partner went with the person who bought Charlie out. Nicky and his partner bought out that man and Nicky is now CEO of a very large investment-banking firm. So, I owe Charlie a favor. How can we help *you*?

"Charlie says you may want to be a Manufacturer's Rep and David has introduced you to some companies. How much research have you done on what it takes to do this?"

When I told him I hadn't done anything yet, but that I had potential customers, all I had to do was get suppliers, Nick said, "You'll have to show a supplier that you have the capital to stay in business. They'll also look at your track record, which you don't have as a Rep yet. Why don't you go to a Rep firm and try to join them? They may even advance you money. You have great credentials. Also, they can advance travel expenses and *their* track record will help get you sales."

Nick had given me the answer to my problem. I'd been a little worried about just going it alone, with no one to show me the ropes.

"I'll give you a list of the Rep firms that call on us," Nick continued. "If you really want to do that kind of work, you can call for an interview. However, Charlie just gave you *one idea*. He has dozens every day. Some are good, others aren't. I once told him to write down all his ideas as he thinks of them. Then, in a few days, consider which had merit and which didn't.

"Why don't you create a *plan* to be a Rep, working for a firm? They may want you to be officed with them, which would require a move. Will your wife and kids be happy with that? Also, you've been a senior executive for some time. A Rep has to schmooze people. Can you do that every day, and still make the calls and close the sales? It's a job requiring a real desire to deal with a lot of different people and many transactions.

"Write down all of the factors you want to consider in a new career. Then the plus and minuses for each factor. Do this *today*. Then, look at it tomorrow and see if you agree with your original thoughts. Look at it the next day and continue this process until you have a balance of positive and negatives about the field you're considering and can make a decision.

"To learn about the field, interview people in it—the Sales Reps themselves. To plan anything, you have to organize your thoughts and resources. Then, you can make the right kind of plan. But don't do anything you won't find very fulfilling. Live with the truth, don't kid yourself."

I left Nick and returned to Sedgefield. David had dinner with me and we became better acquainted. You could see why all the key people *elected* him as their leader. He was smart and really cared for people.

I'd known a lot of smart people who were self-centered and cared only about what *they* wanted to do. If I could talk Pat into moving to Greensboro, I'd apply for a job with ACC.

I was impressed by Nick's relationship with his wife. I commented to David how tough Pat was being on me. She only seemed concerned about the house and maintaining our lifestyle.

David then reminded me, "Isn't that what you wanted? Didn't you want her at home taking care of the kids and running the household?"

"Well, yes, but ——"

David challenged me, "Wait a minute, you and Pat are in a partnership. You focused on your career and she focused on your home and family. You divided the labor. Has she held up her end of the bargain? Did she sacrifice some of her dreams and goals?"

I thought of our wonderful children and the beautiful home that Pat had put together. "Yes, she has. And she has been a rock for our family."

David then told me the story about a retirement party at the company. One of the company's long-term employees was retiring after forty-two years of service. The employee's wife was present and David told me how he was able to thank the wife for staying home all these years so that her husband could be of such valuable service to the company. David told her that the spouses of the men and women who worked and traveled for the company were equally valuable and were considered part of the team.

I knew I needed to really work on my relationship with Pat.

When I told David about my comfort with him, Nick and their company culture, he smiled and said, "You'd have to get an engineering degree or be skilled at the technical work we do to work here. Even though Nick talks about universities polluting minds, he's just kidding. You'd have to go through an apprenticeship program and adjust the way you live. Let's try to help you make a lateral move to maintain your lifestyle. I'll give you my brother's phone number. His company owns an interest in a lot of companies.

"Either Nicky or his partner, Joe Schuchert, can introduce you to CEO's of some of their portfolio companies. But you should negotiate a contract with any new employer or partner to assure you don't have another surprise like the one you just had. Incidentally, Nicky's company makes investments in companies that allow you the opportunity to participate in ownership."

After dinner I returned to the cottage. Organizing my thoughts about the future became my priority. I needed to figure out what I wanted in a career, but I wanted to make my marriage work too. I thought back to when Pat and I had first met. Yes, she had been physically attractive—and still was, but her gentle spirit and dry sense of humor had captured my heart. We had laughed all the time when we dated—and after we first married. We were friends—best friends—and I suddenly realized that I missed that camaraderie. I missed the one-word jokes and the looks we shared just before bursting into laughter. I missed the easy way we used to talk, without anger, frustration and unspoken grievances. I truly wanted to find our way back to the relationship we had once had. Or, to a better one!

I called home, but got the machine. I said, "I'll be home tomorrow." I hesitated a moment before hanging up the phone; I longed for a connection with my family, with Pat. Later, much later, I finally drifted off to sleep.

Chapter 10

Action-Oriented Leadership

In the morning I had an e-mail from Charlie:

> My short stories are just a thumbnail sketch of the life of each of the very gifted men interviewed by members of my Editorial Advisory Board and me. I'll send you a copy of the transcripts of their oral history interviews in a few days.

> In the succinct description of Nick, you'll find the attributes he wants in a new colleague. He is a humanitarian, technically competent, progressive with a desire to keep learning, and healthy (preferably a non-smoker since his company invests a lot of money in training their people, they want to be assured of a good return on that investment). Also, Nick's *secret* is that in addition to all his other attributes, he knows how to organize all of the resources necessary to implement a carefully designed plan. Planning, without organization, is just dreaming.

> One of Nick's heroes, Arnold Palmer once said, "Focus not on the commotion around you, but on the opportunity ahead of you."

Nick's parents were a major influence in his life. I recently read an article about this kind of parental influence:

> Parents' leadership is central to the legacy and inner work of leaders. When asked to consider his past as the prologue for his optimistic framework, Time Inc. president, Bruce Hallett's response was, "I'd have to use my mother," he says, describing a childhood event when he cut off two of his fingertips in his mother's meat grinder.

> "My mother was using a meat grinder to cut up a leftover roast. I asked if I could help. She handed me a wooden spoon, and I remember thinking 'Why do I need a spoon if Mom's not using one?'" he says. "The minute she turned her back, I stuck a piece of roast into the grinder and sliced off the tops of two of my fingers.

> "After the accident, I was hospitalized for several weeks. Here, my mother showed me a model for framing the event. Instead of talking about the details of the accident, she insisted on an optimistic interpretation. There was no *poor Bruce*. Instead, she offered the idea that I had done some good...the accident was not a tragedy or a setback. Throughout my life she told me, 'If you strike out, you will get a hit next time.' She taught, modeled and lived in a resilient way."

Focus on your family for awhile, Ken. They should become a priority for you. Your career will take care of itself in time. Your wife and kids need attention now.

I drove to the airport and took an early flight back to San Francisco. While on the plane I started my tentative plan to be a Manufacturer's Rep, but Nick's comments about having to become a salesman, who is *happy* to be one, made me pause. This job would be an interim step for me, so I made some notes of my thoughts and decided I'd defer my plan to become a salesman. Instead, I'd continue my search. Some people were going to open doors for me. But would those doors be in the Bay Area? I really didn't want to take the kids out of their school and we had friends and family there. Charlie's advice was sound. I had to focus on my family!

So, in writing the Bay Area location down as a major decision factor, I had started to *organize* my thinking and was starting my career *plan*. I felt a little better now that I had made *one* major decision. Everything else would have to fit with that requirement.

When I got back to the house, I had another e-mail from Charlie:

> You're in the process of developing a plan. Nick's organized approach will help you determine the factors you want to include in your plan to find the right career. One of my longtime friends, Bob Midkiff, found himself in the same position as you, at about your age. His *action-oriented* style will be a good example for you so I'm sending you his short story. This will give you an idea about how to go about creating your own company, should you find the right opportunity in the future.
>
> In the meantime, remember my first idea. Having interviews with a number of people in different fields will help you select the one in which you can excel.

I thought Bob's story was fascinating and his decision to make *location* the prime factor in career selection gave me the comfort that I was on the right track.

Pat had come in from a walk and I gave her Bob's story, hoping it would motivate her to want to help out until I landed something. Del had worked until Nick got established. Evanita had sold encyclopedias, then real estate to help Bob. I'd let the short story plant the seed. I didn't want an argument now.

I called Charlie to ask whether Bob might be available for a phone conversation and got his voicemail. So I called information in Honolulu and got Bob's phone number. He answered on the first ring and I told him I was a friend of Charlie Rowe. He said, "Good Man. How can I help you?"

"I've just read your story—Charlie sent it. I have a few questions."

"Charlie's a good friend whom I've known for years. I was wondering what was happening to his new book. He interviewed me two years ago."

"Mr. Midkiff, I—"

He interrupted, "Call me Bob."

"Bob, I'm trying to decide what to do in selecting a new career." Then I told him what had happened to me. I explained how Charlie was helping me by introducing me to some of his friends for possible guidance in selecting the right kind of career position.

"Ken, I'd like to help, but I don't know you. How can I help you if I don't know your background, achievements and greatest strengths?"

He was right. My call was very presumptuous. He was a no nonsense guy. Yet, he had such a marvelous life story. So, I decided to continue to press him for some clues to a direction I could take.

"I talked with Joe Dacey last week. You were mentioned in the story on Joe that Charlie sent me."

"I'll call Joe or Charlie and ring you back, Ken. One of them can fill me in and give me a few hints. Goodbye."

Wow. This was a very organized man who didn't waste time. I read his story again and realized that he couldn't have done so much with his life if he didn't net things out.

I went out for a run to break the tension. When I returned, Pat told me Charlie had called. I rang him back.

"Ken, I'm glad you're taking the initiative. Bob Midkiff just called to ask me to brief him. He agrees with me that you've got to focus on answering those ten questions so that people who are interested in you can help. Bob said he'd be available for another call at 7:00 P.M. your time tonight. However, he wants to see the answers to the questions I sent you first. So you only have a few hours. Can you do it?"

I said I'd have to. I wanted to talk to Midkiff again. Now I knew what dealing with a general or admiral was like. They didn't suffer fools or those who weren't prepared.

I spent some time on a skeleton outline of my answers to the questions and e-mailed them to Charlie. He forwarded them to Bob and I received a call from Bob an hour later, before the time I was to call him.

"Ken, you have a marvelous background and your company dealt with you in a very shabby way. Would you like to come to Hawaii and meet some friends of mine who are always looking for CEO candidates? We've had a brain drain of our brightest and best young people for years, as we're not an industrial state. Many of our gifted high school graduates go to the mainland for college, and there, mainland companies recruit them. So, Go West young man—lots of opportunities here."

I said I'd consider that, but could I ask him a few questions now. He responded, "I called you early because I've been informed we're due at a reception soon. I have ten minutes. Will that do, or should we talk tomorrow?"

"Ten minutes now would be great. My first question: Who is the most influential person in your life? What did you learn from him or her?"

"The most influential person in my life was my father, Frank E. Midkiff. He was a true gentleman, an educator, an innovator, a facilitator and a visionary. I learned from him that I could accomplish anything that I devoted myself to."

"What was your most difficult decision in life and in business?"

"The most difficult decision was to sell my company, American Financial Services of Hawaii. When my selection for successor developed breast cancer, I had to face the fact of mortality, both hers and mine."

"Who are your other mentors? What did they teach you?"

"I had a number of mentors. At Yale, it was Harry Rudin, a scholar of German colonial history, who opened my eyes to the impact of nineteenth century colonialism on the world and the amazing fact that Hawaii stayed independent so long.

"After World War II, I received profound advice from Gen. Claude Herron, who explained the three great decisions in a man's life: one) You can choose your wife, but she will have a great deal to say about that; two) You can choose your church, but your wife will have a great deal to say about that; but three) *You* can decide where you will live. Therefore, I decided to return to Hawaii and get established in paradise."

"Tell me about business disasters, things that didn't work." I was enthralled with our conversation.

"In business there are always a number of disasters. Innovation does not always lead to success. The key is to control the losses and get on with your business and your life."

"You appear to be a risk-taker? Do you think most people in business take as many risks today?"

"I have always been a risk-taker, but I have tried to never get into a fight that I couldn't win. Successful risk-takers need to partner with some bean-counter types to temper their judgment."

"Was it hard for you to give up the reins when you left?"

"Once the decision to sell the company had been made, I never looked back. We sold for cash and I no longer have any involvement. Retirement has been a great opportunity to give back to the community."

"Are you optimistic about the future of Hawaii? What is your vision for Hawaii?"

"As long as the trade winds, the ocean and the drinking water remain unpolluted, the future of Hawaii is boundless. The biggest dark cloud is the revival of racism growing out of the Hawaiian sovereignty movement."

"What advice would you give to someone starting a business today?"

"My advice to anyone starting a business is a saying I learned from Henry J. Kaiser: 'Find a niche and fill it.' You'll have to work long hours, have a lot of wit and wisdom, then success will be yours."

"What would you like to leave as your legacy? What is your most rewarding accomplishment?"

"I would hope to be remembered for three things: At least 30,000 employees of Hawaiian companies got their start toward financial independence through a profit-sharing plan that I encouraged the owners to fund. I served as the catalyst for the Downtown Improvement Association, which led to the design and construction of the Hawaii State Capital, the Financial Plaza of the Pacific, and the restoration of the Hawaii Theatre Center. The needs of my 200 female employees led to my passion for early childhood education and care and the establishment by the Hawaii State Legislature of the Good Beginnings Alliance."

Bob then said, "You'd make a good reporter. My friend Twigg could probably get you an interview with Gannett."

"I read Twigg's story. He's an impressive man. But I doubt that I'm qualified to interview anyone...I just wanted to fill in some blanks, after reading about your life from the perspective of people who know you."

Bob replied, "I've got to go, but I'll e-mail you a story you may want to use in your career search. You'll find a lot of people who are busy will make it difficult for you to get an audience with them. If you have difficulty getting an appointment, e-mail them what I'm sending you. It may open their minds."

About fifteen minutes later, the following message came from him:

> A lady in a faded gingham dress and her hus-
> band dressed in a homespun threadbare suit
> stepped off the train in Boston and walked
> timidly without an appointment into the
> Harvard University president's outer office.
> The secretary could tell in a moment that such
> back woods country hicks had no business at
> Harvard and probably didn't even deserve to
> be in Cambridge. She frowned. "We want to see
> the president," the man said softly.
>
> "He'll be busy all day," the secretary snapped.
>
> "We'll wait," the lady replied.
>
> For hours, the secretary ignored them, hoping
> that the couple would finally become discour-
> aged and go away. They didn't, and the secre-
> tary grew frustrated and finally decided to
> disturb the president, even though it was a
> chore she always regretted.
>
> "Maybe if they just see you for a few minutes
> they'll leave," she told him. He sighed in exas-
> peration and nodded. Someone of his impor-
> tance obviously didn't have the time to spend
> with them, but he detested gingham dresses
> and homespun suits cluttering up his outer
> office.
>
> The president, stern-faced with dignity, strut-
> ted toward the couple. The lady told him, "We
> had a son who attended Harvard for one year.
> He loved Harvard. He was happy here. But

about a year ago, he was accidentally killed and my husband and I would like to erect a memorial to him, somewhere on campus."

The president wasn't touched; he was shocked. "Madam," he said gruffly, "we can't put up a statue for every person who attended Harvard and died. If we did, this place would look like a cemetery."

"Oh, no," the lady explained quickly. "We don't want to erect a statue. We thought we would like to give a building to Harvard."

The president rolled his eyes. He glanced at the gingham dress and homespun suit, then exclaimed, "A building! Do you have any earthly idea how much a building costs? We have over seven and a half million dollars in the physical plant at Harvard."

For a moment the lady was silent. The president was pleased. He could get rid of them now. And the lady turned to her husband and said quietly, "Is that all it costs to start a university? Why don't we just start our own?"

Her husband nodded. The president's face wilted in confusion and bewilderment. Mr. and Mrs. Leland Stanford walked away, traveling to Palo Alto, California, where they established the university that bears their name, a memorial to a son that Harvard no longer cared about.

> You can easily judge the character of others by how they treat those who do nothing for them or to them.

Ken, Malcolm Forbes wrote the above. If I were you, I'd add a note to your e-mail request for a visit to discuss employment and indicate you may be able to make an important contribution to their company; if you're with them more than five minutes, it will be only if they insist. If you have trouble getting an interview, forward my e-mail on the Stanford story. If that doesn't open a CEO's mind, then go on to the next prospect. Good luck and go find out what great opportunities there are for you—and don't forget to include Hawaii!

Bob had sent a copy of the Leland Stanford story to Charlie, and Charlie called a while later. When I told him about my conversation with Bob and that *he* had called me, he chuckled and said, "He's trying to recruit you to help improve the business climate in his own state. They need business leaders."

"Charlie, you've given me all sorts of hints on what makes a good Leader/Mentor. Can you define the term for me? I only have about five minutes to demonstrate that I have these qualities when I first meet the CEO's, providing they set up appointments with me after reading my e-mail."

"Ken, we know it when we see it, but its hard to define and very difficult to bring it into any organization. CEO's know that success is not due to any strategy and that many plans will have to change and probably will. It's about leadership *and* mentoring. Someone has to make a decision that is fully accepted by others due to a trust relationship. In other words, 'Let's cross the river, I'll go first.' Lead by example."

If Charlie couldn't articulate a clear description about the essence of *leadership/mentoring*, maybe it, like charisma, came in different flavors. When I said as much to Charlie, he agreed. He went on to say, "I've been sending you information by e-mail. However, this is a filtered type of communication. You can't communicate trust, spirit and energy through the Internet. Don't make it a crutch. Establish a personal bond with people. Face to face is best. Telephone is a distant second and only works if you have established the bond. You have to *meet* and bond with anyone who could be important to you.

"A fellow once told me: 'Putting off an *easy* thing makes it hard and putting off a *hard* one makes it impossible.'"

I thanked Charlie for his help and prepared my list of phone calls for the next day.

I reflected that I'd put off answering Charlie's questions until Bob Midkiff made it mandatory that I do it, or he wouldn't help! In answering the questions I started to realize that I was a very valuable person for any organization to have as an associate. It made me feel much better about myself.

Vince Lombardi once said, "You must create a winning culture." I had to interview company CEO's to see if they had that kind of culture. And I was going to interview them, not vice-versa.

Bob McKinnon had said, "Show me a good loser and I'll show you a loser." Well, I wasn't a loser, but I had to demonstrate it.

Pat and I took a walk, then had dinner at home. She had a glass of wine—I had a Coke. She was impressed with my determination to stay sober while I dealt with my problems and also commented that if it would help, she could take care of pre-schoolers at our home. Some of her friends who worked had to drop their kids off at a place they weren't comfortable with. When she offered to take care of them, she'd received positive reactions. Would I mind little kids around the house during the day?

I responded, "It's a wonderful idea, but I don't think it's necessary. I'm not going to be home, Pat. I'm focused on my career search, and, we're staying right here. I'll be in great demand once I meet the right people. Also, it was my idea that you stay home and be a full-time mother. You don't have to worry about making money—that's my responsibility in our partnership."

Pat smiled and my world changed. She really did believe in me. That was all I needed. I knew I could go out and establish myself in a new career. I'd read somewhere a Teddy Roosevelt quote: "Black care rarely sits behind a rider whose pace is fast enough."

I was going to get into the saddle Friday and ride fast!

Chapter 11

Controlling the Process

Friday (third week)

I was starting to feel good about my plan to interview a number of business leaders about how *they* had become successful. Charlie and his friends had shared their concepts of the leadership mystique and how it was acquired. I identified with the people I'd talked to. However, I now realized I had not developed my own inner confidence that I could master any challenge I faced without *reacting*, rather than making a thoughtful assessment as to the proper way to respond. But, more importantly, I had to learn how to conduct myself to minimize surprises by *anticipating* future problems.

I also had to take the long view in every decision I made, and that meant I had to overcome my current financial insecurity and make good long-range decisions, even though the short-term penalty might be painful.

I sent an e-mail to Charlie about my thoughts early that morning. Within an hour, I received his response:

> Ken:
> I'm proud of you. I've been where you are a few times and have had to reach the same conclusion. Fortunately, I had a very *Wise Mentor* who spent time

with me everyday when I was in my early twenties and just out of the army.

His favorite expression was, "What were you worrying about one year ago today?" I obviously couldn't answer that question, so he'd then say, "You can either worry or work, not both" and I'd get back to working my plan.

He was helping me *control* my plan—rather than directing my activities.

You've read short stories about some exceptional Leader/Mentors who have all mastered the vital elements involved in the evolution of a real leader—not a driver—of a group of people. I focused on some of these elements in relating the stories of how a person can grow in stature and achievement, from modest financial means, because of the love and support from a number of mentors.

You've had mentors in the past, or you wouldn't have attained your present level of achievement. Everyone who knows you admires you. Don't forget that when you start to feel insecure. You should try to re-establish contact with those people who saw something exceptional in you in the past. That will reinforce your own self-confidence. You're too close to yourself to do it alone.

As you were growing up, you had a natural support group in your family, if it was functional—and since I know your folks, it was! You were asked about your achievements every day. If you made a mistake, you weren't ridiculed—except by your brothers and sisters, who used that opportunity to humble you. When you were in school, you selected friends who helped you reinforce your self-confidence and avoided those people who didn't do that for you.

If you were really lucky, one or two teachers took more than just a passing interest in your life and you performed well so they'd be proud of you. Then, you went into the adult world and started to realize how alone we all are as we start to build our careers, professions or businesses. Your first reaction was a natural one—it's every person for him or herself. You became very competitive, winning at any cost to get approval from almost everyone. Then, if you're lucky, and you were, senior managers noticed you and started to help you win, without losing the respect of your competitors.

After a long period of comfortable winning, you had a minor setback and overreacted. You were punished a little, but you must learn from this experience and turn it around. View it as an opportunity to rise to an even higher plateau of achievement. Self-approval, rather than seeking approval from others, is easier said than done!

All of the *Wise Men* I interviewed have reached that comfort level with themselves. They're now at an even higher level of comfort as they've achieved personal *and* financial success. They're also making their communities, state, and nation better places in which to live and be happy, because they're all philanthropic.

Someday, you'll want to consider *giving back* what you've attained. In the meantime, you have to focus on your family and a career that will give you the means to continue the lifestyle to which you and your family have become accustomed.

The success story of Bodie Bodenheimer that I sent earlier illustrated the importance of *knowledge* and becoming a lifelong learner. This was followed by other stories illustrating the importance of a positive *attitude*, human relations *skills*, the *habit* of finishing what you start, careful *planning* of every action and *organizing* everything necessary to assure success.

Now, the capstone to all this is to *control* the process, as contrasted to controlling another person. Jerry Stone's life story tells how he observed all the essential guiding principles and also made sure that every project he launched was controlled, at every step in the process, to guarantee success. I'm sending you his short story.

Ken, this very talented man has overcome every adversity to reach the pinnacle of success. After you have a plan, I'll put you in touch with him.

All of the *Wise Men* were self-made; their parents had not achieved significant financial success. Nevertheless, their strong characters and the deep interest they had in their children's early development was the launching pad for them to become financially successful.

I enjoyed reading about the life of another exceptional man, and how his father, in *listening* to his son, gave him the early roots of self-confidence to rise to a level of achievement most people only dream about. I especially liked some of his guiding principles. "You can make a bad deal with a good person, but you can never make a good deal with a bad person. Learn to determine the difference between those who claim to be leaders and those who act like leaders. Enthusiasm and passion for what you are doing can overcome most obstacles. A leader sees only delays, not failures."

Jerry believes those who want to be leaders need to adopt role models to emulate. *Who do you want to be like?* Some of Jerry's best teachings include: Fail forward; Don't be afraid to take risks; Work hard, it cures a lot of ills; Seek responsibility; Find something to do that you love and you'll never work another day in your life.

While I was making notes on Jerry Stone's qualities, another e-mail came in from Charlie:

> Jerry Stone observes many rules of behavior, but two of them are: finish what you start and limit your liability. These are demonstrated by his decision to merge a very successful company that he and his partners built to assure continued growth for all concerned. He'd determined, early on, that the unit costs of a merged, compatible company would be lower than his own, stand alone company. As a result, the decline in high-tech stock values did not adversely affect the merged larger company nearly as much as it could have.
>
> I recently read an article about the leadership style of another CEO, who used fear and intimidation to the extreme. The CEO of Bridgestone turned that company around as a radical cost-cutter. When one employee was told he had to retire early, he asked for a personal meeting with the CEO to have him reconsider. After the CEO refused to change his decision, the employee committed Seppuku in front of the CEO, who, it is reported, sent the bill for cleaning his carpet to the man's heirs. This incident was the careful application of terror as a form of communication.
>
> Jerry Stone's leadership style is 180 degrees from that CEO. People *want* to respond to Jerry's leadership control practices, because they know his meaning of

the word *control* is *coordinate*. Every person on the team realizes that *they* must control what they do. People don't care how much their leaders *know* until they know how much they *care*. Jerry's habit of *caring* is to catch people doing something *right*. He also does not give up on people too soon.

There is a story that demonstrates this kind of caring spirit which involves a foot race by kids with Down's syndrome. One of the kids looked to the side at his parents, smiled, then tripped. All of the other kids stopped running and helped him up. Then, they all continued the race.

Jerry *won't* win at any cost, but in any endeavor, he and his partners always seem to win!

Another leader, General George S. Patton, who has gotten a lot of bad press, once said: "I don't fear failure. I only fear the slowing up of the engine inside of me which is pounding, saying, 'Keep going, someone must be on top, why not you?'"

Anyone who has read Patton's biography knows the respect his *troops* had for him. However, he overreacted to what he thought was self-pity by a soldier and slapped him. That almost derailed his career and is an example of an ego out of control.

Jerry has never let his ego control his life. He was raised in a small town and still lives there. He's had the same friends all his life and he adds to that list in every encounter with another person.

I received an e-mail from one of my key advisors concerning friendship last year that may help you focus on the importance of collecting *friends*, rather than an undue concentration on accumulating *wealth*. Although many people who have a wide circle of friends also manage to balance their life and accumulate an independent estate. The e-mail follows:

Eleanor Roosevelt wrote:

Many people will walk in and out of your life, But only true friends will leave footprints in your heart.

To handle yourself, use your head; To handle others, use your heart.

Anger is only one letter short of danger.

If someone betrays you once, it is his fault; If he betrays you twice, it is your fault.

Great minds discuss ideas; Average minds discuss events; Small minds discuss people.

He, who loses money, loses much; He, who loses a friend, loses much more; He, who loses faith, loses all.

Beautiful young people are accidents of nature, But beautiful old people are works of art.

Learn from the mistakes of others. You can't live long enough to make them all yourself.

Friends, you and me… You brought another friend… And then there were three.

We started our group...
Our circle of friends...
And like that circle...
There is no beginning or end...

Yesterday is history.
Tomorrow is a mystery.
Today is a gift.

You might also be interested in a story I heard at a conference in Monterey that our company hosted for some of our clients. One of our distinguished advisory board guests was illustrating the delicate balance you must maintain when showing warm interest in another person.

There can be complications for a warm-hearted, outgoing Leader/Mentor who may attract the attention of those of the opposite sex who seek a mentor/protégé relationship that might not be fully appreciated by the leader's spouse. In *Hamlet*, Shakespeare admonished that we should not "dull thy palm with entertainment/Of each new-hatched, unfledged courage."

This Leader/Mentor was at a cocktail party reception for a client firm by himself. One of the lovely young secretaries of his company was also at this function, and had a few too many cocktails. Her boss asked the mentor to drive this young lady home. On the drive, the young lady told him how much he was admired and respected by everyone in the company. She said she had a lot more to tell him; he should spend some time at her apartment, and not cut the evening short.

The Leader/Mentor said he'd have to call his wife for permission and thought this would send the right message so the secretary would understand why she couldn't have his company that night. However, the next day, there was a *personal* message on his desk, on scented stationery, which read: "You can fool *some* of the people *all* of the time/You can fool *all* of the people *some* of the time/But you can fool around with me anytime."

As a young Leader/Mentor he had learned that *familiarity* breeds contempt, but it can also send the wrong signal and lead to complications.

Therefore Ken, Leader/Mentors have all sorts of opportunities. Some of them come with serious complications, so be careful about how close you get to your subordinates!

I had a good laugh at Charlie's great story—and reflected about the good decision by Ingrid not to get involved with me. I had been vulnerable at that time, but if I'd gone too far with Ingrid, I'd have ruined my relationship with Pat, whom I loved and who was squarely in my corner now.

I got another e-mail from Charlie:

I just finished reading a book, *Wisdom of the CEO*, co-authored by Grady Means. In it the CEO of a large multi-national corporation was quoted regarding how to achieve real freedom of action through encouraging Jerry Stone's philosophy of *self-control*. Niall W. A. Fitzgerald, Chairman of Unilever, PLC said:

Over the next twenty years, three billion people will be added to the world's population. Most will live outside North America and Europe and 75 percent of additional disposable income is likely to come from these regions.

From 1890 to the 1920s, William Lever of
Bolson, England roamed the world setting up
subsidiaries in Asia, Africa and Latin
American, giving capital and goals to local
managers, then sailing off, returning years later
to check on progress. "Best locations, best people, clear objectives—then room to deliver."
Thus was born a business empire of 29 billion
pounds, 260 thousand employees in 300 operating companies in 100 countries.

Lever authored a conundrum that has faced
successive generations of our managers: How
to preserve the benefits of the independent
local units intimate contact with local condi-
tions, while extracting the advantages of inter-
dependence from the total corporation entity's
scale and scope. Stated differently, yet still par-
adoxically, our aim is to be a large corporate
body with many hundreds of small company
souls. That is the way to compete optimally in
international markets: simultaneously have the
attributes of a small company—simplicity,
speed, flexibility, clarity—and the benefits that
arise from size and international spread.
Striking the right balance between these two
goals has been a long (and always unfinished)
learning at Unilever.

Ken, this story illustrates that a large company can be
operated effectively if there is the proper control of the
process, which starts with the proper selection of the
person who can *control themselves*. Your challenge is to
decide whether you want to try again for the brass
ring of a top executive in a larger company or for an
entrepreneurial role in a smaller one.

Good companies push down power at all levels. Jerry Stone did that in all of his business ventures. He also lived by the advice John Gardner gave in one of his books: "We must stop looking at one another as categories and start looking at them as fellow human beings."

I'm sending you Jack Grady's short story, which illustrates his transition to independence many years ago from a senior executive position with one of our nation's largest companies. You'll enjoy his story!

Chapter 12

Self-confidence and Independence

Saturday (third week)

Pat woke me with surprising news. She had agreed to take care of two neighbor children while their mother worked. The family was coming over to get the children properly introduced and she wanted to get the house in good shape. Would I make breakfast while she cleaned up?

We woke the kids and Michael helped me cook Swedish pancakes, his favorite. Julie helped Pat clean. We all had breakfast together, and then Julie asked me if I was going to be a Mr. Mom, now that her mother was the breadwinner. We all laughed, but I realized I'd been unemployed for three weeks, a fact that my kids were very aware of. This realization increased my determination to proceed with my job/career search.

I explained that I was sifting through all my options so I wouldn't make a mistake. Selecting the right job or business was like a business marriage, and a business divorce was almost as painful, both emotionally and financially, as marital divorce. I'm sure this information went over their heads, but Pat understood my situation and chimed in.

"Dad has retired for awhile. Now it's my turn to support the family. He'll help me with some of my household duties until he decides to get back into the business world."

That was not what I'd hoped she'd say, but taking issue in front of the kids was not wise. So, I said, "I'll make breakfast on the week-ends—how's that for pitching in?" Fortunately, the doorbell rang, putting an end to the conversation.

Pat greeted our neighbor's family while the kids and I washed the dishes. Julie tried to get me to wear Pat's apron, but I declined. This role model switch was not one I relished—I made a mental note to be in serious job interviews next week!

Pat came into the kitchen and asked if I'd come and meet our neighbors, the Johnsons, from two blocks up the street. They had two very cute pre-schoolers who were already talking with our kids. After introducing everyone, Pat sent the children into the back yard to play, while we talked with the parents, Don and Mary.

Don started out by asking if Pat had a license to operate a day care center, did she have any medical training, had she ever taught kids three and five years of age?

His wife, Mary, looked daggers at him and broke in. "Grow up! Pat has raised two great kids. We're lucky she's willing to help us. We don't want our kids to be in a day care center. I can drop them off here when I go out and look for work. You travel so much that I'm alone all day and many nights with the kids. I have to start being around adults during the day so I don't start to *think* and *talk* like a child."

Properly subdued, Don retreated into silence—but you could tell he wasn't comfortable with *anyone* but his wife taking care of their kids. I knew just how he felt, so I asked him to come into my study for a visit while Pat and Mary got acquainted.

"Ken, I'm sorry for all the questions, but this is all new to me. Frankly, as soon as I asked the questions, I remembered that my wife's mom took care of pre-schoolers while Mary, her two brothers and sister were growing up. Her mom saved all the money to be sure they had a good education. Her husband saved part of his salary so he could retire early. Now, her folks have a great family who all live nearby, because her mother could stay at home and be a full-time mother for her kids when they came home from school.

"She had five or six kids during the day. My wife and her sister helped out with housework; her brothers helped their father with other chores. They were, and are, a tight-knit family. Forget my questions. Pat is obviously a good mother; we're lucky she's willing to help us. By the way, what do you do?"

"I'm a consultant."

"Oh, so am I. What field?"

"I haven't decided."

At that, he smiled and said, "You're smart. When I was between jobs, I told the same story. Can I help you open some doors?"

"Thanks, but I'm looking for a needle in a haystack and have spent the last three weeks trying to decide what field I want to pursue. As well as whether I want to have it involve travel, if I want to be an employee or an independent contractor, where we should live and a whole host of other issues. I have a lot of people helping me with advice. In fact, I've been fed with a firehose of information I still have to digest."

"Ken, I envy you. I'm so busy just meeting quotas, satisfying customers and my boss, and spending some time with my family that I haven't really ever thought what I'd do if I was forced to resign from my job. Do you mind telling me how you made the decision to take time out to find the *perfect* career?"

I laughed and told him my story. I then told him how Charlie Rowe was helping me with insights into the way to find a good career fit, and that I hoped I didn't run out of reserves before I found it.

"What a great help he is. If I lost my job, I'd be in the same situation. Could I meet this Charlie Rowe sometime? He's a guy worth knowing."

I decided to finesse that question. Charlie was not an out-placement counselor. So instead of answering directly, I said, "I'll do you one better. I'll share some of the e-mails I've gotten from Charlie and a few of his friends. They include biographical sketches of some very successful Leader/Mentors and I've been inspired by their example.

"I now realize that I had illusory security in a salaried position; that I should have lived on eighty percent of what I earned and invested twenty percent! Then I could go back to school and get some formal education to prepare me for a field where I don't have to live on planes and in motels half the time. Incidentally, have you adopted the 80/20 plan?"

"How about our 100/150 plan? We have my next two bonus payments already spent. If I don't make them, our credit card debt will start to consume as much of my income as my jumbo mortgage with a balloon payment due in two years. If my income doesn't justify refinancing, we'll have to sell the house. That's why my wife is out looking for a job. Her folks are on vacation so they can't take care of the kids and we don't want them as permanent sitters. However, Pat is charging us $10 an hour so Mary will have to make more than $1,800 monthly just to pay Pat."

I responded, "$1,800 *after tax*. With your combined income, she'll have to *gross* $3,000 to pay Pat. Then, Pat will only *net* $1,000 because we'll have to pay $800 in tax. The state and federal government will make $2,000 monthly to net Pat $1,000. Your wife will have to earn more than $15 per hour. What are her skills?"

"She was a receptionist at our company until we had our first child. She didn't make $3,000 monthly!"

I could see our neighbors hadn't really thought things through, so I said, "Look, your wife probably needs a break from the kids and Pat has some free time now. Why don't we do a barter deal? We don't need the $1,800 a month yet. I'll have a steady income soon. I have a good resume, an MBA and can command at least $150,000 yearly when I find the right position.

"Let Pat help your wife go out in the job market and try to get $5,000 a month, so she nets $3,000. Then, you pay $1,800 to someone to take care of the kids and save the other $1,200 of her salary. We'll trade time Pat spends with your kids for you and your wife to take care of our kids on weekends, so we can get away by ourselves. Deal?"

He was silent for a while, then said, "Ken, you're a great guy, but we pay our way. We'll pay Pat now, but I know my wife can't find a $5,000 monthly income, she doesn't have the experience and she's not sales-oriented so her job search won't last more than a few weeks. But, I'll tell you what I'd like. When you get situated, I'd like to talk to you about finding a new job for myself. When I do that I'll also need a financial advisor. I'm fed up with my company, my supervisor and my life on the road. I just don't have time to go out and find anything else. Also, you just opened my eyes as to how financially dumb I am. I really need a mentor."

"I'm flattered that you'd accept me as a mentor. I'm also thinking about getting a stopgap job to cover our minimum needs and then learn more about financial consulting. There seems to be a real demand for it, and the people I've met in the field are so busy they aren't taking new clients. I was an economics major at Cal, before I got my MBA. When supply is tight and demand is high, the price goes up.

"However, I'll have to spend at least a year to prepare to even do personal financial planning. Then, four or five years later, I can tackle the corporate market like Dennis, Charlie and their associates. However, Dennis—he's our neighbor—has said that he'll mentor me if I decide to do that. All I have to do is show a budget that illustrates I can maintain my lifestyle for at least a year with just minimal income while I'm in the apprenticeship program."

"Ken, when did you last do any selling?"

"Eight years ago."

"What did you sell?"

"Computer equipment."

"Have you ever sold an intangible?"

"No—that's the rub. So, I've decided I'll just be a birddog for one of Dennis' associates and sit in on the meetings to decide whether I have that kind of skill."

"Great idea! Would you introduce me to Dennis?"

I said I'd do it later and we went in to see our wives, who had made their deal.

After Don and Mary left, I told Pat she shouldn't count on a long-term deal. She responded that she didn't want to make a career of day care work, I'd find something soon. She just wanted to help out until then.

I went into my study and reflected on how lucky I was. At least I had three or four months to decide what to do. Our neighbor had some real pressures, and wasn't even as well prepared as I was to cope with them. Also, he was looking to *me* as a mentor. Maybe I did have the latent leadership skills of Charlie's friends and the *Wise Men*. I wondered how many other neighbors were in the same boat as Don.

If I just charged half the rate my attorney charged me for my will, I could get $150 hourly for doing a financial plan. If I did two plans a week and spent ten hours on each plan, I'd earn $150,000 yearly. Plus, Curt had indicated the investment dollars also earned an average of 2 percent yearly for the advisor for smaller plans.

If I could get a fellow like my neighbor to save $20,000 yearly, I'd make $400 the first year. Then, it would increase as he continued to save money. In five years, his portfolio should be at least $150,000 and I'd earn $3,000 that year on his account alone.

If I had 100 clients like Don in five years, I'd eventually earn $300,000 yearly from just investment commissions. If I got 100 new clients the second year, my income in the fifth year would be even greater and eventually over $500,000 per year. Plus I'd have fee income from new plans and updates on others. All I had to do was recruit 200 clients in two years. Why weren't there more financial consultants? The successful ones could earn more than most corporation senior executives—and they'd have a lot more peace of mind and freedom of action. Also what a difference they could make in the lives of their clients.

If only I'd asked someone like Dennis to work with me five years ago, I wouldn't be in my present uncomfortable financial situation, faced with the possibility of lowering our standard of living for a few years. I'm still young though, and in six to seven years, I'd be in a secure position. I'd just have to focus on getting an interim job so I could go back to school.

While I was considering the future, I got the Jack Grady short story from Charlie. This was one of the best stories I'd read. Not because they weren't *all* high achievers, but Jack Grady had seventy-six years of business experience—starting at age eight!

I called Michael and Julie into my study and read them Jack's story. I especially liked his description of one of his mentors: "When he looked at a wall, he never saw any cracks; he saw the big picture and was an optimist. He was creative, possessing integrity and had a deep interest in everything and everyone."

After I was finished, Michael said, "Are you suggesting we go out and get a job?"

"No, but you are going to do the lawn work in return for your allowance, and Julie will help with housework and with the Johnson kids, after she gets home from school."

"How about my homework?" Julie asked.

"Do that after the kids leave and before dinner."

They both left to see if Pat agreed with the idea. When Pat came in to ask what prompted my attitude regarding our kids having to work for their allowance, I just handed her the Grady story.

She sat down and read it. Then said, "Wow! Don't you wish our kids had a grandfather with Jack Grady's independent spirit? He makes *work* seem like a *game*. I like that. Can I read the other stories that Charlie sent to you?"

I gave her my file and reviewed the e-mail I'd just gotten from Charlie:

> Ken, why don't you pull up the website for the fifty companies you want to investigate. Then, compose an e-mail to the CEO with the subject: "Your website—a suggestion!" Personalize your message to offer a good suggestion on how they can anticipate questions from their prospective customers or employees. Then you can close by suggesting the CEO click on *your website*. You can create an innovative website, with your picture and voiceover that will only take three minutes. Prepare a script and send it to me. I'll edit it, then recommend a good web design company. This is a better way to send your resume out.
>
> If the CEO clicks, you'll know you've gotten his attention. You can then call his secretary to set up an appointment by indicating her boss has asked for information on you. Tell her that you want five minutes on his calendar to answer questions. I'll bet you bat .500 if you do it that way.
>
> Incidentally, Jack Grady's local paper ran an article on Lakeland's most prominent citizens. Here's what they had to say about Jack:
>
> > John P. "Jack" Grady just can't seem to stay retired. The former drinking cup company

executive tried to take an early retirement in 1965. It didn't suit him. After starting and selling a can-making operation in Orlando, the Illinois native arrived in Polk County in 1971. He bought a Lakeland juice plant and transformed it into Juice Bowl Products. Grady sold Juice Bowl, now part of Tropicana, in 1982. Retirement didn't stick that time, either. Grady, now 83, founded the Community Foundation of Greater Lakeland about two years ago. In that time, it has amassed more that $10 million in assets for charitable contributions to various Polk County groups and agencies.

If you want to be an entrepreneur, go down and spend a few hours with a *master*. I've done this every year for over twenty years. It helps keep me charged up. However, be prepared to take the bitter with the sweet. Entrepreneurs make a lot of money and they lose a lot of money. Be sure you can shrug off a loss and start over again.

Also, the nation is full of attorneys with too much time on their hands. They'll sue at the slightest provocation. As a corporate executive, your legal department handles this and keeps all executives in a mode of minimizing legal exposure.

An entrepreneur is his/her own legal department until they get big enough to afford either full-time counsel or a healthy retainer. So, if you decide to become a consultant, or buy into a small business, take a year of business law before you expose yourself to potential litigation for your innocent and well-intended actions.

However, those who are successful in small business activities enjoy the risk/reward of being in business for themselves. Here's a simple three-part philosophy that will help you in your daily leadership activities: Don't sail under false colors. You can't push a string—so lead. Keep a sense of where you are going and where you want to be. Finally, how you pass this on to others is the key to success.

Keep me posted and send me your three-minute script.

I e-mailed Charlie with a request for what it would cost for a personal website and received the following response:

Ken:
You'll spend about three percent of what you earned last year. My own marketing consultant can help you after you draft the script. Incidentally, he helped Jerry Stone and Jere Smith build a billion-dollar company, so he's the best. I'm sending him a copy of this e-mail too.

Even though it was Saturday, I got an e-mail about fifteen minutes later from Charlie's friend:

What a creative idea! We haven't ever done a website like the one Charlie suggested, but it's doable—and, since you're a friend of his, I'll give you his rate. We can probably get it done for under $4,000 if you give us the script.

You'll have to fly up to Portland and use our recording studio and photographer. You can pay us after you have a new position. Incidentally, we're in the corporate website business. If you send me the URL numbers, I'll help you critique the websites you visit and draft your letter with helpful suggestions. Who knows, we may get a few corporate jobs out of your screening. If we get even one, I'll cut your fee by 50 percent; if we get two, I'll waive your fee.

Incidentally, I've reviewed the Grady interview and have extended my retirement date to ninety! I happen to love what I do, so I guess I'm like Charles "Sparky" Schultz who once said, "If I can't draw, then I'm just waiting to die."

Who knows, if you screen fifty websites and decide not to join any of the companies, you may be able to get me meetings with ten of them and we'll probably generate $200,000 of gross income from revising their websites. I can pay you a 30 percent commission—how about that?

This guy is definitely an entrepreneur! I could make money with him. I might become a finder for him and Dennis until I decide on a permanent career. That would allow me to take some classes in law and finance and maybe, someday, be as independent as Dennis!

I had a great Saturday afternoon. That evening I practiced what I'd say in three minutes with Pat and she made notes.

I was developing a plan.

Chapter 13

Achieving Emotional Maturity

Sunday (third week)

When I awoke, I could smell bacon frying and coffee brewing. I'd had the soundest night of sleep since my traumatic awakening three weeks ago when my security blanket was ripped off my back by my boss. I realized my loyalty had been to *a corporate charter*; one or two people above me in the chain of command could determine my financial security.

I felt a new strength after all of my unique counseling over the last two weeks, and my emotions were somewhat under control. I no longer felt alone and isolated. I'd read about some very successful people and talked with some of them because of their friendship with Charlie. I'd even, in one short encounter, started to develop a mentoring relationship with my neighbor.

Money was no longer my preoccupation. I knew I could earn it over some period of time, and that if we had to move, it wouldn't be the end of the world.

My position and title no longer defined me. My common sense, intelligence and bearing would be my badge and ensign of what I hoped was my sovereign mind. I was starting to realize that *tenacity of purpose* was my secret weapon to achieve success.

My family was now the center of my world. My new career would have to fit in with my plans for helping my kids achieve *real* independence and self-confidence. If I left them money, that would be secondary, and if they wanted to go on through college, it would be up to them and I'd help if I could. However, *all* of the *Wise Men* had found their own education in different ways, which made them stronger earlier in life and better able to handle a crisis later in life.

I was treated to breakfast in bed by Pat and the kids. They were showing their support in a very thoughtful way. We all went to Church and the Priest had a closing thought for the day that I wrote down. He quoted Churchill's biographer, Martin Gilbert, "History is concerned with character and humanity, as well as facts and achievement."

When I returned home I e-mailed this quote to Charlie, since he'd indicated he was a Churchill student. I got the following response:

> I recently read an article entitled "The Character of Leadership," by Walter C. Wright, Jr., Executive Director of the DePree Leadership Center. You'll find the following helpful:
>
> > Character shapes leadership and leadership shapes character. So what is this thing called character? Character is the sum total of a person's beliefs, values, world view, and commitments. Character is shaped by what we believe—religiously or philosophically—by what we value and hold dear, by what we commit ourselves to, and by the promises we make. It is that which defines us—that which controls

and shapes our behavior. Character is that which distinguishes us from everyone else. It is the way we see ourselves and want others to see us. Character is at the heart and soul of what it means to be a person—to be the person we choose to be.

Ken, I've been sending you short stories about men of great personal integrity and character. They've also, just incidentally, been a financial success, but that wasn't their primary goal. Other people have been attracted to these leaders because they won't compromise their integrity—no matter the cost.

Ambition, as most people define it, is a word they don't attribute to themselves. However, these men have achieved most of their goals and, if they've failed along the way, they got up and kept marching on. Therefore, persistence and tenacity are their common traits.

Too many people are overly ambitious and crawl over others to attain their goals. The repeat offenders eventually lose the respect of their peers and are seen only as long-term losers, no matter how much money they make. This shortsighted person doesn't gain the respect of intelligent men or the love of children.

It appears you're now focusing on the important considerations in carving out a new business life. Therefore, I'll now send you another Leader/Mentor bio with highlights of the life of Sam Higginbottom. Give me your reaction to his story.

I reflected on Sam's comments concerning the most important attributes for being successful. You must be bright, interested in the world around you, get along with people, have integrity and moral standards, be able to communicate orally and in writing and be a good listener. In addition he said, "You have to like what you're doing and have a passion for what you're doing." He emphasized that you must be able to write and to speak on your feet to be a success.

After reading Sam's story, I asked Pat and the kids to come into my study and I read sections of it out loud. The kids wanted me to read "Robbie Burns" stories to them and Pat said she'd get the book. Pat asked me to read the letter from Sam's wife, Jana, a second time, and then she came over and hugged me. We both made a commitment to start showing how much we loved each other. The kids snuggled in between us and I'd never been happier or more content. It had taken a trauma for me to open my mind to what was lasting and most important—my family.

Sam's gentle family nature and statesman-like behavior in business had made his life very successful. I wrote Charlie about our reaction to his motivating and heartwarming story.

Later, we drove out to the coast and hiked out to the spot where I'd gone the day my life changed, three weeks earlier. I told Pat and the kids of my turmoil, and how even the ocean waves had been threatening to me. Today, they were just waves, and I knew I could surf life's challenges now that I had everything in perspective.

When we returned home, Michael and I barbecued and we all ate a late lunch together in our backyard. That afternoon, while the rest of the family watched TV, I read Charlie's e-mail that he'd sent earlier that day:

> I'm touched by your family's reaction to reading about Sam. He married Jana and took responsibility for helping her raise her three teenagers when most people his age are preoccupied with cruises while

they are still mobile enough to travel. Sam will be in his late eighties before the children in his new family will be out of college.

He spent over ten years caring for his first wife, who was very ill. She passed away a few years ago. Her dearest friend, at that time, was Jana. It was just natural that Jana became a part of Sam's family, while he, Jana and round-the-clock nurses cared for his first wife, Fair.

Sam has had several defining events in his long and very interesting life. However, his life experience demonstrates the importance of being able to speak on your feet. This kind of skill is essential for leadership. So, Ken, if you're apprehensive about meeting a lot of strangers, you might call the local head of Dale Carnegie to start a program to improve your public speaking skills. Also, you will be able to network with other people your age at their meetings.

The first defining event for Sam was the chance he got to attend one of the great universities in the world, even though he was of modest means at the time. His presence and ability to make a positive first impression was vital. He had many other defining events, which reinforces my conviction that communication skills, in addition to intelligence and empathy, are prime ingredients for a developing leader. Then, if that person is committed to lifelong learning, he or she can't help but succeed.

Sam is one hundred percent emotionally intelligent, and few people achieve this ability. Many of us are captive to our emotions from time to time. It's something I work on everyday, and so should you. Sheer cognitive capacity doesn't make any impact unless a person has emotions under control. Our emotions have to be channeled to constructive purposes. In other words, love and happiness are emotions—share them without any restraint. Bitterness and anger should be analyzed to determine how to cut them out of your conscious thoughts, but be sure you don't just suppress these emotions. Talk to someone you totally trust to get your mind straight. This normally helps regain balance.

Incidentally, I recently read a Henry Kissinger biography. One of his early mentors said, "My role was not discovering Kissinger. It was to help Kissinger to discover himself."

Ken, you are discovering yourself. Two things are bad for the heart: running uphill and running down people. You're a gifted person and should now be able to rise above your bitter feelings over actions taken by executives in your former company. Your former boss may not have had any choice in the decision that affected you.

I was being considered for an important position some thirty years ago. My only reference, since I was still a senior executive in a competitive company, was Davis Gregg, President of the American College. When the CEO of the new company appointed me, he told me that Dave had said, "I'm surprised that he's available." That one reference eliminated the need for further reference checking. So, pick as your reference someone in your former company whose position assures credibility and objectivity.

I reflected on Charlie's advice and responded:

I'll summarize my options based on just my prelimi-
nary thinking. I could decide to join a large public
company. The Bodenheimer and Higginbottom examples show that I don't have to compromise my
integrity to rise to the top. They were entrepreneurial
as executives in large companies. If I decide to join a
mid-market private company and eventually buy a
piece of the action, I have the Twigg-Smith, Nickell,
McKinnon and Stone examples to show how they all
became CEO's in that type of company.

If I later want to start my own business, I have the
example of the success of Midkiff, Dacey and Grady. I
now know that there is a need for competent non-
profit CEO's. The Dauer example shows how that
position can be both fulfilling and, if I invest part of
my income wisely, financially rewarding. If I want to
be an independent financial advisor, the Ford example
gives me a roadmap.

Charlie, Monday morning of my fourth week of being
reborn as an entrepreneur is going to be the first day
of the rest of my life!

Chapter 14

Essential Guiding Principles

Monday (fourth week)

That morning I decided to write down for Charlie the basic attitudes and attributes of the *Wise Men* he'd interviewed to illustrate the importance of basic leadership fundamentals. So I sent him an e-mail:

> I am starting to get a sense of what has to be done. After making many notes on a variety of issues, my thinking has become better focused so I can head in *one* direction, not four or five.
>
> You've been referring to the *guiding principles* of a Leader/Mentor. They are the **secrets** to their success. I have written down my ideas and conclusions for each of the *Wise Men*, as you asked me to do in order to help with your book. Let's take them, one at a time, to be sure I understand what you're trying to communicate, and *why* you picked each of the people to illustrate your points. Let me know what you think.

Bodie Bodenheimer

First, let's take Bodie Bodenheimer's story, which illustrates the first principle: *Be a Lifelong Learner*. I was really impressed with Bodie's self-discipline and the way he'd taken control of a failing business he knew nothing about. Bodie got up to speed fast in a new business, because he's had a lifetime of acquiring knowledge. He's a lifelong learner. Knowledge is defined as a clear and certain perception of something; the act, fact, or state of knowing; understanding; enlightenment; learning; all that has been perceived or grasped by the mind; practical experience; skill; acquaintance or familiarity with a fact, place, etc.; cognizance or recognition.

Here are some examples of the importance of being a lifelong learner that I picked up from reading about Bodie. When he considered Zickgraf, he agreed to go there and spend ninety days finding out what was going on—gaining knowledge. Without that knowledge of the company, of the finances, of the banking situation, the company would be gone, along with his great opportunity. Therefore, this example suggests a premise for gaining knowledge. It takes discipline, great effort and sacrifice to learn what you need to know to succeed—a common thread throughout his story.

Knowledge is important to you, but even more so to all others in an organization you might lead. Bodie educated his work force, and thereby made them feel good about themselves. He gave them the opportunity to *learn* which became *power* in their lives.

Learning (the process of acquiring knowledge) became a part of his company culture. Turning hourly people into learners is a great success story. The best scenario for learning begins early in life. If a teacher takes an interest in a child, their life can be changed. In his case it happened several times, both in the military and in college.

Knowledge comes from learning and from serious effort. Genius is not required but motivation certainly is. One thing Bodie came to know early in life was that people are untapped potential. You see it in his early coaching as well as in his recent Zickgraf turn around. He also learned that untapped potential takes various things to release it—access to school, full stomachs, understanding healthy living—life basics. Meeting and working with smart people encourages personal lifetime learning habits. Here is the answer to the question: Why do I need a mentor?

As a leader who wants to succeed by attracting smart people, I'll be aware of the learning opportunities for myself and others, and encourage those around me to grasp those opportunities whenever possible. I'll let them do things that broaden their knowledge base. If they take a course in school, I'll make sure they bring something back! Businessmen are smart, well read, and prepared. They will want those who work with them to be the same. Knowledge is a prerequisite for, but does not guarantee, implementation. Motivation is also required. Being too comfortable stifles achieve-ment potential.

Success in running a company requires continual learning. You always need to know more about your products, processes and markets.

There are three keys to success according to the story about Bodie. First, discipline. Without it I will not learn what I need to know. Second, do not run out of money—knowledge of investments is obviously important. Third, do not try to do it all by yourself.

Knowledge is mandatory, but the ultimate illusion is that you know it all!

Charlie called after reading the e-mail. He asked, "Do you have any other thoughts about Bodie?"

I said, "Charlie, I know now that when I got my MBA I relaxed a bit. I should have taken some additional courses in personal financial planning. We wouldn't be in this tight financial bind if we hadn't lived at a higher standard than my current income allowed. Our mortgage payment wouldn't be so high. We'd own a car, rather than lease it. I'd have saved two months of income for each year of work while I was an *earner*. If I'd done that, I'd have a few years of reserves, rather than a few *months*. Now I'm a *yearner*!"

"Good! You are learning from these mentors. Send me your next essay and I'll call you back."

Joe Dacey

The second guiding principle is: *Maintain a Positive Attitude*. How do I stay positive, no matter what the provocation? A positive mental attitude is one I have to work on every minute, hour, and day of my life. So, here is my overview of Joe Dacey and his very successful life of winning friends, at every level, through a genuine love for his fellow man or woman.

Attitude is defined as the posture or position assumed by the body in connection with an action, emotion or mood. The manner of acting, feeling, or thinking that shows one's disposition, opinion, etc.; or one's disposition, opinion, mental state, etc.

Humility is defined as the state or quality of being humble of mind or spirit; absence of pride or self-assertion; acts of self-abasement; to reduce arrogance and self-dependence.

I have provided both of these definitions because they tie together in Joe's story. If you look at the defining moments in his life, they all required humility to occur.

Joe learned in high school that he needed to surround himself with and learn from those who had what he wanted. It was the same way in the Navy—he chose to learn from others. It takes humility to admit that others have knowledge you don't possess and that you must pay attention to them to gain that knowledge.

Joe had three more attitudinal foundations. The first was his inner strength when his mother encouraged him with his business dreams even as a teenager. The second was his early understanding of the need to save. Conservation of resources, your own and others, is an attitude that you have or you don't. In today's "entitlement" society that attitude is lacking. Third we see humility again when he said, "I always look at it as if I'm lucky...." But he also admits that his luck was bolstered by a lot of study, which once again takes us back to the "no free lunch" rule.

I see in Joe's story humility driving the belief that you owe something to the people who help you define your goals, then help you achieve them. Joe's attitude of giving back seems to pervade his entire history. He established his business with the foundation and built the culture of his company on the principle of sharing, which is the basis for a successful company. Certainly the opposite is true in so many failed companies— "What's in it for ME?"

Joe's values are important. We can *talk* about it all we want, but *living* it is what matters in business. It takes humility to truly live by your values after you are successful, powerful and admired by many.

As Joe talked about those who shaped his life in the early years his attitude of respect was critical. He learned valuable lessons from his teacher, godmother, friend in high school and grandfather. Why? Because he had an attitude of respect for them. Respect in its purest form comes from humility. If you think you're great, you can't learn. Joe discovered the secret to learning from others was showing them the respect they had earned. Would all those people have made him feel good about himself if he had not shown them respect?

Throughout Joe's life, he developed an attitude of lifetime learning. Much of what he learned came from close observation of others. Humility and respect remain the theme in Joe's attitude toward knowledge today: "Learn something new everyday."

Joe ends his oral history interview with two statements which back up this theme of a humble attitude: "No one person can do it all by him/herself. More than anyone else, I know my limitations."

I sent my e-mail and took a break. A few minutes later Charlie called, "The one thing the *Wise Men* have in common is a total lack of *negative* thought. They project an aura of *positive* spirit. Here is another **secret** to their success."

"Charlie," I said, "I've learned that attitude affects everything we do."

"Ken, from now on when you speak of any other person, try to imagine that they are in the room with you. If you write anything about another person, imagine they'll get a copy. Train yourself to imagine that what you *think* is on your lips, and those about whom you think can hear those thoughts. Walk the talk!"

"I've reflected on my initial judgement about my former boss. He really didn't have a choice, and I put him in a tough position. He's been my friend and mentor for ten years and I'm going to use him as a reference."

"I'm glad you've made that decision, Ken. Send me the next essay."

Bob McKinnon

Here's my review of Bob McKinnon's Oral History which illustrates how you can *Create Skills in Human Relations*. As I looked at his story, I tried to distinguish between a *skill* and an *attitude* because they are so very linked. If a skill is a wrench, which we use to fix something, then attitude is the hand, the motivation, and the muscle behind the wrench.

Skill is defined as great ability or proficiency; expertness; an art, craft, or science, especially one involving the use of the hands or body; ability in such an art, craft, or science; knowledge; understanding; judgment; to know; to understand; to be knowing; to make a difference. Synonyms include dexterity, adroitness, expertness, aptitude, ability, ingenuity, and wisdom.

Here's some evidence of skill from the McKinnon story. When asked about his greatest strengths, Bob cited, "perceptive in evaluating situations" and "keeping score." These are skills. However, they must be the result of a rather comprehensive subset of skills acquired over time.

It appears that the skills that surfaced first, and are the key on which all others are built, are *communication* and *understanding* how people think. Bob talks about the ability to deal with people. It's all about knowing people and how to communicate with them. It appears that his schooling in industrial psychology was part of the key to his success.

Bob learned from sports that *teamwork* makes the difference. In school, he began to develop his ability to get things done with others, as opposed to being the do-it-yourself type. Once he understood the basic concept of teamwork, he began to develop other skills needed to succeed.

Bob also began to understand that each person had something positive that he could focus on. He really understood the need for the listening skills he was developing.

Another skill Bob absorbed from his two most important mentors was compartmentalizing his thoughts and learning how to focus. By learning the difference between the urgent and the important, he developed the ability (skill) to solve a problem and make a decision.

Early in his sales experience, he developed his communication skills. He learned to talk *with* people as opposed to *at* people. As I mentioned above, this skill is one of the most critical he learned because he employs it all along his path to success.

He talks about *failing successfully*, which is a skill of sorts. It really comes from an attitude of persistence, which is what I mean about attitudes motivating skill development and implementation.

He sharpened his mental abilities and leadership skills while honing his skill at evaluating people—that is, knowing the difference between *pretenders* and *players*. It is interesting that Bob learned the lesson of how to get the job done through making his boss look good. This valuable lesson is used later, when he carries the same concept into the business by helping his employees—and thus the company—succeed through the ESOP and his people-oriented management style.

You can't overlook the fact that Bob took a year of postgraduate work in industrial psychology, which was a key point in his development. From there he became a master at making things happen through people, and even the union.

You then see his burgeoning success. What were the skills? Knowing people and how to communicate with them! He wanted to make money, but Bob learned that the most valuable skill is the art of understanding what makes people tick—the human mind. Armed with that understanding, he has finely honed his communication skills over the years.

I'm startled at the simplicity and brilliance of the evolution of this leader. What I see are two talents that are tied with an attitude that lead to success. I'm sure it's too simplified, but it sure works for Bob McKinnon.

My conclusions:
Attitude: Caring about people. (Charlie, you told me that he really does care, as opposed to seeing that as a means to an end.)

Skill: How do people think, what turns them on, what are their needs and how can I meet those needs? (Communication is the way I find out what I need to know and how I meet those needs.)
Result: *I know how to make money!!!!!*

The phone rang within minutes. I had been thinking over my conclusions, so I enthusiastically started in, "Hi Charlie, I'm thinking I might add a course in industrial psychology to my *must learn* list. But this is a tough commandment to quickly learn. *Continuous Learning* can be done by anyone with reasonable intelligence. *Staying positive* and avoiding negative people or thoughts shouldn't be hard if I stay focused. But developing the *human relationship skills* of a Bob McKinnon will be tough. All of the people you introduced to me seem to have superior *relationship skills*, so it has to be something I can master. It was certainly the secret to McKinnon's success. Do you have some advice on how to eventually master this commandment?"

"Yes, Ken, learn to *listen actively* and don't jump to conclusions with anyone. The rest will just happen naturally. You have some good basic values. People are attracted to those who have a good value system and to those who listen to others and really hear *them!*"

"Thank you, Charlie. I'll send off the next essay in a few minutes."

After we hung up, I sat in my chair, thinking about my listening skills. When all this turmoil began a few short weeks ago, I wasn't really hearing what others were saying. I had not realized that my boss had been in a precarious position, too. I hadn't heard Pat's fear at having her world turned upside down in a single moment. I hadn't tried to look at things from anyone else's perspective. I had been so tied up in my own anger and fear—in my selfishness—that I had jumped to erroneous conclusions and had neglected to really listen to what others had to say. What was that phrase? "God gave us two ears and one mouth. We should listen twice as much as we talk." I would work on that skill beginning now.

I went into the kitchen and asked Pat if she'd go for a walk with me. I told her I wanted to hear about her dreams for the future. The look of surprise on her face quickly turned to a smile, a smile with eyes sparkling, that I hadn't seen in a long while.

After our leisurely walk, I returned to the computer. I felt calmer and more relaxed than I had for many years. Maybe I was starting to get it.

I reread Curt Ford's short story, then collected my thoughts and e-mailed them to Charlie.

Curt Ford

The really tough fourth guiding principle is *Develop Habits for Superior Performance*. I must finish what I start, and stay the course. Habit is defined as a habitual or characteristic condition of mind or body; disposition; a thing done often and hence, usually done easily; practice; custom; a pattern of action that is acquired and has become automatic; a tendency to perform a certain action or behave in a certain way. Synonyms include custom, practice, usage, and tendency.

Curt's foundational habits were developed young in life. The value of education, and thus the habit of learning, as well as the value of a strong work ethic, and thus the habit of working and enjoying it, are two of the critical habits he learned early from his parents.

Another foundational value that turned into a habit was the proper reaction to circumstances. He learned that disappointing circumstances were only a precursor for the next success.

Curt discovered early in his career that he could learn as much from people as he could from books. The summary of his first jobs shows his propensity to learn from his co-workers, bosses and situations. I'm not sure if risk-taking is a habit, but Curt was not afraid of a calculated risk. He notes that in his younger years he recognized the propensity to get bored and took risks to avoid that boredom.

Curt's story embodies the habit of learning, which may be his most valuable habit. He moved to the home office where he could learn from seasoned people. He employed communication skills and humility when dealing with people: meet them, listen to them, then talk with them. He knew that people, who talk only about themselves, learn nothing from others.

Encouragement is one of Curt's leadership habits. He received it when he was young, learned of its value, and adopted it as a way of life. He still continues to encourage the people whom he mentored and helped become successful. When you become a mentor you take on a big responsibility. If you let your own life become a shambles, you impact your protégés in a negative way. Therefore, every time a successful person becomes a mentor, they assume much more responsibility to be consistent, ethical and to "walk the talk."

Curt doesn't take himself very seriously. This characteristic shows his humility and shapes his habit patterns relative to others. Through his practice of getting together with friends to discuss issues they've all had to confront, Curt has discovered that he can not only learn from others, but be encouraged by them and encourage them in return.

One of his mentor examples, Arjay Miller, once said to him, "To keep yourself intellectually stimulated and motivated, you should re-pot yourself every ten years." Curt believes the term *re-tiring* is more appropriate for him, because of his desire to *hitchhike through life*. A new set of tires periodically makes for a smoother ride. He found a way to re-tire successfully, not only for his benefit, but also for the benefit of those with whom he worked, the company he represented, and the agency he built.

Curt has a practice of taking the long-term view. If you look in the distance, the road is not as bumpy. He has developed a habit of focusing on the outside not the inside and always looking as far down the road as he can. He recognizes good people, associates with them and, if they work for him, he delegates responsibility to them. This conduct illustrates his faith in people, but certainly not blind faith.

Flexibility is the habit of not getting into certain habits. That is Curt's first ingredient for a successful CEO. The second ingredient is confidence that you can get to where you want to go. How do you reconcile looking way down the road, with the entrepreneur's need to get through each day as it comes, while NEVER thinking that you aren't going to make it? There's some magical combination of short-term and long-term thinking going on inside the true leader!

Charlie called again. "You're doing a great job, Ken. Do you have any other thoughts about Curt?"

"Curt's attitude helped him become a true leader and develop successful life habits along the way. Charlie, I've made some resolutions. I will develop the habit of studying, no matter how boring. I'll avoid negative thoughts about everything and everyone. I'll listen rather than talk so much, especially when the person I'm with is intimidating or not too interesting. I'm already working on listening to Pat."

"Ken, don't overwhelm yourself or you won't accomplish anything."

"These are going to be tough habits to master, Charlie. I don't even have a good question for you on how to do it. This time it's up to me."

"Ken, don't worry too much about developing good habits all at once. Decide on one change at a time. Make that new habit a daily process for thirty days. If you skip a day, start at day one again. It takes consistent practice for an action to become a habit. That's the secret to success in forming new and lasting good habits.

"Let me give you an example. I had to work full time, while I was going to college. It didn't take long for me to realize that I could absorb much more knowledge early in the day, so I started getting up at 4:45A.M. every day. After I showered and shaved, I studied for two hours. Then, I had breakfast and left for work at 7:30.

"I could work out at the gym three days each week after leaving my office and not worry about being too tired to crack the books. Two afternoons a week I had classes and returned to my office afterward. Saturday mornings were also study time. The afternoons were spent with the family, as was Sunday. Somehow, everything got done, but the toughest part was the study habits. Early to rise mandates early to bed, so the only penalty for my study routine was that I had to change my party habits. That was how I *planned* my study, school, exercise and family schedule."

I responded, "Great advice! I'm an early morning type, so I just have to sign up for a course—then, I have to complete it. Charlie, you make things sound so simple. I'll e-mail you Twigg's summary now. Call when you've read it."

Thurston Twigg-Smith

Here's the background on the fifth guiding principle: *Prior Planning Prevents Poor Performance.* Thurston Twigg-Smith's life illustrates this attribute. He is a business visionary as well as a strategic planner. He's also the kind of guy who takes the elephant by the tail and hangs on until he tames it.

This story is fascinating; it's a real-life novel that is great reading in its own right. In fact, the story is so good it was hard to concentrate on the issue of planning. The discussion about his family and Hawaiian history shows that, through planning or lack of it, the Islands might have been something other than the 50th state.

A plan is a draft; a map; a scheme for making, doing, or arranging something; a project; a program; a schedule. Planning means to create an outline; to devise a scheme for doing, making or arranging; to have in mind as a project or purpose. Synonyms for plan are draft, delineation, design, project, sketch, contrivance, method, scheme, and device.

Vision is the ability to perceive something not actually visible, through mental acuteness or keen foresight, as his breadth of vision made this project possible. Twigg is an example of a man who had a vision of the future, then planned, acted, planned again, acted again, etc., etc. Twigg's business story began with a lack of planning by others—a good example of what happens when a person is not accountable to anyone. His uncle had sold 49 percent of the family business—the *Honolulu Advertiser*—because of his lack of vision and planning.

As a young man Twigg had a cursory knowledge of the family business before going to Yale then into the Army. While not directly planning for his future, it helped to prepare him for what was to come, by broadening his outlook and expanding his horizons. If it weren't for that experience he might not have had the vision and the will to take on the family oligarch later.

At the end of WWII, no one was thinking about the changing business, or the cultural or technological environment. Twigg's uncle obviously had no vision for the future of the paper. As Twigg continued to get experience working in different departments of the paper, he learned to love the paper and made an effort to do an excellent job in whatever area he worked. Eventually, he envisioned where he could go in that business and what he could do with the paper.

Twigg realized, along with other Board members and allies that immediate steps had to be taken to shore up the paper so it didn't die before they got control away from his uncle. Short-term planning was important here because "if there is no tomorrow, why worry about next week." It's interesting that Twigg responded to his uncle's resistance and defiance by becoming more focused and stronger.

Spurred on by his uncle's rule-by-terror attitude, Twigg planned and executed his strategy for a business coup to unseat his uncle from the paper's leadership position. At this point he had a vision of what the family business could be and, I would guess, he also had a vision of its possible failure.

Once Twigg was in control, his planning mode switched to saving the paper. It was like a football game where the quarterback calls the plays depending on the opposition. His dealings with the Feds, with his uncle and with the Mayor's lawsuits illustrate that he was very deft at playing the game. His planning strategy included a readiness to make quick tactical decisions. His goal was to achieve the vision of what the family business could become.

Twigg had a superior vision and those who sold their stock did not. However, when you are leading the charge it may be easier to have that vision than if you're relying on someone else to guide you.

The negotiations for the joint venture with the *Star Bulletin*, as well as the relationships that Twigg developed and maintained, were all part of playing this game called business as he moved forward toward success. His ability to make quick tactical decisions is evident throughout. It is a study in how short-term planning is used so the long-term vision can materialize—a major secret to his success.

As the story unfolds you can see that he has become an even more effective visionary. He believes that you don't do business with people you don't like—a very sound planning principle.

Conclusion: I think that Twigg is one of the greatest "quarterbacks" I've read about. He's qualified to be the ultimate family business turn-around expert.

When Charlie phoned again, I was ready to discuss ways to use the information. "Charlie, here is a field I know something about. My MBA and my business experience give me an edge. However, I'm used to preparing my part in an overall corporate plan. How do you *plan* for a start up, or for my own career search plan?"

Charlie responded, "Ken, I still think you should follow through with the direct approach to the fifty company CEO's. You've gotten some good advice from my marketing consultant. Sit down and write out, in long hand, how you would describe yourself to a prospective venture capitalist who would finance you, or a CEO who would give you the responsibility for a division. Why should they support you or hire you? Who are you? What have you done? What kind of track record do you have? Are you the horse they bet on to win—not place?"

"Okay, I can do that."

"In short, succinct statements, describe your earliest plan and how you achieved it. Then, the next, etc. Include just a short list of your academic achievements. The important thing is to try to illustrate how you have thought and acted independently. Review these summaries of the lives of the *Wise Men* and you'll get an idea of how it works."

I responded, "I'll get onto that as soon as I finish my reports to you on the *Wise Men* and their *Guiding Principles*. Remember, finish what you start! Call me back later."

Grason Nickell

Now to the sixth guiding principle: *Organizing for Success.* Nick Nickell has another great life story. Every time I read these oral histories, I'm even more impressed with what these men did. One mysterious element that I'm looking for but haven't found is the motivator. What was the engine, the fire, or the catalyst that moved these men? Was it their upbringing, something in their genes, luck? What made these men movers? It will come to me eventually, and then I'll write a book. Maybe you'll agree to be one of my editorial advisors?

Organization is defined as an organizing or being organized; organic structure; manner of being organized; any unified, consolidated group of elements; systematized whole; especially, *a)* a body of persons organized for some specific purpose, as a club, union or society *b)* the administrative personnel or executive structure of a business. Synonyms are systematization, standardization; arrangement, order; coordination, collection; scheme, method, plan; unification, association and partnership.

Nick is a man who is extremely organized, who has a scientist's mind and used it to better himself and mankind. Nick said he has no mission statement for himself or the company. That's not the classic business model these days. On the other hand, his vision for his organization is to "make decisions for the long-term," and he "prefers private companies and shared ownership." Here we see his bias toward his corporate organization.

It is fascinating that this successful scientist and college professor, who obviously has a phenomenal mind, says he doesn't like to read. I suspect that is because he values original thought so much, which is truly a unique form of *mental* organization. He believes his "best producers and inventors have been people who had good technical capability and whose minds had not been 'polluted' by the universities." Two interesting questions about organization come to mind. Is an organization organized around the show of educational degrees like academia, the government and its contractors? Or is it organized around creativity and thinking out of the box like Nick, Bill Gates and so many other creative business leaders?

Nick is a man who was, is and continues to be a teacher. He talks about the importance of teaching in any organization, which parallels his belief in the ability of people to learn if given the right environment.

His father showed him the benefits of hard work, business and organized thought very early in his life. To watch his father create a new business in the middle of the depression must have influenced the blueprints he developed for his future company.

One of the organizational qualities that Nick learned early was the flexibility to respond to the environment. He always seemed to be able to find a new way to make money, another way to get through college, a creative way to solve a problem. One of the greatest secrets to his success is the utilization of creativity within an organization, especially one that deals with engineering and technical issues.

Knowing that no one else was going to support him in his early life made him aware that people needed to be given opportunities in their work. Whenever he was given opportunities, he seized them. His work ethic, organized mind and personal qualities helped him to benefit from every organization in which he worked. Therefore, any organization that expects to get the most from its people must not only give them the environment to succeed, but also be sure that those people have the core characteristics necessary to succeed: integrity, honesty, motivation to do their best, etc.

As I read Nick's story, I realized how he continued to be exposed to all types of organizations, most bureaucratic. In each one of his successes he built a sub-organization to deal with the technical problems that arose. He may be the first person to use a *virtual organization*, one flexible enough to change shape to meet the needs at hand. He assembled the people needed to solve a problem, then went on to the next one and assembled the people to solve that one, too.

Nick values the people that make up his organization. In fact, what is an organization, but people? If you organize a place with an environment to succeed, will the people succeed? Nick seems to have figured out how to make sure that they do.

The phone rang. When I answered, I immediately said, "Charlie...." Then I heard the recorded voice of a telemarketer. I was glad that it wasn't a real person, but I learned to wait for the caller to identify himself before I rushed on.

A few minutes later, when Charlie did call, I told him of my other lesson in life. He said, "Patience is something else you need to learn, Ken."

We had a good laugh before I continued, "Charlie, this story cleared up some of my misconceptions. I can now see how *plan* and *organize* fit together. I *plan* to get my story in front of fifty people. Your marketing consultant will help me present it on my own website. He will help me *organize* my story so that busy people can quickly differentiate between me and the many others seeking investment backing or a senior level executive position."

"That's right, Ken. But once you decide on a plan and organize everything necessary to achieve that plan, you must *activate*. Otherwise, it's ready, aim, aim, aim, etc. You never pull the trigger. The seventh guiding principle is to learn how to *Become an Actuator*. What is your reaction to the Bob Midkiff story?"

"I've been pondering the question about what moves all of these men. I found some clues from Bob Midkiff's oral history, which, like so many of the other histories, is a stand-alone story. If anyone is an actuator, it certainly is Bob; he is a man of action and his life illustrates how to master this principle. I'll send you his summary now."

Bob Midkiff

Actuate is defined: To put into action or motion; to move or incite to action, as, men are actuated by motives; to carry out, to execute. Synonyms are to act upon, impel, induce, instigate, move, and prompt.

Growing up on the campus of a prestigious school, with a father who valued learning, undoubtedly helped to form Bob's early attitudes. His Dad kept him busy with lots of mental stimulation. Bob believes that good genes helped as well. Somewhere in the mix of heredity and environment, he became a man who took action.

He wasn't seen as a "preppy" and had to work much harder to be accepted. Many of the *Wise Men* have similar histories, which may be a key in learning to think independently and take the necessary steps to make your own way.

In his first job, when he was asked to write a manual on recruitment and manning for the Merchant Marine, he applied himself and did the job. Even in his first years in the military, where he was actually discriminated against because of his education, he succeeded by doing the job creatively and correctly.

As a very young man, he took the opportunity to learn Japanese and has used that knowledge throughout his life to succeed and to contribute to his home state of Hawaii. He was a real actuator in the military, quickly learning the system and using it for his own benefit in Japan and Korea. During those military years his self-confidence grew. Can a person be an actuator without self-confidence? Not likely!

When he took action and made the choice to move back to Hawaii, he instigated a defining event in his life. Instead of asking others to help him decide whether or not to give up law school and business school, he made a bold decision that allowed him to begin a new vocation.

It's interesting that he was on vacation when he was asked to gather information on profit sharing plans, which became a major turning point for his career. A self-actuator sees an opportunity no matter where it is, and knows how to turn lemons into lemonade at any time and in any place. Bob even turned chicken pox into a learning opportunity that furthered his career.

Bob looked for opportunities and found a potential answer for another related problem—the deteriorating downtown Honolulu. Again the actuator finds gold in every turn. As long as Bob was leading and negotiating, he could get people to cooperate and make progress. Another trait of a self-actuator is the ability to lead well, earn respect and even get the intransigent to follow.

Bob's time at Amfac shows his ability to lead once more when he had to clean up a mess created by someone else. An actuator can radiate such confidence that people who have been burned or alienated can be persuaded to come back in and negotiate.

I never thought about this before, but one of the real strengths of an actuator is his command of respect. Everyone respects someone who can make decisions with great honesty and integrity. Respect is one of Bob's great secrets to success. It is remarkable that a United States Senator asked Bob for his advice about what committees the new Senator should join.

An actuator/leader also does not let disappointment or setback bother him. Bob created success out of frustration when he didn't get the Presidency of Amfac. Instead of retreating, he built his own company!

Bob saw great things happening, but also had the vision and the will to take action to make them even better. Another trait of the actuator is the belief that things can always be improved.

Bob's story is one of a long steady, *involved employee* approach. Bob says, "I just KNEW that, without all the bank overhead and bureaucracy, I could make a good living if I stayed with the plan." An actuator/leader makes his plan and confidently executes it, taking the personal risk to move ahead. Bob was successful because of his great confidence in the people who worked for him.

Conclusion: Bob Midkiff learned very early that self-ishness didn't work. Giving opportunities to others permeates his story. His life now is totally devoted to the good of the less fortunate; maybe that is also a key to a successful actuator/leader.

As I pondered about the defining events in Bob's life, I realized that the motto, "do it now, do it right, do it right now, and do the hardest thing right now," was the key to becoming an actuator.

When Charlie telephoned, I told him that I had grasped the meaning of the motto and I was going to contact his marketing friend. His response was, "Do it now, we'll talk later." And he hung up.

So, I sent an e-mail to Charlie's marketing consultant:

I'll send you a draft of my achievements and my experience dealing with different kinds of companies. If I'm going to enter a new field, I should have at least some knowledge about it. I'll call you tomorrow to discuss it.

There, the die was cast. I was investing in a personal website. Then, I'd need the right people to click on it. If I moved ahead based upon a well thought out plan, which had been organized properly, I'd succeed.

I wrote the essay on the next *guiding principle*. I was on a roll and we could discuss the summaries after he read this one on control.

Jerry Stone

Control is defined as: to check or verify by comparison with a duplicate register; to regulate; to verify an experiment by comparison with a standard or by other experiments; to exercise authority over; direct; command; to curb; restrain; hold back. Synonyms include restrain, rule, govern, direct, check, curb, overpower, counteract, and dominate.

Controlling can be defined by Jerry's comment about his former partner: "He had the ability to change direction many times in order to keep the company moving toward what the market needed." Here the concept of controlling was setting strategic direction, not micro-managing. Jerry would decide what war to fight and what hill to take then let his well-trained troops go into action.

By taking the hill and winning the war, Jerry learned the difference between those who claimed to be leaders and those who acted like leaders. He believes in managing to a person's strengths, not their weaknesses, and molding his team together into a community. You could call these techniques training, leadership, etc. However, he is really controlling the environment in which good people exercise their talents to move the organization toward a strategic direction. He delegates to qualified people and leads by example.

Jerry discusses self-discipline and controlling yourself. Having passion and enthusiasm for what you do (one of his greatest secrets to success), learning to fail successfully, and seeing only delays not failures are all fundamental principles which are attitudinal in nature. However, one must control ones own thought processes to achieve the attitude of winning as opposed to the attitude of failure.

Effective control is related to the degree of feedback. Jerry's analogy is to "put it on the scoreboard." For example, how long would you enjoy bowling if someone put a curtain in front of the pins and you couldn't see how many you knocked down? Control, motivation, attitude, reward, recruitment of good people and retention of new people all depend upon the ability to give them the score on their efforts.

After I sent off the e-mail to Charlie, I took a break. The house was quiet, so I went in search of Pat and the kids. I found them in the kitchen poring over some of the stories. All three were engrossed in what they were reading.

It was ironic that my entire family was learning from *my* defining event. I was pleased that what I was gleaning from Charlie and his *Wise Men*, I could share with my family and we could all gain insights from the mentoring chain.

Over dinner I asked the kids if they had formulated any plans yet for earning their allowances and helping around the house. I sat quietly, for a change, and listened to their ideas. I offered encouragement, but I didn't tell them how to do things; they needed to learn how to plan, organize and execute their visions on their own.

After dinner Charlie called, "Ken, let me give you an example of how to control a plan. Several days ago you sent me an e-mail on how much money you could earn if, in a financial planning practice, you had one hundred new clients in your first year. They would save or invest twenty percent of their income. Then, you'd repeat it in the second year. You were in clover in your fifth year.

"Yes, some people can build this kind of practice fast, but they are the exception, unless they are part of a *team* of people in a private banking division of a bank or investment house and other members of the team share in compensation. Therefore, I suggest you don't speculate on compensation in a field you still have much more to learn about.

"Too many agents and brokers set unrealistically high goals for themselves. Then, they make little effort to control their plan, which wasn't realistic to begin with. The most powerful force in human affairs is the *realizable wish*. So, the key to controlling your plan is to very carefully plan only what is reasonably achievable.

"I admire your enthusiasm, though, and if you later decide to enter the financial planning field, I'll make some introductions. While unemployed and short of funds, you'd start with two strikes. Get established in a salaried position, build your reserves, then decide whether you want financial backing to start your own business from a venture capitalist or to become a financial consultant."

I thanked Charlie for his sage advice and gave him my understanding of the last two principles. "Charlie, I'm convinced that these last two vital *guiding principles* are essential for success and real happiness in life. I'll give you examples of how they evolve from the life stories of Jack Grady and Sam Higginbottom. E-mail is on its way."

Jack Grady

Self-confidence is defined as confidence in one's own judgment or ability; reliance on one's own opinion or powers, without other aid. Synonyms include self-assurance, security, self-control, equanimity, and composure.

Independence is defined as freedom from influence, control, or determination of another or others; self-maintenance or self-government; income sufficient to make one independent of others; freedom from bias, persuasion or influence. Synonyms include freedom, liberty, exemption, autonomy, self-reliance, and confidence.

Jack Grady grew up in a supportive atmosphere that his father created. He began to develop self-confidence and independence very young with his first "business" as an eight-year-old. Later these qualities helped him finance his college education.

Growing up, people either learn positive attitude habits, as Jack did, or negative ones that can develop into fear of the unknown and unhealthy emotional dependence on others. All leaders depend upon others to do their job effectively. But the delegation of authority is linked with *accountability*. True leaders, like all the *Wise Men*, don't have *emotional* dependence on others.

Jack's experimentation with entrepreneurial ventures after college, before going into the big corporate world, was also the result of his independent spirit, his self-reliance and self-confidence. These attributes were well ingrained in Jack because, after seventeen years in the corporate world, he took the opportunity to start an independent venture.

When Jack took over Juice Bowl, he transformed his self-confidence into a confidence in others. Recognizing that the people at Juice Bowl were his biggest asset, he made provisions for them to participate in the company's success with an ESOP. By doing so he hit upon the true formula for success and his greatest secret to success. Jack's re-acquisition of Juice Bowl (with his family) at age eighty-three is certainly a great example of self-confidence.

Throughout his life, Jack was able to take a problem and turn it into an opportunity. His independence and self-confidence allowed him to recognize hidden opportunities in the well-disguised turning points in life.

Sam Higginbottom

Sam Higgenbottom's story illustrates just about every one of the attributes of a successful person. *Emotional Maturity* is not something you have, but rather something that you show because you are!

Emotional maturity isn't even easy to define. If you take the word emotional by itself it is not generally a positive term in business except perhaps in the context of motivation. But add the concept of maturity to it and it changes dramatically. To be emotionally mature is to be emotionally full-grown, emotionally ripe, emotionally highly developed, emotionally perfected or worked out, in a state of full emotional development. It can also mean emotionally perfect and ready.

After going through Sam's oral history, I believe that there are a few examples that truly show the nature of his emotional maturity. Since this attribute is such an all-encompassing and pervasive part of greatness and success, real life examples are rare.

Sam has developed an attitude, belief and habit of listening to other people. He was able to influence and lead many people with this quality, which is one of his greatest secrets to success. How else can you explain the confidence that management and union workers placed in him? That is an example of emotional security.

When Sam, after some encouragement, agreed to step back in and try to save Eastern Airlines, he exhibited the emotional maturity to do what was right, not what was necessarily expedient.

Another important exhibit of emotional maturity is how he dealt with his wife's Alzheimer's disease. He cared for her and hired loving caregivers to help him. The ultimate emotional maturity is to keep your vows and commitments—no matter the cost. This example also provides insight to Sam's integrity and loyalty, two other secrets to his success.

On the phone with Charlie, I said, "While waiting for your call I looked up some words. Did you know that self-conceit is above self-confidence in the dictionary? Charlie, if you think about it, there is a fine line between one and the other. It truly takes a BIG MAN to maintain a degree of humility, while also having the self-confidence to do what Jack Grady has done."

"Yes, Ken, Jack is also creative, full of integrity, and shows a deep interest in everything and everyone around him."

"And, Charlie, regarding Sam, I can see why you selected his life as an example of a person who has achieved the highest level of Emotional Maturity."

"Ken, if you don't have a sense of the path you should take after the past three weeks of soul-searching, don't fret about it. As you encounter different people or situations, you are better equipped to respond now, after reading and learning from the examples of mentoring and leadership of the *Wise Men.*

"However, at your level of accomplishment you'd reject any spoon-feeding by anyone. You have read about some very accomplished people and have spoken with some of them. Don't hesitate to call any of them to get their reactions to your ideas. They're outstanding mentors.

"Incidentally, Ken, I'll now send you the last short story— mine. One of my editorial advisors suggested that I write my story. It's not as impressive as our *Wise Men,* but some of the challenges I've faced in life might be interesting to you, as you face your present challenges. We'll talk soon, Ken. Good night."

I read his story as soon as it came in. I responded by e-mail since it was late in the evening:

> Charlie:
> Thanks for sharing your story with me. You and Bill Dauer demonstrate the value of persistence. You fellows and the other *Wise Men* just don't give up. In fact, I'm making that the eleventh *secret* or *guiding principle.*
>
> I really enjoyed reading the stories of all of the *Wise Men.* I can see why you are such an advocate of lifelong learning. It also appears that an early struggle to stay independent helps a person form the habit of not looking to others for their personal or financial independence. I have some catching up to do.
>
> I'm up to the challenge and now that I've included Pat in my thought processes and planning—and I'm really listening to her views—she's supporting me emotionally, verbally, and in action. She's willing to go out and get a job, but I want her to stay at home with

the kids for a while longer. Therefore, I am going to focus on creating a plan for maintaining my present income level so we can live in our own home and in *our own world*. When I have the first draft of the plan completed, I'll appreciate your critique.

Chapter 15

Transition to Independence

One week later

I sent Charlie an e-mail to update him on my progress:

> Charlie:
> I've almost finished my plan outline. I described each of the marketing campaigns I developed for my former company and the results. I also called all of the customers I dealt with and asked for testimonial letters as to my role in the planning and execution of the plan. Several of them want to talk with me about a career with their company, which I will do just as soon as I have completed my website.
>
> I'm giving myself sixty days to make a career decision, and I'm not going to touch my 401(k) Plan. My former company has agreed to segregate the assets and give me some time to make up my mind as to whether I want to roll it into an IRA or withdraw it.
>
> Incidentally, my former boss told me that their man in Cleveland is struggling a bit to get the situation turned around. He again asked if I would be willing to consider a transfer. I've also received some phone calls from former colleagues of mine, who are very

concerned about the pressure that the company put on me, without notice, to accept a transfer or resign. They want me to keep them in mind, if I find opportunities that I reject. A couple of them have asked for an employment contract, but have not heard back from the head office.

I will have my website up and running within a week. I'm flying to Portland tomorrow to videotape a three-minute introduction. My education qualifications, company achievements, association memberships, speeches, and articles will be highlighted. I'm going to pay for this site over a twelve-month period, with the first payment starting in ninety days, which is a great deal of help to me now because of my current tight cash flow situation.

Pat has helped me edit my website remarks and her degree in English is really coming in handy. Your marketing consultant indicates that he will have some part-time work for her from home doing some editing for some of his clients.

I had a long telephone visit with Bodie Bodenheimer about a possible career in banking, and he advised that the private banking division of most large banks would be very interested in my background and business connections. He is a proud North Carolinian and invited me to visit his plant in Franklin to determine whether a career with Zickgraf might be in the cards. If I can't find something in the Bay Area to maintain our lifestyle, I am definitely heading for North Carolina.

One month later

I sent another update to my mentor:

Charlie:

The website is really working. Thanks for the recommendation! As you suggested, I sent short succinct e-mail messages to CEO's of companies who might need someone with my background to help increase their sales volume. I review their websites and in the subject say, "My comments regarding your website." Then in the body of the message I describe my background. In other words, I do some homework. I end the short message with, "Click on my website. It will take less than five minutes to determine whether a personal interview would be appropriate."

In many cases, the CEO forwards my e-mail to their human resources person, but in almost every case I am able to get some kind of response. I've had a number of first interviews, a few second interviews and am considering some offers. I guess I'm marketable. That website really helped!

Several CEO's wanted to know who had designed the site since they said it was superior to their own very expensive, but somewhat old-fashioned site. So, I'm stirring up some business for your marketing consultant, who said he'd pay me a commission for any new business.

I also received a phone call from my former boss who had been directed to my website by several of our customers. He said they asked why I was no longer with the company. He now wants me to consider reaffiliation. I told him I wouldn't be ready for that kind of discussion until I finalize some other career opportunities. However, in consideration of the feedback I've had from people who called him for a reference, and received a glowing report of me, I had a social lunch with him.

He offered to take me back in my old job, with a direct track to taking over for him when he retires in three years. He said the head office is now negotiating contracts with several of their field executives and that they will have an employment agreement for me to review prior to acceptance.

I've told him I would like to have you as my consultant so I don't get into conflicts with the company. He's agreed and indicated that if your fee is reasonable, the company will pick up the tab. Incidentally, I've called a few of my other company friends to suggest they might ask you to represent them as well, since you will be already familiar with the company, its benefits program and the culture. However, I'll let you deal directly with the head office on that.

When I make my final employment decision, if I decide to go back, I'm going to insist on a three-year contract with options, and some restricted stock in consideration of all the years I've given to this company.

I'm also going to devote a few hours each week to learning something new. I'm going back to school so I can *transition* to entrepreneurial independence in the future.

In the meantime, some of the younger executives in my former company and some friends of mine in the neighborhood have called to ask me for advice. I'm going to have to learn how to be a mentor, and, at the same time, earn a living.

Giving advice to someone without knowing all the facts of their situation is not wise, so I merely send them the same ten questions you sent me and tell them to call me when they have some answers. So far, I've only had a couple of people take me up on the offer, so it's been a great screening device. It'll probably take some defining event in their lives to cause them to want to answer those questions and get to know themselves better.

You were there for me, Charlie, at a time in my life when I was in the midst of a defining event. I want you to know how much I appreciate your interest in me and the help I received from the *Wise Men* while discovering *their secrets to success*. I learned more from you and your *Wise Men* in the past two months, than in the ten years since I earned my MBA and thought I was ready for leadership.

I now realize that *true* leaders are mentors because they've *been* mentored. I won't break the chain. I'll learn even more when I take on a real mentoring challenge like the one that I became to you.

Charlie responded:

A mentor can accelerate the process for a protégé to reach his or her goals. Also, the bonding that takes place enriches the lives of both people. Great power to you, Ken, as you take control of your own life.

Section II

Chapter 16

Introduction to the Wise Men

The title of this book was selected because of the *secrets* shared with me by the *Wise Men* I interviewed about how to overcome lapses in leadership that result in failure for many thousands of reasonably competent people. If these people had developed early on the habit patterns described in this book, their careers would have been more satisfying, families less dysfunctional, and we would now have a much larger cadre of entrepreneurial leaders in America to build and maintain our unique private capital system.

There are two kinds of people: leaders and followers. Leaders are typically independent and are not born—they evolve! So, how do they evolve into leaders, at what point do they come to a fork in the road that forces them into a decision—*lead* or follow taking the course of least resistance? What are the defining events in their lives that lead to a transition from dependence upon others to independence in their activities and attitude? How can we look down the road of life and prepare ourselves to take the *leadership* turn? What in our early childhood do we draw on to keep us motivated when others drop out?

How can we think logically and objectively about the *critical* issues and determine possible outcomes from potential actions and select, from many alternatives, the *least unacceptable* course of action, after assessing all of the other unacceptable alternatives? Most of the very important decisions a leader makes involve some degree of risk in order to achieve objectives and the ultimate reward.

It is our objective to outline some basic principles which successful leaders, who are also mentors, have adopted to help them make their long climb to *significance* in their lives. It's more important to a Leader/Mentor to be of *significance* to others than to be *successful*.

To better understand how the leadership *mystique* evolves, I interviewed eleven of my friends in their late fifties, sixties, seventies, and eighties, who have become Leader/Mentors for many of their associates. I could have interviewed many other friends who have achieved this kind of success, but deadline constraints and a desire to keep the length of this story manageable made this impractical. I refer to these leaders as the *Wise Men* since the definition of wisdom is "a combination of raw knowledge and experience," and they have both in abundance.

The way to avoid being taken for granted is to remain veiled. However, the *secret* to the success of a Leader/Mentor is to maintain a leadership mystique while getting close to those whom they mentor. One definition of mystique is "mystical attributes of or attitude toward some person or thing." These men are respected by all who know them. They are very knowledgeable and have many years of experience in mentoring other successful people. There are many other *secrets* to the success of the people who were interviewed, and along the way they have developed many *Guiding Principles* which can help anyone bring focus to their lives.

Eight of my younger friends in their forties and early fifties, who have acquired the leadership mystique and also have a natural mentoring attitude, agreed to work with me to add depth to the study of this important subject. They also interviewed these *Wise Men* and shared their perspective and thoughts on mentoring, leadership lessons, and their applications to life. The following are short biographies of these entrepreneurial editorial advisors:

- David Binns is in his early forties. He was formerly the Executive Director of the ESOP Association and is now East Coast Director of the Foundation for Enterprise Development.

- Bill Chetney is also in his early forties. He recently sold his interest in a $3 billion asset company he and his partner created in 1991.

- Ralph Christie, in his early fifties, is President of Merrick, one of the nation's fastest growing architectural engineering firms. He has created a unique stock purchase/option program for his key people.

- Paul deVille is in his early fifties and is CEO of Pomare (parent of Hilo Hattie stores). He was formerly President of Persis Corporation, which owned a chain of newspapers and real estate all over the country.

- Steve Love retired at age fifty and sold his interest in one of his companies after building it from scratch. He recently graduated from an Executive MBA program and now owns an interest in several businesses.

- Brian McShane is in his late forties and is President of the Advertising Checking Bureau. He developed a turnaround strategy for ACB, which included management investment.

• Scott Sangalli is in his early fifties and is CEO of Morrison Supply. He has built a $15 million company to over $300 million during the past fifteen years.

• Mike Scherr, in his late forties, is the former General Agent for Mass Mutual in Hawaii. He built it into one of the largest agencies in the Islands. Mike is now our Managing Director—PCC Hawaii.

Chapter 17

Bill Dauer

Retired Senior Executive
Chambers of Commerce
Lodi, California

For those who have accepted the reality of change, the need for endless learning and trying is a way of life, a way of thinking, a way of being awake and ready. Life isn't a train ride where you choose your destination, pay your fare and settle back for a nap. It's a cycle ride over uncertain terrain, with you in the driver's seat, constantly correcting your balance and determining the direction of progress. It's difficult, sometimes profoundly painful, but it's better than napping through life.

The future is shaped by men and women with a speedy, even zestful, confidence that, on balance, their efforts will not have been in vain. They take failure and defeat not as reason to doubt themselves, but as reason to strengthen resolve. Some combination of hope, vitality and indomitability makes them willing to bet their lives on ventures of unknown outcome. They also have staying power.

Nothing is ever finally safe. Life is tumultuous, an endless losing and regaining of balance, a continuous struggle, never an assured victory. We need a hard-bitten morale that enables us to face these truths and still strive with every ounce of our energy to prevail.

The previous quote is from John Gardner's book, *Self-Renewal*. In his Hawaii Executive Conference presentation in April 1999, he describes the ideal leader as a person who improves the *society* where he lives and makes a difference in the lives of those in the community. Few politicians are able to accomplish these goals, and, unfortunately, most business leaders are afraid to tackle them. While reviewing the highlights of Bill Dauer's very successful life, I realized John's remarks described Bill, one of my longtime friends and influential builder of the San Francisco Chamber of Commerce. He, like John Gardner, believes that people who think like capitalists should be involved in building the very important non-profit sector of our society. Bill has dedicated his business life to making the communities and cities in which he has lived better places for everyone to live.

When I first came to San Francisco, in the early 1960s, Bill was already making a difference in this great city where I would have my office for thirty-five years. He organized and participated in twenty-seven International Trade missions. The first business groups were invited to the USSR and China. These trade missions attracted eighteen international banks and sufficient headquarter companies to keep office vacancies to 3 percent or lower annually. He also organized teams of top San Francisco executives to visit major cities in the United States to sell San Francisco as a good place in which to do business and establish their headquarters.

In his interview with David Binns, a member of our editorial advisory board, Bill said:

> I'm basically a salesman and a fundraiser. I was able to analyze a city and assess its strengths and make contacts with business leaders to organize them around common themes of economic development. I was able to establish peer-based relationships with business and political leaders, so they perceived the

Chamber itself as a problem-solving organization. It was definitely on-the-job training. I did not even know what a Chamber of Commerce was when I applied for my first job at the Lexington, Nebraska Chamber!

In San Francisco he attracted the top business leaders of our region, and nation, to serve on his board and executive committee. People like Steve Bechtel, Sr., Chairman of Bechtel Corporation; Cyril Magnin, Chairman of J. Magnin Company, the City's major philanthropist and Patron of the arts who *adopted* Dauer and made the Chamber his favorite cause; Walter Shorenstein, whose company owns or manages many of the high-rises in our city, (he was also Bill's partner in many real estate ventures); Sherm Sibley, Chairman of PG&E; and Ben Biaggini, Chairman of Southern Pacific. He built a ten department, fifty-five person staff and funded an increased operating budget six times the largest in the country. Through voluntary contributions by the business community and proceeds from projects—not subsidies from government—he accomplished this great feat.

When David Binns questioned Bill about the biggest challenges he has had to overcome, Bill replied:

When I took the job as President of the Chamber of Commerce in San Francisco, the city had a shortage of luxury housing. A housing construction boom soon followed that resulted in a glut of luxury housing. To avoid the same boom/bust dynamic in regard to commercial construction, the Chamber approached the Planning Commission and offered to take on the role of determining how much space should be built out each year AND recruiting businesses to fill that space.

During my twenty years as President of the Chamber we never had a boom/bust cycle in commercial real estate. But to meet our growth goals we had to take trade missions to Europe to promote San Francisco as a business-friendly location. I led delegations of CEO's from eighteen to thirty prominent SF companies for three-week tours to three countries and five cities. We focused on developing relationships with banks on the assumption that they would be the likely source of advice to companies looking to set up operations in the U.S. The strategy worked—we never had more than a 3 percent vacancy rate in commercial space during my twenty-year tenure at the Chamber—though the vacancy rate has risen to as much as 20 percent in subsequent years.

I first met Bill, through our mutual friend, the PR whiz, Art Blum, when we were both involved with the Convention Bureau as vice presidents. Bill was hosting CEO luncheons at one of our city's finest hotels. These groups of twenty to twenty-five CEO's would meet from time to time to discuss the city's problems and come up with solutions.

When Bill left the Chamber, he joined us as a Principal. He also went on five boards of directors of local companies, including Blue Shield of California, headed by his long-time friend and fellow ex-marine, Tom Paton, who had built the largest Blue Shield organization in the nation. However, old friends in Springfield, Missouri finally convinced him to move to that city to create an Economic Development Corporation and oversee a consolidated Chamber, Industrial Development Commission and Convention Bureau, which he did before eventually moving back to California.

A sports enthusiast, Bill co-chaired the movement of the Dallas Texans to Kansas City as the Chiefs football team. He is currently a director of the San Francisco Sports Hall of Fame, an organization that he and the former president of the

San Francisco 49ers, Lou Spadia, created in 1979. Their group has raised more than $2 million for youth sports equipment.

Bill went into semi-retirement in 1988, built a beautiful home in Lodi, California, and volunteered his services to the Lodi Memorial Hospital Foundation. Their fund, which had taken ten years to build to $165,000, was at $9 million as of December 31, 1999. He is currently on the board of four non-profit organizations in Lodi and is always selected as finance chairman. This man knows how to raise money!!!

A true *venture capitalist* for the *non-profit* world, he is also a legendary mentor of chamber presidents all over the nation—there are 3,600 chambers in the country. Bill was president of the American Chamber Executives Association with 2,600 members and is now a life member. He was also the first chamber executive to be elected to the board of the United States Chamber of Commerce. Other leadership roles include director of the National Chamber Litigation Center and director of the Arbitration Council of the San Francisco Bay Association. He was also on the Mayor's Fiscal Advisory Committee.

While he was doing all this good work to stimulate *business* as head of several Chambers of Commerce, Bill became a prudent *investor*. It has been many years since he has had to *work* for a living. But he does it because it's fun!

I showed Bill my list of ideal qualities of a Leader/Mentor (LM). They are not necessarily in order of importance. Depending upon the situation, one quality might be deemed more important than another; however, a person that does not have *all* of these qualities in some measure will have a difficult time building an organization that endures.

• LM's must be people of *integrity* who are proud of their accomplishments; their word is their bond; they are consistent in their behavior toward others and can build long-term friendships and relationships. They have compassion for their family, friends and associates as well as a passion for their work. They also contribute to the society in which they live.

• LM's are *loyal* to their associates, but they expect outstanding performance from anyone to whom they delegate responsibility. They recognize their associates' strengths but constantly challenge them to work on improvement. They help their associates learn how to delegate to others. When they are sure that the associate is competent, they freely delegate to those people who are treated as *partners*.

• LM's are *lifetime active learners and listeners*; they are *dreamers* and *visionaries* of what is possible. However, they are very careful about what they *plan* to accomplish, as they are tenacious in *achieving* what they plan. They are able to *focus* their energies and *finish* what they *start*.

• LM's have a strong will to win, but will only do so by playing fair and square. They are *flexible* and *adaptable* to changing times and events and can bounce back from disappointment. They regard *failure* as merely an *idea that did not work*. They do not feel that because the *plan* failed, *they* are failures.

• LM's will take a *calculated risk*, but they are not gamblers. They are willing to invest in their own ideas and take responsibility for financing an enterprise on a *conservative* basis, keeping plenty in reserve for emergencies.

• LM's have a genuine *humility* and believe that *anything can happen* when credit for an achievement is publicly shared with others, who helped assure the success of a plan.

Bill, who for over twenty years was one of the most influential people in San Francisco, agreed with me on the essential qualities of a Leader/Mentor. He added, "Leaders must trust their own instincts almost totally, then select associates with skills that are superior to their own in certain areas." Bill always looked for highly intelligent people who would be stimulated by working with each other. He also made room at the top for the young hard-charger. If a person was not able to fit in, Bill helped them locate a position where they *could* be successful, and then promoted a more qualified person. Because of the care he took in helping people find positions for which they were best qualified, some of Bill's best friends are former associates.

Donna Shaw, Bill's assistant, shared the following with me:

> Bill Dauer is one of the most important people I have met. It tells you something about a person when he retains so many friends and contacts throughout the United States. It always surprises me that he stays in touch with so many previous business associates, employees and friends and that each and every one of them is very friendly and personable.
>
> Bill is the kind of boss who builds confidence. He will give me a project and let me run with it. If it is not quite perfect, that is okay. He will give me pointers for next time. As a boss, he does not have to demand perfection, he makes you want to be perfect. As his assistant, I want to do my best and give my all.
>
> Bill is truly a wonderful mentor and I feel lucky to have been able to work with him for the last six and a half years and hope to remain by his side for many years to come.

Bill Dauer was raised in Lincoln, Nebraska in a small railroad town and graduated from Nebraska Wesleyan University with a BA in finance and management. His father, who was a railroad boilermaker, lost his eye in the height of the depression in an accident and lost his job. He then had to walk seventeen miles each way to work on a road gang to support his family. Bill's mother was a housewife. Both his parents were educated through the sixth grade and then had to work. One of Bill's early memories is watching his mother set aside *pennies* so that she had 25¢ for the Metlife man. Bill decided, early on, that he wanted to have a *quarter* ready and he has been a big believer in insurance, from an early age.

Bill grew up in a very loving family, with parents who sacrificed so that he could have the best. His friends envied him for his parents. In the 1930s, during the depression, money was not plentiful and a weekly movie plus a few radio programs were the passive relaxation for most people. Reading a good book could generate excitement. Language and communication skills were developed through dialogue among children, their parents, aunts, uncles, etc. Bill said his family were *talkers*, which helped Bill in his present command of the King's English—one of the secrets to his leadership success. He truly valued the time that his parents spent with him and he spends quality time with his children. In raising his own family, he has followed his parents' example. Bill and Shirley's kids are their favorite people.

My interview with Bill was very helpful in identifying another *common denominator* of all gifted leaders: their total focus on *approval of self*, as contrasted with the need most people have for *approval from others*. When I questioned Bill about his childhood, I shared with him my growing conviction that the way we are treated in the first few years of our lives has a major impact on whether we will be able to take life in stride, or whether it will be a struggle. Bill answered that "he was *surrounded* by the love of his parents, even though they were not affluent." In response, I reflected upon my early childhood and the love that came from my own family, my aunts, uncles and cousins during frequent family get-togethers—especially our family picnics.

The self-confidence, that ultimately allows us to find happiness in our lives, is created in our first few years of life, because of the acceptance that we, as children, feel. The greater the acceptance, without spoiling the child, the more the child learns to stand on his or her own two feet. "Tommy" gets his first bike by earning half the cost, which is matched by affluent parents, or *all* the cost because his parents do not have the money, but have a lot of love to share. A child who is raised this way will easily climb up the mountain of life to a peak of *contentment*.

Many of the tragic failures in leadership I have observed involve a second or third generation heir taking over a fine business. The coddled heir runs it into the ground when suddenly faced with having to make a tough decision and having to rely upon the advice of others, who do not have to take responsibility. It is very lonely at the top of the decision-making tree and the seasoned business leader must have an abundance of self-approval. He or she may not be able to *earn* the approval of associates, because they do not like a particular decision.

As Harry Truman once said, "The buck stops here!" Truman's early childhood training in self-reliance resulted in his ability to make the tough decisions himself, after getting input from his talented cabinet who were attracted by his inner strength of character. There's a lot of Harry Truman in my close friend, Bill Dauer.

Bill told David Binns during their interview that he considers Major Lonni Hill one of the most important influences in his life. Major Hill, a tough Marine uncle, inspired Bill to join the

Marines. One defining event in Bill's life was his decision to enlist in the Marines, where the discipline and self-confidence he developed helped him become tenacious in accomplishing his goals. In his words, "I felt they could be smarter, bigger, better looking, but I was hungrier and could outrun them." He was a Marine Raider during WWII and served on the Staff/Command Board in San Francisco. Bill still keeps in touch with the surviving members of his Marine Rifle Company in yearly reunions. Although he was seriously wounded during WWII, it does not diminish his appreciation for the Marines and how they helped him control his own destiny.

I could write another book on all of Bill's accomplishments. He spent his life promoting the image of the business chieftains, who formed his leadership cadre in the various chambers he built, by helping them attain *civic* leadership. He *involved* them in making their city, state and nation a better place in which to live and build business organizations to employ people, who could be self-sufficient, educate their children and become better citizens.

I once read that "the *group* becomes the sum of the knowledge, experience and integrity of its members, who should be carefully selected." Bill carefully selected his leadership groups from the business leaders in the city where he assumed the responsibility for guiding the Chamber of Commerce. These leaders helped him choose effective board members, and then recruited *activist* Chamber members. His carefully chosen, trained and mentored Chamber staff could then tap the collective wisdom of the board, and many of the members, to create and implement plans to make their fellow citizens more business oriented. This arrangement, in most cases, resulted in more *business people* running for and getting elected to *governmental* positions of power.

Bill said his feeling of *relentless searching for problems to solve* did not go away when he retired. He is now committed to making Lodi a better place in which to live—because that's where he lives!! Bill's recent project was to retain as much *social capital* in Lodi, California as possible. He organized the leaders of all of the worthwhile non-profits in Lodi so that their *collective* fundraising resulted in appropriate allocation of capital and income to support *private* sector efforts providing better education, health care and social services. Police, fire, environmental issues, effective zoning and many other community services and issues can only be addressed and provided through *laws* that can be enforced.

If all of the nation's non-profits could do *their* jobs effectively, our tax burden would be reduced. If responsible people could be motivated to serve their turn as *citizen* politicians, *bad* laws would be repealed, *good* laws would be passed and young people would again start to believe that we have a system that really works.

There are a few really good *career* politicians, but they are in the minority. Most have been in office so long that they have lost touch with the reality most people face each day. Political *families* have emerged, where it is considered a *birthright* for the children to follow their parents and grandparents in government service. A loyal network of campaign contributors for members of both our major parties assures the gusher of dollars needed to get elected to even a minor office.

Media costs are astronomical and their profits come from *paid* advertising. The Supreme Court has determined that *money* is speech. Therefore, trying to get campaign finance reform will be an uphill battle as long as more *have-nots* in our country than *haves* vote. Powerful interest groups that want to maintain the status quo influence most of the have-nots. Incumbents and those who inherit the large *networks* of campaign contributors will not try to change laws that allow them to stay in office or be elected to a higher one.

I do not know whether the following was a creative thought by a writer or based on historical fact: "Nobility is defined by our actions, not by birthright." There are few *noble* politicians today, as politics has become *very big business!* Committed Chamber of Commerce leaders can change this. The *entrepreneur* is the heart of American business. Most business leaders are independent-minded and it takes a very strong Chamber Chief Executive to *attract* and *keep* their attention. In my *good old days* of San Francisco, Bill Dauer spoke for and was backed by the business community. Business leaders supported George Christopher, who is considered San Francisco's greatest mayor. He cleaned up corruption in many city agencies and turned over a well-managed city *that worked* to his successor. He became one of the greatest mayors of *any* city.

After Bill left the Chamber, it was difficult to fill his big shoes fast enough. Today, one of the great cities in the world struggles to be considered a good place in which to do business. The citizens of the City have always been fairly liberal and compassionate. Most of the business leaders and their staff are also commuters and, therefore, do not vote. Bill Dauer, George Christopher and their leadership teams managed to keep all of the various factions together in a *common cause*. It was a unique partnership of a *non-profit* and *for profit* leader. George was a successful businessman before he became mayor, and he also built an unbeatable city government *team* to solve problems.

We moved our offices from Montgomery Street to Marin County in 1998 to solve the frustrating commute nightmare of our associates who had to spend up to three to four hours *daily* just getting to and from our office. However, I still miss the excitement of the City and try to get to San Francisco

Rotary meetings on Tuesdays when I'm in town for my *San Francisco fix*. But it is still not like the good old days in San Francisco that Bill Dauer helped create!

Chapter 18

F. P. Bodenheimer
CEO, Zickgraf Industries
Franklin, North Carolina

I know no such unquestionable badge and ensign of a sovereign mind, as that tenacity of purpose which, through all change of companions, of parties, of fortunes, changes never; bates no jot of heart or hope, but wearies out opposition, and arrives at its port.

Ralph Waldo Emerson

Almost everyone, at some point in their lives, has a special teacher in school who takes an interest in them and encourages them as no one has before. That is one reason why teachers are so important today—they can influence so many lives for the future. "Bodie" Bodenheimer's most important non-family mentor was a very gifted teacher who made him feel that he could do anything he set his mind to do! She also helped instill a very disciplined work ethic, while influencing many aspects of his life, including a lifelong habit of *reading to learn.*

The former president of France, Poincare, said, "Discovery favors the prepared mind." Bodie started preparing his mind at an early age. He enlisted in the Navy at age seventeen where another important mentor entered his life, a commander, who recognized Bodie's talents and elevated him as an enlisted man, to an officer's job to learn navigation. When Bodie got out of the service, he started at Appalachia State and ultimately became Chairman of its Board of Trustees. In his first year of college, a physics teacher warned him that he was going to fail in that subject unless he worked hard and had a *learning breakthrough*. He ended up teaching this course, which he said helped him learn how to think through complex issues; the study of physics requires one to *believe in laws* and *examine results*. He used this thinking process to become a highly successful leader in banking, the military and in the business he bought, before he had a deep knowledge and understanding of that business. However, he had the benefit of previously learning solid principles of *coaching* and *mentoring*.

After graduation he coached football at Appalachia State, then at a high school in Charlotte, NC. Many of the kids in Charlotte were from the other side of the tracks and both parents worked. Working with these kids helped Bodie understand human nature and in the first year his team won nine games and lost only one. They had a few bad years after that, but Bodie said, "Those guys never lost the fights they had after the game, as they loved to fight!"

One of his friends, the boxing team coach, who later went into business and became very successful, took his team all the way to the finals in New York, beating everyone along the way. When the reporters asked the coach how he motivated his team, he said, "Very simple. Before they go into the ring, I tell them: all those who win today, eat." The most popular explanation for lowered motivation is "too much prosperity." The old adage that a hungry fighter is hard to beat is a valid one.

Bodie relayed another story describing the poverty of some of the students. "Clam" was a young man with a big head and even a bigger mouth. Bodie was trying to teach the kids on his team to *eat right* so that they would *think right* and their bodies would *work right*. The kids would buy a donut on the way to school for their breakfast. One day Bodie bought one, squeezed it in front of his team and fat came running out. He slammed his hand down on this glob of fat and made it into a pancake. He then said, "See what's happening to your stomach when you eat this stuff." Clam raised his hand and said, "Coach, are you through with that donut? I'd like to have it." The lesson Bodie learned was that these kids were hungry! He remembers Clam's request when he is tempted to tell people what they *should* do. He discovered there are forces of nature that he could not control!

One of the nation's greatest football coaches, Bill Walsh, recently addressed my San Francisco Rotary Club and described the way he built the 49ers into a world class team. Walsh spent time, alone, at his own *planning retreat* to plan every *minute* of the six-week training session. He did this each year!

Walsh also planned every play *before* each game. Then, afterward, he determined whether any play needed improvement. His cardinal rules were the key to his *team building*: the coach must suppress his ego and listen to others, and the players must do the same thing. Every person on the team must do the best at *their* job; some will move to a different slot and will do better in that position. Each player can win or lose a game by their performance on each play, so concentrate on quality delivery. He also described the disciplined practice of Joe Montana and Jerry Rice. Montana practiced every week with Walsh at Menlo College; Rice practiced alone each week, running pass patterns so they became automatic and habit.

Bodie used his coaching skills in his business and military career very effectively. He was on active duty in the reserves and an officer in the National Guard for thirty-nine years. During this time, two generals were mentors. He still frequently sees General Cecil Adams. Bodie and Cecil developed an ROTC program when Bodie was commandant of the North Carolina Military Academy at Fort Bragg. They conducted a six-week training program during the summer for ROTC students from all over the country. This program is now considered one of the best courses in the world and is similar to a *mini* Harvard Advanced Management Program, sponsored by Harvard, Yale, Stanford and many other universities.

Steve Love, one our editorial advisors, also interviewed Bodie. His perceptive comments add insight to Bodie's character:

> The first thing that came to my mind after interviewing F. P. "Bodie" Bodenheimer, retired Bank President, ex-Brigadier General and current CEO, was that *this is a gentleman who commands respect*. What might come to mind when you read the words *Brigadier General* and the phrase *commands respect* is General Patton played by George C. Scott standing on stage dressed in his uniform and barking out orders. It is not that Bodie would be incapable of that type of leadership, if needed, but that is not what impressed me about the man.
>
> Bodie earned my respect through his high moral and personal values. He understands the importance of education and lifelong learning. Bodie has had many successes in life—mainly through helping others. He believes in people and that, given the right opportunity and education, they will be successful. He continues to prove that every day at his company in North Carolina.
>
> Bodie is very focused and goal-oriented. He is very clear that there are right and wrong ways to achieve one's goals. Integrity is paramount to Bodie and he

instills that in others. He has been described as an *uncommon* leader. It's too bad his leadership qualities are not more common. The world would be a better place and definitely more educated.

I too am very goal-oriented and one of my goals is to go to the hill country of North Carolina, meet Bodie and tour his company—Zickgraf Industries. Heaven forbid, but if we ever do go to war again, hopefully we will have more uncommon leaders like General F. P. "Bodie" Bodenheimer.

Thank you Bodie.

Bodie attributes much of his success in his various endeavors to lessons learned in the military about management, motivation and leadership style. He has some firm concepts about *leadership*. Most people have the capacity to lead, but lack commitment. They get comfortable with the status quo. Their commitments lack execution or implementation. The most important part of leadership is the habit of *finishing* what you *start*. Once a person has this habit, then the next skill is to learn to develop a plan. However, the greatest planners in the world, without learning the discipline of *finishing* what they *plan*, will not succeed. Bodie feels that until someone starts worrying about something, nothing happens. Discipline leads to concern, then to developing ways to eliminate worry. The more experience you have, the more confidence you develop.

When Bodie retired as President of First Citizens Bank of North Carolina in 1987, he joined us as our North Carolina Principal. He had also just retired as a Brigadier General in the North Carolina National Guard. A couple of years later, one of our clients, Grant Zickgraf, President of Zickgraf Industries, decided that it was time to consider retirement. He was seventy-nine years old and had just terminated his

COO, after a very bad year. Grant decided it was time to *sell* the company, because the plan we had designed a few years earlier could not be effective without a very competent CEO successor—a fatal impediment to a perpetuation strategy.

Bodie and I spent over a year trying to locate a buyer who would pay a fair price for a company that was losing money each month. I eventually suggested that Bodie consider buying the stock owned by Grant, which was 37 percent of the company. Our venture capital fund board declined to co-invest with Bodie because this was a turnaround situation. Therefore, Bodie negotiated a 90-day option for extensive *due diligence* before agreeing to acquire Grant's stock and elect a new board. He invited J.T. Hunter, my longtime friend and client, who had introduced me to Bodie, to join his board and then orchestrated a rapid turnaround.

We had designed an attractive Supplemental Executive Retirement Plan for Grant to give him a retirement income. That plan was a liability Bodie had to assume. Bodie also had to cope with an established ESOP that had been installed by another firm. Zickgraf had not installed an ESOP funding plan at inception and the ESOP repurchase liability was becoming a problem. We had designed a Management Stock Ownership Plan (MSOP) and an Incentive Bonus Program for the managers, but since there had been no profits for a few years, Grant had made *discretionary* bonus payments to help the executives pay their bills.

Bodie also had to deal with the bank that had loaned too much money to the company to finance the sale of stock to the ESOP and additional money to keep the company in business during the loss years. Fortunately, Bodie—as a former senior banker—was able to build a solid long-term relationship with the bank. He informed the banker: "Guess what? We're partners. If you pull the plug, we'll both lose money!" He also informed the managers that *special* bonus payments would only be made from profits, and that if they kept their shares they would have to guarantee their share of the bank loans. No one took him up on that offer so the company offered to buy the managers' shares for 20 percent over the fair market value. Everyone took that offer.

The ESOP participants were also insecure about their ESOP accounts as the loss in market value had been substantial. So Bodie assumed still greater risk and pledged personal assets to guarantee a bank loan to buy back ESOP shares, at the same 20 percent premium!

This former banker and retired general then started a weekly, four hour each way commute from Greensboro, where his wife said she wanted to continue to live, to Franklin, where he immersed himself in a very different business than he had been accustomed to.

From $8 million in sales produced by seventy-five employees in 1991, Bodie and his associates now generate $50 million in sales with 250 employees. They changed the mission of their building supply division and closed down all but one branch, focusing on sales to contractors and subcontractors, and *just-in-time deliveries* to reduce the amount of inventory they must maintain. They set up a computer-tracking program so that each piece of wood, as it comes into the gate, is followed all the way through the cutting, drying, flooring, shipping and collection process.

They have two teams who monitor production: one on *waste control*, where they track any waste back to the manufacturing unit, then help that management team refine the system; and one on *quality control*, where they're able to improve the quality of the product while minimizing waste. It is called "The Mountain Man Quality and Waste Management Control System." Each one-percent of waste they cut, adds $200,000 to the bottom line!

Bodie also created a Design Center to demonstrate the products they sell and recruited interior decorators to work with customers from all over his market area to plan for new kitchens, living rooms, bedrooms, etc.

His experience in the military gave him a real appreciation of the importance of international trade and a respect for the typical international businessperson, who is normally highly educated, well read and very smart. Therefore, to tap the European market of 365 million people, Zickgraf now buys wood in China and sells it in Europe to satisfy the European demand for wood products. Russia and some other former Iron Curtain countries are suppliers of large quantities of wood, but they are not a *reliable* source to the Europeans. Bodie considered manufacturing in Europe until he analyzed labor costs in Germany, where an employee costs $22 per hour, with only $10 going to the worker, due to their very high taxes.

At Zickgraf he developed the Zickgraf Educational Program, which started in their lunchroom for three hours, twice a week. Bodie is convinced that you have to make people *feel good about themselves*. Employees who have not graduated from high school can come in with their spouses and children and each is paid $7 an hour for attendance. He also provides a meal. The first class had twenty-three people. They now have seventy-five people in the process of finishing high school.

He also set up the Zickgraf Health Services Plan. The company pays for annual medical exams and all shots. They conduct clinics on how to quit smoking and chewing tobacco with a cash bonus of $500 for those who actually quit. He has a long-term commitment to building a *world-class* company and knows it will take lots of people who are highly committed, and then some time.

A great football coach in the 1950s, Bud Wilkinson, taught my good friend, Don Curran, two excellent management rules. Don used these rules to build a world-class career in broadcasting. The first was "Prior Planning Prevents Poor Performance." The second was "Give the Play Time To Work."

In seven years, Bodie's basic game plays (a little more complex than when he was coaching a football team) are working well. Bodie is truly an uncommon leader. It is a continuing pleasure to see him excel in his third very successful career.

Chapter 19

Joseph Dacey
Chairman Emeritus, A. H. Hansen Sales, Ltd.
Honolulu, Hawaii

That man is successful who has lived well, laughed often, and loved much, who has gained the respect of the intelligent men and the love of children; who has filled his niche and accomplished his task; who leaves the world better than he found it, whether by an improved poppy, a perfect poem, or a rescued soul; who never lacked appreciation of earth's beauty or failed to express it; who looked for the best in others and gave the best that he had.

Robert Louis Stevenson

Starting when he was age seven, three women and three men had a significant influence in shaping the habits and attitudes *Sunny* Joe Dacey has today at age seventy-six. His mother, although not well educated, made Joe feel good about himself. She listened carefully to him and constantly told him he was going to be very successful. Her nickname for him was "Sunny Joe," she said, because "he brings sunshine into every life he touches."

Joe, the eldest of four children, developed a positive attitude about almost everything and everyone from his caring mother. His mother also suggested that when he got older, he save part of every dollar he earned. Today he still saves a portion of his considerable investment income from a portfolio he personally manages and has built into a significant personal estate.

The second woman in his life was a teacher, a nun, who taught him to listen very carefully and not interrupt others who might be trying to listen to a lesson. After being distracted by Sunny Joe's enthusiastic whispered comments to another student while she was teaching class, she stood him in the corner so that others in the class could concentrate on what she was saying. An embarrassed little Sunny Joe learned how to pay attention and focus on every person who had something to say and to learn from everyone he meets. The third woman was his godmother who lived in an area without electricity or running water near Joe's upstate New York hometown. Her home was just a summer farmhouse where he spent part of the summer each year. He looked forward to his visits with her as she taught him how to chop wood, pick ripe tomatoes and pump water. Her big smile and cheerful disposition made him feel special. When he did a good job of pumping water, her beaming acceptance of that accomplishment made him view work as fun, an attitude he has today as he enjoys anticipating the markets, economy, and company performance in the management of his own investment portfolio.

The first male mentor in Joe's life was his father who drove a milk wagon and allowed Joe to help him on school vacations. Joe sat next to his dad and watched the way he handled the team of horses pulling the wagon with a firm, but gentle hand. Joe's leadership style was developed from his early life experiences and was used when he was an officer in the Navy during World War II, then CEO of his own company and president of the Pacific Club and Waialae Country Club (the Sony Open is played at this beautiful club). He leads with a firm but gentle hand.

The next male mentor was his grandfather, who had eight children and was a hard working chauffeur for one of the town's wealthy families. He taught Joe the virtues of hard work and staying on the straight and narrow path of good behavior. If Joe strayed from that path just the slightest, a frown from granddad was all that was needed to straighten him out. Frowns and smiles let Joe know at a very young age which kind of behavior was going to make him feel the best about himself.

His third male mentor was his Uncle Mike, a priest, who helped Joe with his facility in English. Words are the handles by which conversation is controlled. Joe mastered this art over many decades. Some call it *persuasion*; others call it *selling*. With Joe, it was a complete understanding of what the other person felt and wanted. Joe tried to help people *get what they wanted.*

At age twelve, Joe decided to help his father pay the rent of $30 per month. He sold magazines at 5¢ a copy and earned enough to contribute five dollars a month to the family and still buy nice clothes. In today's dollars, it would be the equivalent of a twelve-year-old boy earning $100 per month to help his family. How often do we expect this contribution from our children? In Joe's case, the experience of earning money to help his family made him feel *even better* about himself.

While in school with kids who came from wealthy families, he was proud of how he looked and talked. He was his father's *partner* in taking care of *their* family, and his Uncle Mike's tutoring gave him an edge when dealing with other kids who could not really express how they felt. Joe was becoming a self-confident leader.

No welfare system in the world could have helped Joe grow into a leader before he entered his teens as a mature, self-sufficient, honest and cheerful person. It took the personal relationships Joe developed with six different people (*not a village*) at a very early age, to give him the platform for a life that ultimately affected—in a very positive way—countless other people, including his family, company and employees.

At age fifteen, he secured a job as a waiter in an Italian restaurant. The chef, who could not speak English, took an interest in Joe because Joe took an interest in *him* by bringing him a beer from time to time. *Sunny Joe* became a popular waiter and his earnings from tips when added to his modest salary were $50 per week. About that time, Burton Kaufman, a schoolmate who was from a wealthy family, became a close friend. He advised Joe not to worry about the modest lifestyle of his family. He said, "Just do the right thing and people will admire and notice you." Today, according to our mutual friend Bob Midkiff, Joe is one of the most admired men in Hawaii. Coming from a man like Bob, that is the ultimate compliment.

Joe's perception of himself has not changed, though, since he was seven or eight years old. "Scratch the eggshell veneer of every person you meet, and you will find the seven or eight year old child they will always be." Those early lessons Joe learned were vital. Burton just reinforced them, as did others whom Joe met during his lifetime. Many friends also opened doors for Sunny Joe. He took advantage of *opportunities*, not *people*!

The positive attitude that Joe adopted early in life was a major factor in the creation of a solid food wholesaling business that Joe and his partner built from the $2,000 they invested in it in 1953. After working for others all his life, Joe joined Art Hansen who had just started Hansen Foods (A.H. Hansen Sales). Joe wanted to be rewarded for his own hard work, do things on his own and control his own destiny.

Following Art's retirement many years ago, Joe continued to build a fine company. Joe and Art started out sharing profits with everyone who became their partner-employees in a plan installed by Bob Midkiff.

We helped him sell the company for over $6 million after the person he had selected as his CEO successor moved to the mainland. The departure of his CEO left Joe with a very productive employee group—most of them with very large profit sharing accounts—but no CEO to assume Joe's financial and leadership role in the company. Again, the fatal perpetuation flaw.

Joe gives much credit to Art Hansen for the growth of their company from one employee to over 100, and for the loyalty, personal growth and success of their employees:

> Right at the beginning of our partnership, Art told me that he wanted to share any success we might have with our employees. I shared his feelings and had sent several suggestions about employee benefits to the large Chicago meat company I had previously worked for.

> Sharing with employees, in addition to the profit sharing plan, included health insurance for the employee's whole family, scholarship money for every child of an employee who attended college, as well as student awards to the local university and community colleges. We provided mentoring help to some who needed it and hosted quarterly meetings with all employees regarding their profit sharing plans, where a guest from the bank or an investment group was often available to help the employees with their own investments.

The firm became very family-oriented, and our employees' good fortune grew as the company grew. It was a winning philosophy that helped the employees as well as the company, much like the effect that ESOP plans now have.

Joe's *sunny* disposition, in Hawaii, is called the *Aloha Spirit*. His comments to his employee associates in November 1993 at The Royal Hawaiian Hotel show the depth of his concern for the people who helped him build the company and for the successor CEO he selected to provide guidance for his *second family*.

> Our founder, Art Hansen, started this company on a shoestring with $900 and Art's minister's help and prayer. When Art had just lost his job, his minister, Eddie Spirer, made Art kneel down right in the parking lot and told him to ask for the Lord's help: to start his own business, to always treat his customers honestly and to treat his employees fairly and to share with them.

> Thus was created A.H. Hansen Sales and two winning components: suppliers that put almost everything on consignment and probably the greatest group of employees that any company has ever had.

> I applaud the wonderful memory of Art Hansen—and I wish he were here tonight—and I applaud also our employees who have made this all come together.

> It is you, the old-timers—and we have a lot of them still with us—and the new people who have combined to make Hansen Sales the leader in the food service business in Hawaii. Without the kind of commitment that you have made, it never could have happened. So

I personally want to thank you all from the bottom (and the top) of my heart.

For me it has been a wonderful experience working with a group of devoted people—warm and feeling people—talented and hard working people—who have helped Art and me to put this thing together. I will never forget one little part of it—even if my memory one-day fails.

So, on to the future and my good wishes to all of you. I think with the talented supervisors and officers of our present company—with the business acumen and the warehouse facilities that our new owner, Mike Clifford, has—that this company—and all of you— will continue to grow and prosper—and that is my wish to all of you. "E Keia Maikai Ahi Ahi"—maikai meaning good or wonderful. Aloha no—a hui ho— warmest wishes and see you soon.

Mike Clifford, a prominent Hawaii businessman, acquired Hansen Foods and continues to run the company as an independent entity. Joe's daughter continues as their leading sales representative. Most of Joe's former employees continue to enjoy a good work environment and participation in the 401(k) Plan, which replaced their profit sharing plan. My daughter, Julie, provides advice for the employees who now make their own investment choices.

When Paul deVille, an editorial advisor for this book, interviewed Joe, he discovered many interesting aspects to Sunny Joe's outlook on life. Joe believes the key to business success, and success in life, is in understanding people, getting closer to your customers, and sharing the wealth with your employees. These keys to success blend well with his simple, but important goals: to enjoy life, to make money, and to help the people with whom he works.

Another lifelong learner, Joe believes the secret to growing is to learn something new every day. He likes to read history, especially Hawaiian history, and enjoys studying languages. Political, financial news and current events are also daily topics of interest. Learning is one constant that can have a large positive impact on your life.

Joe has always had the ability to observe and learn from those around him. One of his greatest strengths is his understanding of people, which was enhanced by a good education. Joe looks for people who can learn from their own experiences, who can clearly distinguish between right and wrong and who are good listeners.

Though it is not necessary to be charismatic, Joe thinks a mentor should be knowledgeable and accomplished. Encouraging the mentoring philosophy in his company, Joe focused on illustrating how people performed their jobs well, in order to encourage others to grow as individuals, and as employees. These employees, who are like a strong family, describe Joe as a caring person and someone who is very young at heart.

Today, Joe and his wife Mary Ann travel all over the world and spend quality time with their children and grandchildren. And Joe continues to mentor those who come to him for advice and counsel.

Chapter 20

Bob McKinnon
Former Chairman and CEO, CV Industries
Newton, North Carolina

We live in deeds, not years: In thoughts, not breaths; In feelings, not in figures on a dial. We should count time by heart throbs. He most lives who thinks most, feels the noblest, acts the best.

Aristotle

Bob is one of the youngest of the eleven current or former CEO's interviewed. His background is very similar to the other people included here. His family had a moderate income, and he grew up on a farm in a small community near Burlington, North Carolina. His dad made him toe the line and this upbringing helped Bob develop a work ethic and a *do it now* and *do it right the first time* attitude. His mother was a spiritual and calming influence and a good balance to his father. She helped him develop an unselfish interest in other people and the traditional manners of a southern gentleman, including ethics and common sense. For example, if your friends are considered bad, then so are you. Today's youth, who respond to the wrong kind of peer pressure, need this type of advice from their early mentors, whether they are family or just a caring, interested adult. *You are known by the company you keep*, and *you become like those with whom you associate most.*

According to another member of our editorial advisory board, Ralph Christie, who interviewed Bob McKinnon, many of his strengths were encouraged and developed when young. Bob believes his greatest strengths include a strong conscience. He is perceptive in evaluating situations, does not operate on fear, but does keep score. As a competitor, he also believes that calculated risks should be taken.

At age nine, Bob was mowing lawns and helping farmers harvest. Later, he worked in a service station and gristmill. He was becoming self-sufficient at an early age. Competitive, he excelled in baseball and football, where he learned even more about discipline and the necessity of teamwork. He was also a good student and active in student government in his small high school. His grandmother, a major influence and example for him, took the necessary time to listen to him on their long Saturday walks during some very special visits. She made him feel good about himself!

I have had the opportunity, over time, to see Bob relate to a number of people. He always finds something special about each person upon which he can develop a positive focus. This attention makes other people *feel good about themselves*. Bob, an optimist, looks for the best in others. His habit of careful *active listening* leads to an *understanding* of the other person's point of view. When a person feels his or her position is understood, most will reciprocate and try to understand the situation from *your point of view*.

The people he looks up to and those who have influenced him in business and in his life share some important traits. He told Ralph Christie that a common theme of those who influenced him is "people who have inner strength, are very perceptive, are excellent listeners, and take facts before motion." He believes that "successful people can deal with champagne or beer people and understand the differences and appreciate both." In business or in life, someone he would trust would be someone with whom he would share a foxhole.

Leaders are very careful about whom they adopt as a mentor. Bob's two most important mentors were very different people but had a few common attributes: they were both very perceptive, highly educated and could compartmentalize their thought processes so as to focus, without distractions, on a number of activities at the same time. They also avoided staying so busy with the *urgent* that they neglected to do the *important*. One of Bob's most successful protégés, my associate, Joe Wisniewski, has another graphic way of expressing this idea: "Don't stay so busy chasing ants that the elephants get away!" I am reminded of the expression, "Don't bring me anything but problems, good news weakens me," when I think of Joe. He and Bob have worked together in business and Joe is now one of our partners.

In his interview with Ralph Christie, Bob described how his mentoring relationships work. He prefers a one-on-one situation with the protégé, and it usually involves more than one meeting, because a lot must be done to change behavior. When correcting or reprimanding someone in a way that mentors the person, Bob believes it should be done privately. "Don't do it when you are mad. Have a separate meeting after emotions have calmed down. Say, 'We have gone through this before….' Don't shoot from the hip; help them understand your expectations. Someone fired should not be surprised." To build confidence in a protégé, Bob says, "Show them your honesty. Have open communications. Be consistent."

Those people with a high IQ and PQ (People Quotient) will be successful in almost anything in which they have an interest. Bob developed his PQ early on as a roofing salesman, while working his way through Elon College—starting at age nineteen. He was the first in his family to graduate from college. One job was as a door-to-door, *cash with order*, roofing salesman. Bob initially struggled with what all of us who started out in direct sales felt: *hot doorknobs* or *call reluctance*.

This experience helped him develop through trial and error a process to solve almost any problem and make a decision. Bob uses the same process to this day: (1) define the *problem;* (2) *get help* to understand all possible options and alternatives; (3) assure that those who must make things happen *agree* on the best alternative; then (4) make a decision, or get one! He also learned to never paint himself into a corner where there was no escape, and to always leave room for an alternative. If alternatives are not viable, cut your losses on the project and move ahead with the next.

He analyzed every unsuccessful roofing sales attempt and decided that he was *talking to* a prospective buyer rather than *talking with* them. He then developed a *dialogue* method of communication as contrasted to the *monologue* that so many people use to try to communicate. Bob would make an observation then ask a question. He would *listen* until he understood the other person's situation a little better. Then, he would make another observation and ask another question until eventually the prospect began to respond to his or her own conclusions so Bob could discover what they wanted. Then he did the necessary research to create a roofing project to meet their needs and fulfill their desires.

His gentle probing resulted in the prospective customer identifying goals, which Bob could help them achieve. He also developed a very effective way to get an initial *small* decision, which led to a *chain* of decisions. For example, his questioning process would establish that the prospect wanted to eventually have a new roof, but either did not have enough money to pay for the whole project or was reluctant to commit to a large expenditure. Bob would then focus on discussing that part of the roof that was in the worst shape. He would then quote a price for *that* section and suggest they authorize that *small* project, which was very affordable, then wait awhile before considering starting the next.

Bob also learned the value of persistence and not becoming *discouraged*—ever! He understood that he might be *disappointed* from time to time, and, therefore, learned to *fail successfully*.

He compared his early sales experience to playing football and said that he could not just play the ball between the twenty-yard lines, that he would have to push it in from the twenties and over the goal line. One of my associates, Mike Scherr, the highly successful former General Agent for a major financial services company, has recently taken up boxing. His description of those who *play between the twenties* is they are *dancers*, not *punchers*!

Bob has another graphic description for those who do not *walk the talk*, they are *pretenders* not *players*. His years of dealing with people at every level have helped him identify the *pretenders* and concentrate on helping the *players* reach their potential. He learned this skill from his mentors. In addition, after he left the Army, he took a year of postgraduate study in industrial psychology then started his business career in industrial relations and human resources work. Now, he has formal education in *understanding human nature*.

After he graduated from college, where he developed additional leadership skills and mental toughness, and pushed himself to limits he did not know existed, Bob joined the Army. At age twenty-four, five weeks after graduating from Officers Candidate School, he was appointed a company commander. Bob used good common sense in dealing with his First Sergeant, a highly decorated Korean War veteran, who had a very unusual but reasonable request, which Bob granted. The result was more freedom of action for the First

Sergeant than is usually permitted. Bob allowed this irregularity, but only if the company performed at the highest level, which they did by becoming the consistent honor company in his battalion. This risky decision resulted in Bob's promotion to First Lieutenant and Battalion Executive Officer when he was twenty-five years old. The Lieutenant Colonel, who had become Bob's first non-family mentor, recognized Bob's natural leadership and mentoring capabilities and gave this promotion to Bob, a job that normally goes to a major. The Lt. Colonel was tough as nails but could also be very forgiving. On occasion, he would put his arm around Bob's shoulder and show real compassion.

Just before Bob left the Army, the Lt. Colonel had a career crisis and was about to resign because he had been passed over for promotion. Bob gave him some solid counsel—be patient. The Lieutenant Colonel was promoted to full colonel shortly thereafter and Bob had become a mentor to his mentor! Bob was awarded the Army Commendation Medal at the end of his brief military career.

His next mentor, Cyrus Cooley, was a division president of Burlington Industries, a $3 billion company in the 1970s. Bob, at age thirty, became a senior executive in the industrial relations department of a 2,600-employee division. His success in this and other jobs resulted in a promotion to manager of labor relations at the largest *organized labor* manufacturing facility. It was one of the worst profit centers, but became one of the best, generating over $20 million in profits (in today's dollars about $60 million). However, Bob started to try to improve the performance of other departments in his division and was reined in by Cooley who announced, "That's my job." Bob apologized, but then asked for, and got, a meeting every week at a specific time. As the person responsible for the continuing productivity of the 2,600 people in this division, he wanted to understand Cooley's objectives, so he could help Cooley and his other management associates achieve their goals.

When Bob took over as the Labor Relations Director it was a tough, undisciplined place with fifteen cases in arbitration and fifty grievances unresolved. There were sit-down strikes, cars being turned over, shootings, etc. He asked Cooley, "Do we try to co-exist with this union or break it?" They decided that co-existence was preferred, so Bob invited the union leader to his office for a cup of coffee. There, Bob gave the union leader his home phone number and, in return, received his phone number and an agreement that they would contact each other immediately and nip in the bud any problem before it escalated. They negotiated a truce. This kind of offer had never been made and the union man accepted! In eight months, attendance went up to 88 percent and efficiency up to 96 percent from 72 percent. There were no cases in arbitration or grievances on file.

Bob was offered an opportunity with another public company, Riegel, with 7,500 employees, to initially become Director of Human Resources, but to eventually head one of their divisions. He performed and they rewarded, which led to a friend of the Shuford family suggesting that Bob meet with the Chairman of Shuford Industries, one of the largest private companies in North Carolina. When Mr. Shuford asked Bob what he did best, after some thought, Bob responded, "I know how to make money." Mr. Shuford also administered a unique character test. He asked whether Bob played golf. When Bob said he did, Shuford asked his handicap (twenty at the time). He later called Bob's Pro to confirm the handicap. Another candidate for the same job said he had a ten handicap. His Pro said the fellow had never broken 100! Shuford decided the other fellow was not to be trusted! Bob got the job as President of Valdese Weavers, a small company they owned. Harley Shuford, Jr. recruited Bob when Bob was thirty-eight years old, then gave him total autonomy and eventually became his most important mentor.

Bob developed a surrogate son-to-father relationship with Harley Shuford, who spoke fluent French, piloted his own plane, and was a top ranked tennis player, a scratch golfer and a member of Augusta Golf Club. In his interview with Ralph Christie, Bob said the person he most admired was Harley Shuford, because "he did not set rigid standards, he told stories on how he did things, and he explained things to his people." Bob learned to stretch his mind and became even more disciplined. He also learned how to select and deal with highly motivated managers. When Bob would describe a complex issue for Mr. Shuford, he would not receive any *direct* advice. Instead, Mr. Shuford would describe his own experience in a comparable situation with a similar problem, then, he would tell how *he* had solved that type of problem. He *never added*, "Why don't you try the same thing." He gave Bob plenty of space and the freedom to solve his own problems and set his own goals.

The most powerful force in human affairs is the *realizable wish*. Bob learned from his greatest mentor that people respond best to their *own conclusions* and work hardest to achieve *their own* goals. Bob has achieved world-class excellence in running a very large private company. His knowledge and experience in sales, marketing, human resources, general business and financial management resulted in Valdese Weavers having a 1,700 percent increase in profits during the years he ran that company. After two years of running the combined companies—CV Industries, which also includes Century Furniture—profits increased by 400 percent on revenues of over $250 million. Bob considers this job one of his biggest challenges to overcome: he had to assume control of a non-profitable company, was able to make money within one year and continued the profit for sixteen years. "I hired good people, had good communications, and gave the organization some freedom."

Our company worked with Bob's senior people to install a large ESOP in 1996. The $75 million employee trust owns 38.5 percent of the company. Bob indicated that efficiency in the wood plant was up by 40 percent during the first year of the plan. They could more easily deal with their employees as *partner/ESOP participants*, who have common objectives with management in the achievement of sales production and profit goals. The participants increase their own net worth as beneficial shareholders, while enhancing values for the shareholders.

Bob assures that his management associates value their time and his by arranging specific time for meetings with them. He also practices *management by walking around* and gets a lot of comments from employees regarding their enthusiasm for the ESOP. The most common question from employees is: "How's our stock doing?"

The ESOP makes it easier for his management associates to ask their production people for an extra two hours Friday night to fill an order and have it to a customer on Monday rather than Tuesday. This teamwork makes the sales rep a hero and increases the potential for new orders, which increases production and profits. The CV employees do not build crutches for customers to use in complaining about the quality of their products or *not-on-time* deliveries as a reason to defer orders or get other quotes.

Bob's primary message for his management associates is, "Recruit, recruit, recruit—you never know when we may need new talent, so take names and keep in touch." Bob feels their ESOP has helped them attract and retain talented people. One of the most successful of Bob's protégés, Bob

Maricich, is now President of Century Furniture. He sent me the following note:

> Thank you for sending me an overview of your new book. I thoroughly enjoyed the reading. My mother used to tell me that "you are judged by the company you keep." After reading the eleven short bios, I can easily say that according to her standard you are doing very well!
>
> You mentioned a number of times "Emotional Intelligence" as a key ingredient in mentors. I thought if you hadn't seen the article on Leadership that I've attached that you would also find it [relevant] to mentoring. I have always felt a key ingredient of successful mentoring was someone who sincerely wanted to be mentored. Leaders with positive characteristics, described as emotional intelligence, are very attractive to those of us looking to leverage our ambitions and skills by associating with a mentor.
>
> Good luck in completing what looks to be a terrific book. I can hardly wait to see the end product.

As a young man Bob learned how to properly sell roofing. Now his associates are selling the ESOP in the same way. They communicate with those people who can make things happen and do not rely on posters or speeches! In my three decades of observing ESOP company operations, Bob's team, when he was CEO of CV Industries, achieved real excellence in having his 2,700 employee partners understand their *opportunity* and *responsibility* for increasing bottom-line profits. What you measure and reward, you get! Too many company CEO's adopt an ESOP, then sit back and wait for something to happen. It will not.

One of my former mentors, who recently passed away, built a fine private company in North Carolina and felt good about enhancing the net worth of his 1,400 employees. He also taught his management associates to view the ESOP we installed as their greatest incentive program for increased productivity. Our assignment in 1976 was to help management understand the ESOP. The managers would then make sure that their employee associates would know how to make a difference.

I have become acquainted with Bob's lovely wife, Ray. During his interview, Bob described the important role she has had in shaping his life. When Ralph Christie asked him what he believed was his most significant accomplishment, Bob said, "I feel I'm a good father. I've always worked hard to achieve goals and most goals were achieved. And companies have always been better after I have been involved." He also described the unique CV Industries *educational program,* which has increased the percentage of high school graduates to 78 percent of the workforce, up from 50 percent in just two years.

The only thing in life that you can control is *who you are!* Bob McKinnon is a natural leader who inspires others to excellence by the example he sets.

Chapter 21

Curt Ford
General Agent Emeritus
Northwestern Mutual
San Francisco, California

If anything goes bad, I did it. If anything goes semi-good,
we did it. If anything goes real good, then you did it!
Paul William "Bear" Bryant

Curt Ford is one of the greatest *coaches* in his profession. He built a team of top agents with a team spirit much like the legendary Bear Bryant built his teams. His creed was the same as Bryant's quoted above.

As with the other successful current and former CEO's I have interviewed, Curt's first mentor was a member of his family, his mother, a nurse who was born in a two-room, thatched-roof cottage in Ireland and immigrated to the United States as an orphan when very young. She married an Irishman whose grandparents had left Ireland to escape the potato famine of 1848. As one of six children, Curt worked his way through college and law school on a full academic scholarship, with odd jobs as a waiter and a referee for basketball games to pay for food and other necessities.

In his interview with Bill Chetney, a member of the editorial advisory board, Curt explained that his strengths include:

A positive attitude and confidence. Every time something bad happens to me, right around the corner there is something good, so I assume when something bad happens I can anticipate something good from it.

When asked where he got his positive outlook from, if it is something he was born with or learned from experience, he said:

I think it is a combination of the two that happened to me. My mother was born in Ireland and came here as an immigrant. I was the first generation Irish guy. I got to go to both college and law school on full academic scholarships. I've always thought positively, and I've been encouraged to do so by my parents, especially my mother.

Curt discovered the importance of mentors early on, and when he was praised or encouraged by them, he tried to live up to that praise. In doing so, he felt good about himself. One of his earliest *non-family* mentors was a Harvard Law School graduate, Hugh Mackay, who taught him how to prepare and present estate planning briefs for agents and clients of a major insurance company. He later went into that field and became general counsel to an outstanding estate planner in Tampa, Florida.

At age thirty-two, Curt became an agent with one of Northwestern Mutual's legendary General Agents, Gene Koch, who became his most significant mentor. He said that Gene "really cared for his associates. He *showed* he cared, so that they *knew* he cared." In response to my request, Gene contributed the following to this story of Curt Ford's life:

He's good natured, bright, very literary, always on target with the ability to see the big picture. He recognizes that *the best way to proceed is to promote one's mentor!* We were associated in the management and development of a scratch agency and Curt made the experience exciting and fun. His good-humored presence, thoughtful concerns and undertaking contributed greatly to the success of the operation that was split into three, and ultimately four, general agencies for the Northwestern Mutual Life.

Curt joined the Northwestern Mutual (NWM) home office in 1965 as a Senior Marketing Executive. Another mentor, Harold Gardener, taught him to "invest time like you do money."

After becoming one of the youngest General Agents (GA's) at age thirty-seven, he joined three study groups, including a group of four GA's in San Francisco, of which I was a member. I was GA for another major company at the time. His fellow study group members taught him to have a long-range perspective concerning the building of his agency and not to get frustrated with slow progress. Also, he learned to anticipate turnover of agents, financial challenges, tax law changes, and personnel problems—these help a person grow. And it is important to relax and have fun while getting the job done.

When asked about the people he admired most and how he dealt with problems, Curt told Bill Chetney:

> The people I admire the most have been in my own business. Bill Earls was a great mentor to me. I was in a study group with him and several other people who are superstars. They brought me in at age thirty-eight and a lot of the other people were a lot older than I was. They had gone through a lot of different issues and experiences. They took me under their wings. It was just a tremendous opportunity for this little guy from Massachusetts to be a part of this group.

I learned that they all had the same problems I did. I was not going to overcome everything that I came up against. Those problems will still be there and continue, but I just learned to cope with them. People expect certain things from you. My parents did. Those folks who were older than I did. So, if people expect certain things from you, you live up to it. That's what I did. I always felt that I had to live up to their expectations.

Curt built his agency through mentoring talented people, and then assuring that his agency had a motivating atmosphere of caring support. All motivation comes from within, so he did not attempt the typical motivation techniques, which are customary in most financial service organizations. His description of a mentor is, "you must show that you know what you're talking about to generate credibility. What you seem to be on the outside must be the same as what you are on the inside to demonstrate integrity." He backed up these fine character traits with solid training and education. He reads a lot of history books and learns from them too. Winston Churchill and Thomas Jefferson are but two historical figures of interest to Curt.

Curt is one of the most admired financial professionals in America. Here is his list of attributes of a good financial advisor: knowledge, experience, and the ability to communicate complex concepts in business and tax planning. The ability to listen and ask lots of questions is paramount because people tend to respond to what is said, rather than what is meant. Therefore, he trained his associates to learn how to listen by paraphrasing and asking for more information. For example: "What I think I heard you say was.... Is that what you meant?" Or "I'm not tracking you. Would you run that by me again?" These are important techniques to be an *active* listener versus a *passive* listener.

I was at the head table for a recent Bankers Club CEO Forum and had a chance to get acquainted with another outstanding *mentoring leader*, David Pottruck, Co-CEO, Charles Schwab. The following excerpts are from his presentation:

> Last week I read a story about Frank Carubba, the head of the Hewlett Packard Research Laboratory in the late 1980s and early 1990s. When Frank took over the lab, he was determined to create the best team possible. So he conducted original research on team effectiveness. He compared teams that failed to meet objectives with teams that attained good results, and then looked at teams that consistently exceeded expectations...and discovered that the factors that made the difference between mediocre teams and good teams were *motivation* and *talent.* Clearly, the good teams had better quality leadership and better-qualified researchers.
>
> But the difference between the good teams and the superior teams could not be accounted for by these two factors of talent and motivation. What is really impressive was that he judged the difference between good teams and superior teams to be in the range of 40 percent. What made the difference? Carruba found that it was in the *quality of the relationships between team members....* That this 40 percent increment in team performance was accounted for by the way they treated one another...the degree to which they believed in one another and created an atmosphere of *encouragement rather than competition.* In other words, in this high tech and competitive industry, vision, talent and motivation could carry a team only so far. To fully optimize and expand performance, personal values, such as caring for their teammates and communicating with integrity and authenticity, made the

difference between plain success and extraordinary results. <u>Relationships are everything</u>.

What he discovered suggests that talent alone might be insufficient to really assure the best results of a team. It takes a generosity of spirit to bring out the spirit of the collective, and, therefore, the best results for the team. Now you should know that I'm like you. I know how easy it is to get caught up in the tactical day-to-day of operating the company. I know how easy it is to move from graciousness to selfishness. But since I'm a little new at this, I realize that my job demands that I spend a fair amount of time considering what Chuck Schwab and I stand for and how we want to have that reflected in our company.

It is unthinkable to me, at this point in my life, that we would allow our company to drift from the values that are important to us. I want the best parts of myself to be reflected in my work. And, as a result, I need to be in the company of people who support the idea…that the best part of ourselves can be expressed in business, and that profit can flow from those principles. This is managing the business with strength of character. It is not our technology, our clever plan or our innovation that keeps us in front. Our success is built on the same foundation as the Hewlett-Packard lab, or the winners of the great athletic competitions.

Curt is a leader and gifted communicator who believes in the kind of team-building described above. He said, "The most important five words are **I am proud of you**. The most important four words: **What do you think?** The best three words: **I love you**. The best two: **Thank you**. The least important: **I**."

Curt Ford retired at age forty-seven and turned over one of the largest insurance agencies in the company he represented to the man he had recruited a few years earlier to eventually replace him, Ed Tippetts. With a law degree and home office executive experience, Ed became a successful agent and then served for three years as Curt's assistant. Curt and Ed perpetuated a large financial planning services organization of sixty to seventy professionals—a very difficult task and rarely achieved in the financial services field. Most highly trained, well-compensated financial advisors drift off into smaller organizations when their original mentor moves on or retires. Curt built the kind of organization that, under the right kind of successor CEO leadership, could continue to grow and flourish, which it has! Over a ten-year period, Curt increased sales by 500 percent from 1970 when he took over the organization. In the past twenty years, this agency continued to grow and is now many times larger than it was when Curt passed on the General Agent's baton to Ed.

Curt's career path was shaped by a *mentor example* provided by Arjay Miller, former president of Ford Motor Company, who gave up a successful career in business to become Dean of the Stanford Graduate School of Business. After that, he headed up the World Bank. Mr. Miller's advice: "To keep yourself intellectually stimulated and motivated, you should re-pot yourself every ten years." Curt has re-tired himself periodically. He never intends to *retire*!

When asked by Bill Chetney what his biggest challenge had been in life, Curt responded:

> Being a leader of an organization was really hard for me. The CEO who preceded me was very successful but more of a cheerleader type—very dynamic. I'm the quiet type. It was difficult taking over from a person like that. I had to find out what I was good at, and what I wasn't good at, and understand that. I tried to

emphasize the positive and find someone else to do the things I wasn't good at doing.

I also recruited my successor. The agency did not miss me at all. He was a Home Office lawyer in his early thirties and worked with me for three or four years. We had a mentoring relationship.

He initially wasn't sure if he could work on a commission. I guaranteed he would make as much as he did in the home office his first year. If he did not, I would personally make up the difference. I did not have to, as he was very successful. So it's a matter of recruiting: finding people who are good and being able to choose them. It's important to understand with whom you are dealing and what kind of business you are in.

There are a lot of phony people out there and there are a lot of good, genuine people who don't know how good they can be. You might just have to find the people who don't know how good they can be, and help them be as good as they can be.

So, it's about being able to see the talent in people. People have seen that in me, and I have tried to see things in them, and it works very well.

When looking for a mentor, Curt wants to see that "they are successful and have integrity. You can tell they are really interested in you, and they are not trying to be a big deal. They are real, and willing to be helpful." Integrity, though, is the cornerstone of a good mentor.

Curt did a good job mentoring his two sons and is currently mentoring his grandchildren. He feels that we owe our children two things: roots and wings. He also believes that there are only three things to do with money: earn it, save it and then, give it away! He has made lifetime gifts to his children and grandchildren and is now in the process of giving away the considerable estate that he has built during a highly successful career in a very challenging business.

Bill Chetney also asked Curt what his greatest fear was and how he overcomes something he fears. His answers are insightful:

> The thing that makes me successful in many ways is the fear that I will not be successful, and I think this is the greatest motivation.

> I used an organization psychologist. It's said that the vast majority of great successful people—the top executives in many corporations—have a small fear that people will find out that they are just like everybody else, and that they are not extraordinary, even though that is how they come across.

> I always assume in my relationships with my associates that I am just an average guy. I happened to have this job, but as far as I was concerned, as a General Agent, I was working for the agents, and they were not working for me.

> I think I've been successful in whatever I've done because I have credibility. People felt I knew what I was doing, that I could do the things I was saying they could do.

> That's very important. If you just do what you do, you will be successful.

> I have worked a lot of joint cases with agents, and they say, "Hey, this guy knows what he is talking about."

During his many years working with people, Curt has discovered a great deal about relationships. A profound belief of his is: "There are two things bad for the heart: running up hills and running down people!"

Chapter 22

Thurston Twigg-Smith
Chairman & CEO, Persis Corporation
Honolulu, Hawaii

A company can never become what its people are not. The work place must become a place of high quality relationships, based upon a shared commitment to ideas, issues, values and goals. These relationships enable work to have meaning and be fulfilling.

Max DePrees

Thurston "Twigg" Twigg-Smith shares the previous philosophy about building a business with Max DePrees, retired CEO of the Herman Miller Company, one of the better-managed companies in the nation. Twigg, along with the other *Wise Men*, believes that it is important to make people feel good about themselves in *all* aspects of their lives.

When Twigg was ten years old, his grandfather, Lorrin A. Thurston died. Twigg only knew him as a large fellow with a big mustache "that tickled when he kissed me good night." Lorrin A. *did not* tickle Queen Liliuokalani when, in 1893, he orchestrated the overthrow of the last Hawaiian monarch in a bloodless coup. He received no land, government job, or power after the overthrow. His sole objective was to annex the kingdom to the United States, rather than see the Hawaiian Islands become part of the British or Japanese empires. The strategic importance of the Islands to America's defense during World War II, and the current role of Hawaii as a gateway to the Far East, illustrate the importance of this annexation. Twigg's grandfather also bought the *Honolulu Advertiser* for $5,000 a few years later. He became a working publisher and was a self-made man, as is his grandson.

When Lorrin A. died, his two sons and Twigg's mother inherited his interest in the *Advertiser*. Twigg's Uncle Lorrin (Lorrin A.'s son) was CEO and Twigg's Uncle Robert was National Advertising Manager. There was serious conflict among Twigg's mother, his Uncle Robert and Lorrin as the paper was spiraling downward, making a few dollars one year, losing the next. Lorrin was selling shares to employees and a few investors to stay in business, eventually diluting the family ownership to 51 percent. But Lorrin retained the largest share of the family ownership.

Mike Scherr, another Editorial Advisor for this book, interviewed Twigg. His insights are included throughout this life story.

> Obviously very intelligent, Twigg grew up with no money around people who had it. He probably came to the conclusion early that he was as good as and most likely a lot better than others were, which gave him confidence and an optimistic outlook.

During my interview with Twigg, I told him of the general perception in the Islands that he had been born with a silver spoon in his mouth. He laughed and said, "More likely a pair of homemade chopsticks." Twigg was a scholarship student and the first of his family who made real money. An engineering student at Yale, he worked his way through college as a baggage transfer agent and a printer. While in the Army, "he was given a tremendous amount of responsibility in France and Germany in June 1944 through May 1945. After being an artillery officer in the thick of the Battle of the Bulge, fighting serious Germans, he would not be intimidated by an incompetent uncle in a boardroom fight" (from the Mike Scherr interview). He left Army service in January 1946.

At age twenty-four, Twigg returned to Hawaii, where he was asked by his mother and Uncle Robert to become involved with the paper to turn it around. He started at the *Advertiser* as a Retail and National advertising account salesman. He then transferred to Circulation, Business Management, and the Editorial departments during the fifteen years before he acquired operational control and became publisher.

Mike Scherr discovered:

> A less optimistic and tested man would have run, or walked, away from the paper that was losing money, literally doomed to failure with a family member who stood exactly in the way of saving it. He did what he had to do. He worked till 2 A.M. at all the jobs in the newsroom, and when his uncle paid him back by bringing in an outsider to be the new editor, what did he do? He saw it as an opportunity. He made him an ally. He could have quit or tried to subvert or whine. Instead he saw this guy as a pro around whom he could build a new team. He used the newfound credibility to sell the financial backers on financing the stock purchases.

Getting the cold shoulder from his Uncle Lorrin, Twigg was backed in his efforts to improve profits by two of his early mentors, Uncle Robert and George Chaplin. Chaplin was an outstanding editor who had been with a New Orleans newspaper and *Stars and Stripes*, a military paper, before coming out to the Islands in 1958.

Twigg, Chaplin, and Buck Buchwach, a gifted editor, tried to rebuild the paper, but realized that a joint operating venture with the leading Honolulu daily, *The Star Bulletin*, was vital to the *Advertiser*'s survival. However, the family owners of the *Star Bulletin* would not deal with Uncle Lorrin, so Twigg orchestrated *his own business coup* and unseated the family monarch, in 1961, when Twigg was thirty-nine. "He gathered his allies in a sort of Grand Alliance and went after his targets with the precision of the artilleryman. He had a vision of how things ought to be at the newspaper and created it out of necessity" (from the Mike Scherr interview).

Twigg asked Uncle Lorrin to stay on as Chairman when he took over in March 1961 as CEO and publisher. Lorrin only lasted a year before the situation became intolerable, and he retired for good. Twigg's brother, David, was his strong ally in the battle for control, and, in Twigg's words, "was our thinking man." Dave and Twigg are very close friends, which is not always the case with brothers sharing ownership in the same business. During the control battle in 1959 and 1960, Walter Dillingham, an *Advertiser* Director, became a strong mentor for Twigg and encouraged him in his efforts to unseat his uncle.

Twigg negotiated the joint venture in 1962 with the new *Star Bulletin* owners. Bob Midkiff, his long-time close friend, organized this group, which included the successful real estate developer, Chinn Ho. The *Star Bulletin* was much better financed with almost twice as much circulation at the time. It had an outstanding team of businessmen and attorneys, including Marty Anderson, a good friend of both Twigg and Bob, who is now Senior Partner of one of Hawaii's largest law firms. Twigg had only one legal advisor, Russell Cades, to advise him in the negotiations. Russell is currently Senior Partner in another fine Hawaii law firm.

Chinn Ho had been an early mentor for Twigg and helped him acquire his 50.2 percent interest for his family and allies. Chinn Ho's son, Stuart, became President of Gannett Pacific, owners of the *Star Bulletin*, in the 1970s.

From his interview with Twigg, Mike also learned:

> Twigg knew how to get (and take) good advice and was blessed with some great business, financial and legal counselors. They showed him the tactical moves for his strategy. This strategy is seen when he bought an option on a large block of stock owned by a cantankerous old lady. That move sealed the takeover of the paper. Chinn Ho financed the takeover, then made the deal on the joint operating agreement after buying the other paper from the former owners. There was certainly more than a little luck here, in that the Farrington Family wanted out of their paper when Twigg was ready to make the deal. But the joint agreement was no foregone conclusion. His uncle wouldn't speak to the Farrington's when he was in control...and the joint operating agreement was technically illegal.
>
> They moved the pressroom literally overnight so that it was a done deal by Monday morning. THEN they went to DC for permission. It was a calculated risk that the politics of two papers and jobs would outweigh "doing it by the book." They knew it was harder politically to close them down than to deny them permission in the first place. Twigg had received good legal advice and provided good tactical execution.

Twigg and his brother, David, have made sure that all members of their extended family have significant net worth. He is now giving much of his share of the estate he has built to a number of educational, charitable and cultural institutions.

Private Capital Corporation designed and installed a $42 million ESOP for Persis Corporation, which became the parent of the *Advertiser*, in the mid 1980s. Millions in benefits were distributed to ESOP participants prior to the sale of the *Advertiser* to Gannett for $250 million in the early 1990s. Then, the ESOP share of the net sale proceeds (approximately 24 percent) was distributed to the employees. Twigg and David considered them part of their *extended* family, illustrating one of their many philanthropic activities.

Twigg has written an excellent history of the overthrow of the monarchy entitled, *Hawaiian Sovereignty: Do the Facts Matter?* Lorrin A. Thurston's grandfather, the Reverend Asa Thurston, arrived with the first group of missionaries in 1820. Those who say that "the missionaries came to Hawaii to do good—and did well" do not know the facts. None of the *men of the cloth* made money. Some of their descendents took advantage of opportunities, as did a lot of business people who migrated to the islands after the missionaries had been there for some time. Asa's grandson, Lorrin A., inherited only a bible, which his father, Asa Goodale Thurston, inscribed on his deathbed at age thirty-two.

I recently read *Faith of Our Fathers* by Senator John McCain. This outstanding hero, who has become a statesman politician, graduated from the Naval Academy, as did his father and grandfather before him, both of whom ended their careers as four-star admirals. Senator McCain retired a few years after his long imprisonment in Vietnam as a Captain. He was then elected as a Congressman and, eventually, as a Senator.

McCain's father was his primary mentor, but many other mentors helped him develop the strength of character to take on the entrenched interests who oppose his efforts to reform campaign financing. "Adversity, if it doesn't kill you, makes you stronger," believes McCain; he is one strong fellow! In his book he referred to the following "Qualifications for a Naval Officer," written by John Paul Jones:

It is by no means enough that an officer of the Navy should be a capable mariner. He must be that of course, but also a great deal more. He should be as well a gentleman of liberal education, refined manners, punctilious courtesy, and the nicest sense of personal honor.

He should be the soul of tact, patience, justice, firmness and charity. No meritorious act of a subordinate should escape his attention to be left to pass without its reward, even if the reward is only a word of approval. Conversely, he should not be blind to a single fault in any subordinate, though at the same time, he should be quick and unfailing to distinguish error from malice, thoughtlessness from incompetency, and well-meant shortcoming from heedless or stupid blunder.

In one word, every commander should keep constantly before him the great truth, that to be well obeyed, he must be perfectly esteemed.

Twigg was one of the founders of the Hawaii National Guard; he served on active duty in the Army and retired as a Lieutenant Colonel in the Guard. He has all of the qualifications of an officer (or any leader) described by John Paul Jones.

I was involved in negotiations for the large Persis ESOP, the acquisition of a chain of newspapers by Persis, and, eventually, the sale of the *Advertiser*. Twigg is quite a strategist, but keeps everything very much above board. Bob Midkiff, who is the person most responsible for our PCC Hawaii activities over the past twenty years, worked closely with me, Twigg and Paul deVille, who at the time was President of Persis Corporation—the former parent company of the *Advertiser*—

in all of Twigg's projects. Paul is now CEO of Pomare (Hilo Hattie Stores) and Persis is now a real estate investment firm.

In 1991, Twigg was elected by the Yale class of 1942 alumni group to be chairman of what became the most successful class reunion fundraising project in Yale's history. Twigg, Bob Midkiff and other people on his committee raised over $52 million, some of it in charitable remainder uni-trust contributions. Bob recommended this sophisticated gifting program, as he had started to promote this type of philanthropy through American Financial Services (Bishop Trust and American Trust). Twigg was a co-founder of this company with Bob and twenty other friends about thirty years ago.

Twigg's business philosophy is uncomplicated: to be in business with people he trusts and who have fun at what they do. He believes in the *Boy Scout* precepts: Clean, reverent, and trustworthy (his words). In short, he surrounds himself with people of strong and ethical character.

Twigg is now considering retirement at age eighty-one. When he was running the *Advertiser* he had great influence in the islands—his opinion mattered. The *Advertiser* is now part of the Gannett chain and others determine the editorial policy. Nevertheless, Twigg still has significant clout because of his continued involvement with the business community in Hawaii.

Some final thoughts from Mike Scherr include:

> The key to Twigg is that he takes it all as it comes and DEALS with it. He does not waste time or argue about things that are not likely to change. He makes lemonade out of the lemons. He does not seem to be self-reflective. He does not care why things are as they are, as much as how he can make them how he wants them to be. There is some downside: he sacrificed

family life when he was young. Today he seems con-
spicuously well balanced, though, with family and
business, art and collecting. He has learned from
experience.

Twigg paid the price of success, but does not take himself too
seriously.

Chapter 23

Grason Nickell
Chairman, AC Corporation
Greensboro, North Carolina

The leader who can win a battle, dazzle an audience, or smash electoral opposition has something the journalists and historians can write about. How many have ever written about the bonds of trust that George Marshall forged so quietly.

John W. Gardner

The insights into attributes of a world-class leader, that John Gardner writes about above, apply to Grason Nickell. "Nick" Nickell started working with his first mentor, his father, in the family coal and ice business. When not shoveling as much as ten tons of coal in a day, he helped his Dad make the ice. His father also taught him the basics of the refrigeration process. By the time Nick was fourteen years old, he knew what went on inside the refrigeration pipes. Observing his father's humanitarian treatment of people shaped Nick's values, even though his father was a little too kind-hearted to insist on payment from those who were down and out during the depression. One day he commented to Nick that he would find a business where, if he could not collect for the product, his family could eat it.

His father leased sixteen acres of cultivated ground for $10 a year, bought a $10 mule and purchased a used tomato-canning factory for $50. He also had a yard where wood slabs were cut up for use in cooking stoves. They put aside a slab with three good sides and called it a "board." When they had enough of these boards to build the canning factory, Nick, with the help of two laborers, built the 30' X 60' structure. They also did the wiring and installed all of the necessary steam and water piping using manual threading equipment. The only available automatic tool was an electric drill.

Nick experienced all aspects of the farm, from planting the seeds, growing the ten-inch high seedlings, to transplanting them into the fields, which were plowed by the $10 mule. The opportunity to work with the laborers in the fields gave Nick an understanding of the black race and a respect for their culture and deep faith.

Nick's mother kept the books and her interest in math left an impression upon him. Nick remembered his father's experience with accounts receivable and AC Corporation now has a very solid credit policy with virtually no bad debt.

When Ralph Christie interviewed Nick, he asked who his top three mentors were. Nick's response is enlightening:

> I can't limit it to three. The training from my father was marvelous. I had good mentors in school. I woke up about half way through high school to the idea that it was being conducted for my benefit, not as an obstacle to me, so I buckled down and started working and learning. I had a good mathematics teacher and I was especially fond of a physics teacher.

In high school, this physics teacher, who was also a magician, would allow him to assist, as long as Nick was a good physics student. Because he was an adequate magician's assistant, he was awarded a Bausch & Lomb science award. This award later helped him get a job so he could work his way through college. He received excellent early technical training and a scholarship to the University of Virginia (UVA). His background in physics qualified him for an undergraduate teaching position with naval students during World War II.

Nick also helped another mentor, a professor at the university, produce a manuscript and a pre-thermodynamics course that is still in use today. The UVA student-run honor system gave him a great appreciation for the truth that has been unchanged throughout his life. Recently, someone asked him what his company did. He told them, "We do anything that is honorable and profitable, and the priorities are in that order."

He served in the Merchant Marine during World War II as an Engineering Officer. With the exception of ships blown up in convoys and a few Kamikaze attacks, the war was fairly uneventful for him. In between trips at sea, Nick was married and found a supportive partner and mentor in his wife Del. She taught pediatric nursing and helped in earning money for college expenses when Nick returned to college. In her own way, she has been a significant mentor to Nick through her personal example. After he graduated, he taught for a year at North Carolina State.

Nick described his work ethic and accomplishments to Ralph Christie:

> I'm a work-alcoholic. Fortunately, I had a good partner as a wife. I also had a pretty good relationship with my children. I taught them to swim and encouraged them to play golf as early as they felt like doing it. Both of them play fairly well in the high 70's and low 80's. I'm happy to be celebrating my 56th wedding anniversary and I have two sons who are not on dope.

In 1948, Nick joined Air Conditioning Corporation (ACC) and met his most important, non-family mentor, company founder, Sturgis Siglar, a self-taught air conditioning specialist, who gave Nick lots of freedom to develop business in his own way, which resulted in many new and unique projects.

One of them involved a client, Sloan Sherrill, who became a mentor and had virtually no turnover among his engineers; he would just keep working with the people until he helped them find their own niche. Sloan Sherrill was an executive at Western Electric and a great innovator, who thought *outside the box*. For example, one of his inventions involved a *just-in-time* serving system for a cafeteria that could handle 2,000 people in twenty minutes. He developed the system using separate lines for each food type and multiple check-out lines, rather than the typical, slow-moving cafeteria where people stand in line to select their salad, then their main entrée, vegetables, then dessert.

Nick was selected by Western Electric Company (WECO) to design and construct the first production-size *clean room* in the world. It was needed for the assembly of gyroscopes for the Nike guidance system. His team even selected the type of clothes that were worn by those who worked in the clean rooms to eliminate the dust that normal clothing would generate! He had demonstrated to WECO that he could design and produce complex air conditioning systems, so they asked him to produce a clean room system that had never been done before. The filtration technology was available from the Manhattan Project; however, there the filtration was used to capture the radioactive dust particles to protect the personnel at Oak Ridge. Here, this technology was used for the first time to provide a better atmosphere to produce products with close operating tolerances. Our astronauts recently replaced six gyroscopes on the orbiting telescope.

Another project involved the first air-conditioned display space in any of the national furniture markets. It was a system for 100 different locations in the Southern Furniture Exposition Building in 1955. The landlord could not afford the capital investment, so Nick arranged for his company to buy, install and lease the equipment to the 100 furniture manufacturers who used the space, thus creating the ACC lease program.

Nick became one of ACC's senior people when it was a very small air conditioning contractor. They are now a manufacturer/contractor with a number of specialized divisions: Air Pollution Control; Plumbing; Electrical; and Process Control, which installs electronic components and computers. The company name is now *AC Corporation* and they have developed many proprietary systems, such as air scrub equipment to control odors in rendering plants. They have clients in most major industries including synthetic fiber plants, textiles, electronics, fiber optic cable and pharmaceuticals.

Nick and three other senior employees acquired company stock from the founder, who eventually selected thirty-five people who would own the company. Today, there are many more key people who own stock and participate with over 600 other employees who have *beneficial* ownership of the company through the ESOP installed by Private Capital Corporation (PCC) in 1976. When asked for his criteria for a leader, Nick responded, "He must be a humanitarian, technically competent and healthy, with a desire to keep learning."

When asked if there was someone who would be his hero, he told Ralph Christie:

> Churchill. This country wouldn't exist in its present form without Churchill. He controlled the destiny of the free world. It was totally in his hands and he did

this with great style and considerable ingenuity and I
don't think he was looking for fame.

Even though Nick taught at two universities and most of his
top people are well educated, he believes, "ACC provides
opportunities for those unique, self-educated individuals
whose minds have not been *contaminated* by some college."

Nick may be on to something. In the February 11, 2000 *Wall
Street Journal* article entitled, "Home-Schooled Pupils Are
Making Colleges Sit Up and Take Notice," it was interesting
to note that "Stanford University…accepted 27% of home-
schooled applicants—nearly double its overall acceptance
rate." The Senior Associate Director of Admissions was
quoted as saying, "Home-schoolers bring certain skills—
motivation, curiosity, the capacity to be responsible for their
education—that high schools don't induce very well."

Home-schooled students appear to be doing well in college.
Those enrolled at Boston University in the past four years
have an average 3.3 grade point average (GPA). Georgia's
Kennesaw State University reports its home-schooled students had higher than average GPA's as college freshman.

Home-schooling is an early form of mentoring. There are
now 1.5 million kids being educated in this fashion. Charter
schools get all the publicity as an alternative to public school
education, but there are only 400,000 students attending
those schools.

Marlee Mayberry, the author of a book on home-schooling,
says the jury is still out on the overall effectiveness of this
educational alternative. She states that research shows a
small class size, individualized instruction, and a disciplined,
nurturing environment are the key elements in effective education. These are all characteristics of home-schooling. Nick's

management style is similar to this form of schooling, and his management protégés are lucky to have such a mentor.

Ralph Christie asked Nick if he had a different mentoring approach to blue-collar and white-collar workers. His response was:

> I hate to even use that term. They are not a blue-collar worker, they're another partner in our company. And the value with some of those so-called workers is so great that some make more money than white-collar ones. Their contribution is greater and they deserve to make more money.

Nick is a shrewd judge of people and his company operates like a big partnership with a great spirit of goodwill toward each other. After years of preparation, his son David was selected as President of ACC a few years ago, through a third party, anonymous poll of their top sixty-plus key people. An almost unanimous decision selected David as Nick's eventual successor. David's humanistic and consensus style of leadership is now taking the company to even greater heights.

The company has a policy, established forty-five years ago, that you must be an employee to own stock. The company has an option and a right of first refusal on all shares owned by departing employees. Therefore, the company acquires the Employee Stock Ownership Plan (ESOP) shares after termination of service.

Contributions to the ESOP provide broadened ownership for all employees. ACC makes periodic discretionary contributions to the 401(k) Plan installed by Private Capital Corporation (PCC) in the early 1990s. They also continue to fund a solid *corporate* ESOP program to assure that ACC has the cash to *make a market* for all shares that are owned by employees, because ACC has no interest, at this time, in going public.

Nick has been my partner in many ventures and made it possible for his son, Frank "Nicky" Nickell, to join us in 1977. Nick also became a limited partner in Kelso Investment Associates in 1980 and in MBR Investment Associates in 1987. His son, Nicky, was Treasurer of Kelso when I was Chairman and has now become one of America's top investment bankers. He is now CEO of Kelso & Company and was recently elected a director of Bear Stearns.

Nick has built one of the finest companies of its kind in America, with divisions headed by very special people he has mentored, including both of his sons. He believes that an effective mentor is "someone who is willing to select and place trust in an individual whom they think is capable of being mentored. You have to be willing to be a teacher."

During our many visits over the years, we have discussed the differences between those who become the *marathon runners* in business, as contrasted to those who are the *hundred-yard dash sprinters*. He has created a strong bond with his associates, key customers, and longtime friends. Nick believes his greatest strengths include:

> Coming to a decision that is fair and workable and one that I'm willing to live with. I don't have problems making decisions if I know the facts. I have the ability to evaluate the employee's ability to handle difficult assignments. My main weakness is that I am probably too soft, too forgiving, and short on greed.

Nick's mission statement is to "perform work that is honorable and profitable. If you do that well, you will be suitably rewarded for your efforts."

Chapter 24

Robert Midkiff
Retired Chairman, American Financial Services
Honolulu, Hawaii

Maturity is understanding your impact on others.
                                    John Gardner

Bob Midkiff's most important mentors were his father, an educator, and his mother, who was a Kamaaina descendent of Amos Starr and Juliette Montague Cooke. Amos and Juliette came to the Islands with the seventh group of missionaries in 1837 and were asked by the King to found a school for the children of Hawaiian royalty.

Bob's father was born in Illinois and came to the Islands to teach. He later became a trustee of the Bishop Estate, which owns one-seventh of all the land in Hawaii. Bob grew up on the campus of the Kamehameha School and graduated from Punahou School at the head of his class. He then went on to Yale where he was a Phi Beta Kappa. One of his professors encouraged his interest in colonial history and Bob studied Hawaiian history from the colonial point of view.

In Mike Scherr's interview with Bob Midkiff, he discovered Bob's yen for new information:

> The main theme of Bob's success was his willingness and capacity for learning. When faced with a problem, whether it was learning pension plans, learning about

land development, or Hawaii history, he would delve into the subject.

First he would consult a mentor about *what* was required, then he would do research about how to do it. Then, with the can-do confidence of many of his generation (he was on MacArthur's staff during the occupation of Japan), he goes out and does it!

Sounds simple. He possesses a confidence in the ability to LEARN and DO.

After graduation, he worked for a year at the War Shipping Administration, where he researched and wrote a manual on World War I lessons for recruitment and manning for the Merchant Marine. At age twenty-three, he joined the Army, went to Officers Candidate School and returned to Yale to study the Japanese language, culture and history. He was ultimately assigned as an aide to the military governor of Japan.

Upon his release from active service, he received some solid advice—for a single man—from a retired army general. "You will make three great decisions in your life—whom you'll marry, but your wife will have a lot to say about that; what church you'll attend, again your wife will help make that decision; but *you* can decide where you want to live." So, he returned home to Hawaii and started with Hawaiian Trust Company as a trainee at age twenty-six.

When he was thirty-two and in New York on a long vacation, which his wife, Evanita, helped finance by selling World Book Encyclopedias on a part-time basis, the president of Hawaiian Trust cabled him to ask that he research profit sharing plans. A client wanted to install one in his company and needed information. Bob did the research and installed three plans that year. One year later, while recovering from chicken pox at home, he relaxed by reading a three-inch thick pre-ERISA text on profit sharing plans, in order to become one of the most informed experts in Hawaii on the subject. He eventually became one of the nation's foremost authorities on this unique kind of incentive and retirement plan.

In the next eleven years, Bob helped over 1,000 Hawaii and mainland companies install trusteed profit sharing plans. He believes that over 30,000 employees have enhanced financial security due to his pioneering efforts.

In 1964, he was invited to become Vice President for Corporate Planning and Real Estate for Amfac Inc. one of Hawaii's legendary Big-Five Corporations. The Kaanapali Destination Resort on Maui and Silverado Country Club in California are two of the projects he shepherded to success.

During this period Bob worked closely with a lawyer-legislator, Sparky M. Matsunaga, as a Congressman and then as Secretary of his Senate Campaign Committee. Bob became a close friend as well as an active supporter and advised Sparky to ask for positions on both the Senate Finance Committee and the Labor Committee, two committees that were vital to retirement plan legislation. Sparky was successful and helped to pass very favorable legislation for all small businesses. The Small Business Council of America honored Bob for his efforts. When Bob and I were working to get favorable ESOP legislation in the 1980s, we used Sparky's office as our base of operations.

In 1968, Bob was invited to become the President and CEO of the third largest bank in Hawaii. Three groups of local Chinese investors had gained control of the bank stock and were looking for a sales-minded and trusted local "Haole" (Caucasian) businessman to become the independent leader of a multi-cultural, multi-ethnic Bank.

As a marketing tool, Bob obtained a State License for the Bank to do a trust business. He developed a new concept of the "custodial trustee" to hold the securities of client retirement plans, to keep clients out of trouble and to hold their hands, but offer no investment advice. Success was immediate with two new accounts flowing in every week.

In 1973, however, one of the Bank investor groups obtained majority control and elected to go with their own group of officials. Bob then experienced his *defining moment* and resigned to become an entrepreneur. He started a new and independent trust company offering corporate and individual clients custodial trust and agency service. He was confident he could succeed; he had thoroughly tested the details of the new concept at the Bank.

Building on the success of the custodial concept, Bob ultimately formed American Financial Services of Hawaii with ESOP financing for the purpose of acquiring the old, traditional full-service Bishop Trust Company. The illness of one of Bob's senior people, who was ready to step into his shoes and run the company, ultimately caused him and the American Financial Services board to decide that it was time to sell the company.

Bob built American Financial Services, over a twenty-year period, from three employees and $550,000 of capital paid in by him and twenty-one friends to 300 employees holding $4 billion of assets. The company was sold to Bank of Hawaii (now Pacific Century) for $53 million, which was shared with his employees, management partners and the founding shareholders. He got an agreement that all of his employees would have employment with the Bank after the sale.

During a recent visit with a friend, Jeffory Morshead, who built another fine company, we discussed the concept of this book. He wrote to me about the four-letter word so essential in building a company:

> Most "how to" business books I have read don't discuss it, but from my observation, it is fundamental to how well a group functions. Groups tend to become families. Offices become family units, with shared babysitters, birthday celebrations at the office, going together to movies, even romances (some under the table, some out in the open).
>
> The four-letter word is "love." No "how to" author ever talks about it. Japanese companies emphasize a form of love by the way they care for employees into several generations. Managers who can love their group get the group to function effectively. They share rides regardless of rank and eat lunch together. The manager manages by walking about (versus memos), and an energy of camaraderie develops within the group.
>
> People crave love. When a manager goes by the book and has no heartfelt relationships, the group withers. People will work more productively for love in their business relationships than for money or the chance for promotion. Yet no one ever talks about stability, harmony and the resultant profitability of mentoring loving relationships.

I sent him a note saying, "In Hawaii, they call the *love culture* you describe, the *Aloha Spirit*!"

Bob Midkiff built American Financial Services with the *Aloha Spirit*. His job description of a mentor is:

> They must lead by example, support those who support them, and get everyone involved in major

activities by practicing bottom up management. The CEO should only get involved after each project has been thoroughly staffed by those who will have the primary responsibility for implementation after the decision is made. Then, when the CEO says, "let's do it," everyone is on board because they were part of the decision-making process. They know how to make a difference. Each associate must be helped to plan simple, achievable objectives.

Bob also managed by *walking around*. He looked for potential leader/mentors who had some or all of the following attributes. They should read a lot, like to teach, have a good home life, be involved in their community, have strong character with a history of ethical behavior, and, most of all, *they must care about people.*

Bob's new projects keep him even busier than when he was running his business. They include President of the $100 million Atherton Foundation, which distributes over $4 million yearly; Board Member, National Council on Foundations; Chairman of the Hawaii Theatre, which he helped renovate as a result of a $30 million fundraising effort; and Chairman of the Governors Commission on Early Childhood Education and Care, which is now known as The Good Beginnings Alliance (TGBA).

His great passion is his newest project as President of the Good Beginnings Alliance, which is building a constituency for young children. Their goal: "All of Hawaii's children will be safe, healthy and ready to succeed in school."

Twenty years from now when Bob will be celebrating his own centennial, he will probably be jogging two miles a day and playing golf with a decent handicap. His two current mentors are his wife, Evanita, who recently gave up her very active real estate sales career to spend more time improving her handicap, and Thurston Twigg-Smith (Bob said they mentor each other).

Thousands of people live and work in downtown Honolulu because of his leadership in the Honolulu Downtown Improvement Association. According to Mike Scherr, Bob is the man to go to if you want to raise $9 million for charity. While working on the downtown improvement committee, "Bob learned that the best way to develop is to get anchors like a new state capital building or a new headquarters for a major bank."

After I completed my interview with this long-time friend and one of my most important mentors, I decided to send a transcript to a few of the people he mentioned as key influences in his life. A summary of their comments describes this uncommon man, who has done so much to make a positive impact on the lives of millions of people through his pioneering legislative work for the Profit Sharing Council and ESOP Association.

> One of the most creative, innovative and energetic men I've ever known.
> > Ed Carter, former President of Bishop Trust, an American Financial Services subsidiary.

> A wonderful gentleman. So kind in word and so obviously caring, with the mind of an intellectual giant, a doer and developer of action plans.
> > Michael Keeling, President of the ESOP Association of America.

Bob's leadership of the Downtown Improvement Association, and mine with the Oahu Development Office, were important for the transformation of our city. He was the most inquisitive person I knew during my thirty-two years in Honolulu. Bob was always

seeking answers, always trying to make Hawaii a better place in which to live, work and visit.

> Aaron Levine, one of America's finest city
> planners.

He taught me how to align my interests with the
client, which makes for a very profitable relationship
for all involved. Integrity and trust are critical to the
long-term client-advisor relationship, not just a simple
financial transaction.

> Robin Midkiff, Executive Vice President,
> Bank West.

Mike Scherr describes Bob's unusual, but highly successful,
work ethic:

> It seems he did not know anything nor did he have
> any particular background to prepare him before he
> started projects. But, rather than throw up his hands
> in the face of the obstacles, he put them to work. He
> does not think like those who see only obstacles when
> they consider a major undertaking. His attitude is "I
> can do it. I only have to learn how…and I know I can!"

Few people are legends in their own time. Bob Midkiff is one
of them and he will certainly leave Hawaii and our nation a
better place in which people can enjoy their lives.

Chapter 25

Jerry Stone
Former Chairman, Claremont Technology
Cape Girardeau, Missouri

*There are men and women who make the world better just
by being the kind of people they are.*

John Gardner

Steve Love, a member of our advisory board, also interviewed Jerry. His insightful comments are a great introduction to the life of Jerry Stone.

After my recent interview, it did not take me long to
figure out why Jerry Stone has been so successful
throughout his career. He has the unique ability to put
one at ease very quickly. You immediately feel comfortable talking with him and realize that he is sincere
and interested in what you have to say. Jerry is quick
to credit others for his accomplishments. These are
rare qualities that I have found are more the exception
than the rule for most leaders.

He is family-oriented and believes in people. He also
values integrity more than his accomplishments. His
leadership style is to give people responsibility and
the ability to learn from mistakes without constant
supervision and criticism. Jerry has always realized
the importance of mutual respect among one's colleagues and peers.

If I were asked to briefly summarize a list of characteristics that I would value in a leader, the leader
would be: Intelligent, articulate, respectful, modest,
enthusiastic, passionate, goal-oriented, fair, successful, a good listener and a willing mentor. These are the
characteristics of Jerry Stone.

I feel blessed having the opportunity to meet and
interview him and am looking forward to our next
opportunity.

Thank you Jerry.

Jerry was born in 1942 and grew up in a small town in
Missouri. His father was fifty years old and a disabled World
War I veteran when Jerry was born. He spent a lot of time
with his father who was a strong, compassionate man. These
early talks had a long-term impact on Jerry's development.

He joined the National Guard as soon as he graduated from
high school in 1960, where he developed an early understanding of the leadership and organizational skills that he
had to acquire. He spent thirty-one years in the Guard and
Reserves, retiring as a Lieutenant Colonel.

Jerry married young, at nineteen, and helped his wife get a
teaching degree. His first full-time job was as a collector for a
small loan company. The manager, Sid Wilson, became one of
his first non-family mentors. He taught Jerry how to work
with people under adverse circumstances, such as repossess-
ing their car! He probably learned one of his favorite expressions during this first work experience. "You can make a bad
deal with a good person, but you can *never* make a good deal
with a bad person."

At age twenty-four, he went to work for a small savings and loan bank and by age forty was Executive Vice President and a board member. Jerry had a number of different jobs in the bank during his sixteen years with them. The bank bought an insurance agency and Jerry attended a New Orleans seminar to learn how to generate fee income for the bank by marketing tax-deferred annuities. Jere Smith, Chairman of Marketing One, was the speaker. Jere had co-founded a small annuity marketing company. He eventually became Jerry's most important mentor after the bank board decided to reject the opportunity to represent Marketing One. Jere Smith then recruited Jerry Stone as an independent contractor.

After some hesitation and concern about not having benefits and having to *eat what he killed*, Jerry became one of the top producers for Marketing One and eventually became National Sales Manager. When Marketing One was sold, Jerry assumed the Chairmanship and CEO responsibility, and when his contract was up, the company was generating premium income over $1 billion per year.

Jere Smith had negotiated a very lucrative incentive performance contract for his protégé, Jerry Stone, when he became a senior executive with Marketing One. Jere was ready to walk away from the sale if the buyer did not assume it. At closing, when the buyer balked at honoring the contract, Jere Smith got up and started to leave the room—and the lucrative transaction. Integrity first! The buyer quickly accepted and the deal was consummated.

The proceeds from Jerry's contract allowed him to become, in a short period of time, an *adventure capitalist*, taking a more calculated risk than in traditional investments. One of his first investments was to back an entrepreneur who created some unique *information technology*. This person had lost his first company and wanted to return capital to his original backers and build up his own net worth again. Jerry and his partner built one of the fastest growing companies of its kind, Claremont Technology, Inc., which, when it merged with CBSI, had a market cap of $280 million.

Jerry then went on the board of another fast-growth public company in the information technology field until the two companies were properly integrated. He described his former partner as a real visionary, who had the capability to change direction many times in order to keep the company moving toward what the market needed.

The three most important mentors in Jerry's life were his dad, who Jerry emulated in developing a compassion for others; his first employer, who taught Jerry to respect everyone, regardless of their situation in life; and the great Jere Smith, who is also one of my mentors.

In the seventeen years I have been privileged to know him, Jere Smith has become one of my most valued advisors. He motivated me to write my first book and helped me reorganize our company to focus on providing more comprehensive service than designing and implementing ESOP's, which had been our basic mission. He also taught me some very basic concepts, including one of my favorites, "Don't get ahead of your headlights." Jere's father gave him some good advice as a boy, "Know your product; be on time; tell the truth."

Jerry's experience in the military exposed him to a large number of micro-organizations. He made contact with many effective (and ineffective) leaders who helped him learn to differentiate between those who *claimed* to be leaders and those who *acted* like leaders. He mastered tried and true leadership principles while in the service and developed a number of cardinal rules. He deals with people by understanding and appreciating their differences; manages to a person's strengths, not their weaknesses; and understands that behavior modification and personality changes are almost impossible—we cannot change who we are. In the organizations he has built and run, he has molded his team together into a *community*. It becomes a *collective* effort.

Jerry believes that *enthusiasm* and *passion* for what we are doing can overcome almost all obstacles. With passion for what we do, we do not see the mountains quite so high; we see only opportunities. We see delays, not failures.

He feels that every experience, good or bad, teaches us something. Sometimes, the bad experiences teach us more important lessons than the good. A failure is as important as a success if you learn how to *fail successfully*. The great Latin American Liberator, Simon Bolivar, spent a lifetime of "turning adversity into good fortune," as he repeatedly lost a battle and an army, only to return and raise another army to fight again.

Jerry believes that people who want to develop into future leaders should find and adopt role models to emulate. Who would you like to be like? He also believes strongly in measuring performance. Performance pays! It has to be fair measure though. In other words, do not tell someone what you are going to do, just "put it on the scoreboard."

As a major shareholder in CBSI, Jerry has had an opportunity to observe the actions of their CEO, who has a real passion for his mission, an ability to focus on vital goals and an ability to identify, attract and retain talented people. This CEO delegates to qualified people and leads by example.

Jerry feels that hell on earth is *responsibility* without *authority*. His advice to aspiring young people is to "fail forward; don't be afraid to take risks; work hard, it cures a lot of ills. Seek responsibility. Find something to do that you love and you'll never work another day in your life."

Jerry Stone has a unique ability to focus on the *important*, rather than the *urgent*, to cut through the chaff and address the real issues, and the ability to deal with people and motivate them. He also has a solid sense of *fair play*.

Jerry built his life on a number of bedrock principles and I was reminded of some of them, and Jerry, when I met Fred Weyand and again, when I heard a impressive presentation at a Change of Command Ceremony.

To get a star in the army is a real achievement. To get more than one is rare. I interviewed eleven business generals, including Jerry Stone. Some were also retired reserve senior army officers. During the time I was writing this book, I also got acquainted with a retired four star general, the former Chief of Staff, Frederick Weyand. Fred has made the transition to the world of business in the same way he made the transition from the University of California at Berkeley to Chief of Staff (he was not a graduate of West Point). Because of his unique type of leadership, he is now, and has always been, a *mentor*.

According to my longtime associate, Joe Rafferty, who served under Fred in Vietnam and at the Pentagon, General Weyand exemplified the finest mentoring skills in both combat and peacetime. Fred is now a business leader in Hawaii and was recently selected to receive the George Marshall Award. He was described as a true patriot and soldier's soldier, who is known for his diplomatic and legislative skills. He served his country with distinction—fighting in three wars and leading our Army during extremely controversial and challenging times.

My son Brian, a reserve Lt. Colonel, recently assumed command of a civil affairs battalion. His Brigade Commander, Colonel Bryan J. Golden, who is now a PCC associate, made a moving speech at the Change of Command Ceremony, which included the following:

Distinguished Guests, Soldiers, Families and Friends of the 425th Civil Affairs Battalion. Today is truly a great day to be in the Army because today we celebrate one of the most important and significant events in the life of a unit—the passing of the unit colors from the outgoing commander to the incoming commander.

In the time-honored tradition that dates to the very origins of military organization, we honor the departure of the outgoing commander and the arrival of the incoming commander with the symbolic transfer of authority and responsibility embodied in the passing of the unit colors. These colors, like the responsibility of command, are sacred. They occupy a position of honor, second only to the national colors.

In the same way the commander assumes the sacred trust of leading, teaching, mentoring, and caring for the unit—its soldiers, family members, equipment, and readiness. Few have the desire, strength of will, stamina, and endurance for this awesome responsibility. Even fewer survive the selection process to become commanders. And so it must be, because the unit and its soldiers, each one of you, deserve nothing less than the very best commander possible.

In ancient times, the commander was selected by Darwinian methods—survival of the fittest. The commander was the strongest, most cunning, toughest and smartest...and won the right to command by defeating his rivals in tests of battle skills and field savvy...sometimes through a fight to the death.

Today our commanders are selected through a somewhat more civilized means, though still similar in
many respects to the ancient ways. The path to command lies over tough ground, with many obstacles,
tests and rigors along the way. Even today, only the
fittest survive to become commanders...and so should
it be...we cannot afford anything less than the very
best.

Lt. Colonel Buxton has shown that he is the
fittest...now he must prove that he is the best. LTC
Buxton, these colors, and the sacred trust that goes
with them, are now yours. Now I challenge you to
earn them.

One of the *Wise Men* said, "Discipline opens up all opportunities." Another said, "If you have a screwed up financial
program, it will screw you up." All of the *Wise Men* have the
habit of finishing what they start. And they all have earned
the respect of their families, business associates and the communities in which they live.

Chapter 26

Jack Grady
Founder, Juice Bowl Products
Lakeland, Florida

If you can dream—and not make dreams your master;
If you can think—and not make thoughts your aim;
If you can meet with triumph and disaster
And treat those two imposters just the same;

Yours is the Earth and everything that's in it,
And—which is more—you'll be a Man my son!
From "If" by Rudyard Kipling

Jack Grady was raised in Topeka, Kansas. His first mentor, his father, financed Jack's first business venture when he was eight years old with a $5 loan for a soda pop stand. Jack and his brother, who was six years old, built a prosperous business selling Cokes to members of a paving crew during a hot summer. His brother did some market research and they added a nurse's dormitory to their customer list. They were soon selling four or five cases of Coke each day at a 1.5¢ per bottle mark-up. Their $2.50 per day in 1924 dollars has an approximate value of $50 today, not bad for an eight-year-old!

Jack had his first business reversal a few months later when the paving crew finished their work and moved to another part of town. He also learned a valuable lesson. In retail sales you need a solid core of repeat customers!

He became an Eagle Scout and his second mentor, his uncle, balanced his *idea-filled* life. Jack said, "When he looked at a wall, he never saw any cracks; he saw the big picture and was an optimist."

His father was an entrepreneur and had a number of successes and setbacks. When Jack was ready for college, money was limited. Therefore, he worked his way through college in a number of jobs, including picking cherries and forming his own band: "Jack Grady and his Highland Hotel Orchestra." He played drums and booked his band at Polish weddings, Bar Mitzvahs and a number of taverns. One club was in Cicero and was owned by the Mob. Jack learned another important lesson: the customer is always right. When one of the club's owners, Murray "The Camel" Humphrey, requested a song, all other requests took a back seat!

Jack graduated with a degree in Economics, then went into a number of entrepreneurial ventures before going to work in an ad agency. His first big job was with Chase Bag Company. He then spent seventeen years climbing the long hill of big company, corporate management. He joined Johnson and Johnson in 1963 as head of their Permacel Company, a "turn-around" opportunity that did not work out. So, at age forty-eight, even though he was earning big money, he resigned to seek an *independent* opportunity.

Scott Sangalli, another editorial advisor for this book, also interviewed Jack. Scott's impressions are revealing. He says:

> As a person, Jack is very thoughtful and deliberate. There is definitely something to be learned for his approach in that no matter how grave the circumstance, there is almost always a little time to step back and think before acting.

Jack's wife had inherited a house in Winter Park, Florida, and it served as a base of operations while he weighed his options. A few weeks in Florida convinced the couple they had found a place where they wanted to live. That narrowed the search, and soon Jack had teamed up with a major citrus grower to organize Citrus Central, a marketing and supply cooperative, to serve five major processing cooperatives.

After buying an orange concentrate can-making plant and building a steel can manufacturing plant, he tried to get his co-op board to buy a small specialty cannery from Mead Johnson, but they declined. Mead Johnson then offered Jack the opportunity and the financing to acquire it himself. So in 1967, he founded Juice Bowl Products with an aged factory on fifteen acres, no source of fruit, and little sales. But there was an asset, which did not show up on the balance sheet—thirty-five dedicated employees.

Kelso & Company installed an ESOP for Juice Bowl in 1973, which was among the first, if not the first, ESOP in Florida. The employees owned 22 percent of the company when it was sold to Campbell Soup in 1982. When I met Jack in 1978, they had 200 employees and the company was very profitable. He was a founder of the ESOP association and became a partner of mine in Kelso Investment Associates in 1979, then my partner in MBR Investment Associates in 1987.

In 1981, Jack asked me to help him recommend legislation for a Small Business Sub-Committee he served on for the Department of Commerce. We came up with the concept that was later adopted in 1984 as IRS Section 2210, whereby an ESOP could assume the estate tax liability of an estate which qualified under IRS code section 6166. This section provided for a fourteen-year term for estate tax payment on non-liquid estate assets, such as farms and private company stock. During the five years IRS Section 2210 was effective, some of the largest private companies in the nation adopted ESOP's.

There is current legislation pending to reinstate this important tax provision.

Jack developed a *partnering culture* in his company. He learned it from one of his important mentors, Bob Conners, Executive Vice President of Chase Bag Company. Conners had the unique ability to give a subordinate constructive criticism without directly challenging that person's opinion or decision. He would allow people to respond to their own conclusions after they heard Conners describe, "Some other fellow who had a challenge much like yours."

In his interview with Scott Sangalli, Jack spoke at length about mentoring:

> Almost every successful leader can recall one or more "turning points" that vaulted his position or company to a new level. Many times those "turning points" came well disguised as problems rather than obvious opportunities. Over time, the successful leader knows that the greatest opportunities usually appear in a very subtle form, and they know how to recognize them when they appear. This combination of instinct and experience is the mark of every successful executive.

When asked if mentoring could accelerate the development of instinct or could shorten the time required to accumulate the necessary bank of experience, Jack responded:

> Problems are the crossroads that either sealed or spoiled the relationship. Relationships are created through problem solving. One should be instructed to never run from a problem. And, problem-solving situations are best served by "throwing people together."

When asked to rate the percentage of importance of the following to the mentoring process, he said, "Forty percent on the capabilities of the protégé, twenty percent on the mentor's approach, and forty percent on the chemistry between the mentor and the protégé." Jack then elaborated:

> Every successful executive that I know had an incredible ability to quickly and continually bounce back or realign after setbacks. Business today moves much faster than it did a decade or two ago. "Change" is the norm, not the exception. It's very apparent that you personally possess the ability to embrace change. However, and with all due respect, I am afraid that the pace today is much faster. In our day, it was possible for a company to somewhat "settle in." Our current and future executives cannot afford complacency. As a mentor, you must recognize that there will be a fine balance between "the cutting edge" and "over the edge."

And when asked to assess on a scale of 1 –10 the importance of each tangible characteristic a protégé should possess as foundations, Jack responded in the following table:

Category	Jack's Rating or Comment
Appearance and/or charisma	8+
Educational background	Very high for young persons
Competitiveness	Essential to success
Communications skills	10
Strong work ethic	10
Ethics and morals	10
Sense of "fairness"	10
Economics	High but not vital
Finance and Accounting	Essential for a CEO
Marketing	It depends

Systems and Technology	Should have a good understanding

Jack worked to develop methods of helping others to reach their potential during his long business career. In 1982, a serious illness caused him to decide to sell Juice Bowl to Campbell Soup. His 200 partner-employees all shared in the sale proceeds. He has spent the last fifteen years in small ventures and in philanthropic activities. In his eighties, he is again involved in a major business venture. Jack reminds me of the great Satchel Paige, who said, "How old would you be if you didn't know how old you was?"

A while after Juice Bowl was sold to Campbell Soup, Dole bought a multi-national company, acquiring Juice Bowl in the bargain. In 1995, Tropicana, then a subsidiary of Seagram's, bought Dole, and again Juice Bowl was part of the package. In 1997, Pepsi Cola acquired Tropicana and along with it, Juice Bowl.

Tropicana recently decided to sell Juice Bowl. It was still the same company Jack had incorporated to buy the old Bib plant from Mead Johnson in 1967. On December 29, 1999, the Grady family—Jack, his two sons and daughter, his wife, the rest of the family, and Terry Simmers (former VP of Operations) closed the deal to buy back Juice Bowl. It began producing product under its new owners on January 3, 2000.

Sixteen of the current employees are "BC's" (before Campbell). They have spread the word about the old ESOP and Jack, who is Chairman and very active, has assured them it will not take six years this time to get another one going.

Jack, Betty (his second wife), Grason Nickell and I get together every year just prior to a golf tournament in Lakeland, Florida at Lone Palm Country Club, which is owned by Publix Supermarkets, the largest privately held supermarket chain in America. Members of the George Jenkins family and present or former employees of Publix own the supermarkets. Mr. George, as his 75,000 plus employees referred to him before he passed away, also believed in shared ownership.

Jack has a wonderful *marriage partnership* with Betty. We discussed how she helps him respond to the mood swings most creative people have, "I find myself either trying to get her excited when I'm high, or hanging on to her when I'm low." He could have been describing my relationship with my own lifelong dearest friend and marriage partner, Betty Buxton.

Every time we visit, Jack has a new and interesting project to discuss. Jack, Betty and his daughter, Susan, returned recently from a trip to Ireland where all three were researching their roots.

Jack's creativity, integrity and deep interest in everything and everyone reminds me of Kipling's poem, "If," part of which is quoted at the beginning of this chapter, describing how a boy becomes a man. Jack Grady is a unique and very special *man*!

Chapter 27

Sam Higginbottom
Retired Chairman, Rolls Royce –North America
Miami, Florida

Believe that everything in life is the will of the Lord, but study and work as if everything depends on you.

Sam's early spiritual foundation and continuing thirst for knowledge reminds me of the succinct advice above, recently given by a very articulate priest in the church Betty and I attend. Sam was born in a small town in Ohio and lived there until he was two. His father worked for a railroad. His Scottish grandmother emigrated, all alone, from England when she was fifteen. She started a sewing school for the wives of Welsh miners and earned enough money to go back two years later to bring her parents, sisters and future husband to the United States. She had nine children, seven of whom grew to maturity and were successful. She was also Sam's first mentor. He spent two to three weeks every summer with her, helping her in the garden and listening to her recite "Robbie Burns." She was quite religious and Sam still has the Bible she brought from England 135 years ago and which she read every day of her life.

Sam's mother and grandmother read to and discussed ideas with him from the time he was four. They made him believe he could do anything he wanted to do and overcome all obstacles. They were a close-knit family. However, they were not affluent, so Sam, too, had to work his way through college. Columbia University loaned him money for tuition, and then helped him with scholarships and financial assistance until he graduated. Sam has been a dedicated alumnus ever since, culminating with his election to the Board of Trustees. He was chairman when I met him in 1986.

It is a great pleasure to have been Sam's friend for these past fifteen years. Every time we meet, I learn something new and inspiring. Sam started his airline career as a service engineer for TWA at age twenty-five, progressing through the ranks to a very senior level. In 1963, Floyd Hall who was general manager of TWA, joined Eastern and convinced Sam, who was forty-two at that time, to join him as head of engineering and maintenance at the competitor airline.

In Sam's interview with Brian McShane, an editorial advisor, he talked about two of his most significant business accomplishments. One is discussed here:

> When I went to Eastern Airlines, the airline was plagued by delays, and six to nine percent of the flights were cancelled each day for mechanical reasons, which in turn was delaying up to thirty percent more. We arrested that in a matter of weeks, reversed it totally in about six months, and after a year we were running the most reliable and on time airline in the country.
>
> We focused on what was causing our problems, provided the assets to correct them including physical resources, human resources and management resources. We installed systems to track and control the operation on a real-time basis. And we brought in some bright young mathematicians to help overhaul our various inventory management and scheduling problems, including where to allocate spare equipment, how much to allocate, how to schedule flight

crews more efficiently, how many spare engines were required and where to place them, etc. And as a corollary benefit of producing a quality operation, we very significantly reduced our costs.

Sam eventually became President of Eastern Airlines at age fifty, but left three years later due to philosophical differences with Floyd Hall, who was by then the CEO. Sam had decided that fuel shortages and the downturn in passenger traffic made it essential to institute strict cost controls. Hall wanted to increase customer service and costs to increase market share. Since the COO reports to the CEO, Sam felt he had no option but to leave. Frank Borman was eventually elected CEO and Eastern later went out of business. They should have listened to Sam!

I met Sam in 1986 when I was the interim President of the Eastern Airlines Acquisition Corporation. We formed this company after being retained by the board of directors of three international unions—Airline Pilots Association, International Association of Machinists, and Transport Workers Union—to try to keep Eastern independent. The Eastern board had recommended that their shareholders approve a merger with Texas Air, headed by Frank Lorenzo. The employees owned 25 percent of the company through an ESOP. One of our missions was to find a replacement CEO, so I could settle back into my more comfortable role as a consultant. Sam agreed to take my place and work, without current compensation, to secure the financing and help the employees become partners with the public, in what would have become the largest ESOP ever installed. When I introduced Sam to the heads of the three local Eastern unions and he accepted the CEO position, the *Miami Herald* ran a front-page headline and story. The reporter said the employees now had a chance to save the airline.

Unfortunately, after we had gotten $1.1 billion approved in a financing commitment, contingent upon the board agreeing to sell to the Eastern Airlines Acquisition Corporation ESOP, the Eastern Executive Committee decided that they could not back away from their agreement to recommend the Texas Air offer. Our acquisition corporation and the employee coalition sued the board, but we could not get a Temporary Restraining Order before the annual shareholders meeting. Since the board could not entertain any other offers due to their prior agreement, Eastern was acquired by Texas Air. About a year later, Eastern went into bankruptcy.

During the period that Sam and I worked together to try to save the airline, I was impressed with his leadership skills and good judgment. We became friends and he eventually became a partner in our MBR Associates limited partnership.

I also observed the respect the union leaders had for Sam. He came out of the engineering and maintenance end of the airline business, so the machinists had confidence in him. The pilots also had a lot of trust in him. It is unusual for machinists and pilots to agree on anything.

Sam learned early that one key to a successful airline was to have happy, cooperative pilots. Just like the CEO of a mid-market company, they operate all alone from the time they leave the gate and have no supervisors once they are in the air. The CEO of an airline must listen to them, pay attention to their problems, and make sure they have good equipment, along with ensuring good communications with all other players in the airline system. When communications with all employees are open and honest, an airline makes money!

Sam became a committed ESOP advocate after I explained the plan we had designed for Eastern. He believes the ESOP helps unions and management to sit down together and agree on goals, eliminating many of the adversarial feelings each side has for the other.

Another great airline CEO, Herb Kelleher, installed an ESOP when his company was just a small regional airline. My first exposure to Kelleher's creation, Southwest Airlines, was during a meeting with Howard Putnam and Al Feldman in 1981. Al was CEO of Continental Airlines and Howard had just joined Southwest as President after a very successful career with United. Continental had retained us to design an ESOP for them. It was to be an *equity owner* alternative to Frank Lorenzo's Texas Air hostile takeover of Continental. Al wanted to determine whether an ESOP could be viable for an airline. I introduced him to Howard, who had told me about their very successful plan.

An airline stock is influenced by energy costs, capital investment and payroll. Al was concerned about asking the Continental employees to take pay cuts in order to acquire 50.1 percent of the airline if *increased productivity* would not assure bonus income for all employees and increased stock values.

Howard, whom I had known when he was United Airline's Regional Manager in San Francisco, cited the Southwest Airlines experience with an ESOP and gave Al the assurance he needed to recommend our ESOP to his board. The financing of the Continental ESOP ultimately fell through after the 1981 air controllers' strike. Al committed suicide shortly thereafter, so the Continental ESOP, which had been approved by the board and employee groups, was not installed.

However, the United Airlines ESOP was installed a few years ago under the direction of the CEO, Steve Wolf, who was an executive of Continental during the 1981 takeover battle. When the pilots of United Airlines determined that they wanted to have an ESOP, they asked Sam if he would advise them. Sam, in a videoconference interview, urged the employees to work with management to create what was at that time the largest ESOP in the world. New company management and employees are now working together to rebuild their airline after serious dissension over the past few years.

Southwest Airlines has grown under Kelleher's creative leadership. At a recent meeting of The Foundation for Enterprise Development, a marketing executive for Southwest Airlines shared some of their philosophy concerning the impact of employee ownership in increasing the value of their shares. A $1,000 stock investment in 1973 would have been valued at $1.5 million in 1999!

Southwest *hires* people for their attitude, and then trains them in the skills required. They have a number of slogans. "Southwest attracts thoughtful, committed people who are fun to be with, and who have a Positive Mental Attitude which is contagious." "Is your *attitude* worth catching?" "You don't have to be happy to laugh—laugh to be happy!" "A negative attitude is like a *toxic* spirit—it contaminates the entire organization." "We only hire people with a sense of humor."

In 1998, they had 134,000 applicants and conducted 62,000 interviews to hire 3,054 new employees—2.5 percent of those who applied were hired!

Kelleher discovered in 1973 that owners *think outside the box.* He also realized that almost any airline could copy their formula of using only one kind of airplane (the 737), which reduced maintenance problems and spare parts inventory. They also created a short hop route structure, low cost seating, and ticketing arrangements. Therefore, he decided to create a *world-class employee ownership culture.* Other airlines would have a difficult time trying to replicate his idea! He determined that loyalty to and from his associates was the vital factor, as it would build customer loyalty, which is priceless.

Employee satisfaction begets employee retention and quality service, which results in higher load factors and customer satisfaction due to on-time schedules. It adds to profits and stock value for the employee partners and the *public*, who own the majority of Southwest shares!

Leadership at all levels fuels employee satisfaction, and everyone is empowered to contribute to the common goal: customer service and profits. Their partnering *culture* is the *driver* of this broadened ownership leadership motivator.

They create business literacy for all employees. For example, if a pilot seeks a higher altitude and different vector, savings of $7 per trip is possible. With their large fleet and trip schedule, this translates into $5 million a year in fuel savings!

Sam and Herb Kelleher took a page out of the Jack Welch book. This most successful of CEO's built GE to its present size and profitability with the following management philosophy: "All we do is bet on the people whom we pick. So, my whole job is picking the right people."

After teaching at the Graduate School of Business at the University of Miami for a brief period and doing some consulting, Sam joined Rolls Royce and became the first foreign director of the parent company. He formed a close friendship with Kenneth Keith, who later became *Lord* Kenneth Keith. Sam left Eastern, where he was responsible for 35,000 employees to join Rolls, which had 30,000 employees when he retired. Sam and Lord Keith rebuilt Rolls after the reorganization.

302 Dickson C. Buxton

Sam also discussed his second most important business accomplishment with Brian McShane:

> When I started at Rolls Royce, they were still recovering from bankruptcy and the disastrous introduction of the RB211 engine. Customers all over the world were upset with Rolls. The parent company chief executive and I visited the airlines and made substantial warranty reimbursement. We focused on rapidly correcting the engine problems, in anticipating problems that could become major technical problems, and developing and implementing effective corrections for them. We ended with a very reliable engine and happy customers. We did that in a fairly short period of time.

The 757 airplane was a joint project between Boeing and Rolls Royce. Tex Bouillon, President of Boeing, and Sam, who was on the board of Rolls and ran their operations in North America, teamed up to make it happen. According to Sam, Tex was the world's greatest airline salesman, who left the seminary just before he was to be ordained to go into the world of business. After Tex retired from Boeing, he helped start a company that was recently sold for over $100 million. Tex and Sam remain close friends.

After Sam's retirement as Chairman of Rolls Royce-North America, he remained on the Rolls board until their mandatory retirement age. He has just retired from the board of directors of British Aerospace.

In 1988, Sam was elected Chairman of the Conquistadors, an organization founded in the 1930s by CEO's of the major airlines, who decided to throw a party to thank those who saved their airlines with mail contracts during the depression. They had such a great time it became an annual event, enjoyed by 125 people, all leaders in the aerospace industry.

Sam believes strongly in delegating authority and responsibility. He required his associates to set high but achievable goals. He made sure that progress was frequently measured against those goals including discussions of performance at all levels. After assuring that each side understood the commitment, Sam and his management associates listened carefully to employees and honored their commitments, building mutual trust and respect. He feels that if everyone communicates well with each other, then policies and strategies will evolve that are appropriate for the company, helping it to grow and prosper.

He is a great believer in training at all levels, as the airline industry must operate twenty-four hours a day. In many cases, fairly junior level people make major decisions. If you have ever waited an hour for your baggage to arrive at a carousel, you will know how the baggage handler can influence future passenger load levels. A ticket agent, who ignores long lines while casually chatting on the telephone or with another agent, can also adversely impact operations.

Sam developed his management teams by recruiting very bright people, who were respected by their peers, willing to work hard and were self-starters. His senior management checked backgrounds carefully to assure that a trust relationship could develop. Sam feels management people should be well educated and able to express themselves orally, extemporaneously, and in writing. He also believes that words are the handles by which you control or direct conversation. Sam is an advocate of recruiting well read people.

To Brian McShane, Sam spoke about balancing family and career, his spirituality, and his life purpose:

> When my wife and I were raising our three children, a major portion of that burden fell on her because I was

away from home a great deal. And what made that really hit home for me was the time when my son was completing eighth grade, and my wife said, "Let's talk about where he should go to school next year." When I asked what was wrong with where he was, she replied that the school only goes through grade eight! That made me stop and think! I don't know how, but if I had it to do over again, I'd certainly spend more time at home.

I was raised Presbyterian. I converted to Catholicism when I was thirty-five. I'm a reasonably participating Catholic. My wife was Catholic and my children were raised Catholic. When my youngest daughter was six years old, she, her mother, brother and sister were headed to church one Sunday morning, when she turned to me and said, "Daddy, I want to be a Presbyterian." I asked why, and she replied, "So I can stay home with you and eat breakfast and read the funnies." That really caused some introspective examination by me, and I ended up taking instruction and converting to Catholicism. I strongly believe children should have regular exposure to some organized religion and that it must be part of their home life with full family participation.

I'm eighty years old, and, looking back, I believe I've done a commendable job with the help of my first wife in raising three children. We provided the necessary means and instilled in them the desire to acquire a superior education. All three have turned out to be outstanding individuals contributing in many ways to society and mentoring and raising children, who show every promise of being a real tribute to their parents. After my wife died, I married a much younger woman who has three teenage children. I hope to be equally successful with them.

I asked Sam's wife, Jana, to comment on my oral history interview with him and got the following letter, which adds another dimension to the life of this gifted man:

Dear Dick:

You asked me to send you some comments on Sam, and here they are.

I think that one of the nicest things about Sam is that family is a very important matter in his life. He enjoys spending time with his grandchildren, sometimes building tree houses or just teaching them how to work with tools. He also helps my children with their homework.

Being his wife is a very special place to be, because he knows how to make a woman feel loved and cared for. It's a blessing.

He is a very fair person, very organized and neat. He loves to be with friends, to play golf, to fish, to read with the dogs curled up in his lap.

Life with my husband means a lot of fun, and my kids and I feel very happy that he is in our lives.

> Sincerely,
> Jana Higginbottom

Sam is dedicated to his spiritual grounding, his family, continual learning, and the people whom he can help, whether through an ESOP program for a company or through mentoring people to excel.

Chapter 28

Charlie Rowe
(a.k.a. Dickson C. Buxton)

The greatest compliment that was ever paid me was when someone asked me what I thought, and attended to my answer.

Henry David Thoreau

I have been a mentor for many people during my life, and, although Charlie Rowe is a fictional character like Ken Wilson, his life story is mine. My interest in helping creative and talented people determine how to best channel their energies to achieve happiness and financial security started early in my life. The following overview of my life will illustrate how I transitioned from dependence on others to independence. It all started on December 7, 1941 with the attack on Pearl Harbor.

A few hours after the attack, my father, mother, brothers, sisters and I were gathered around our breakfast table in Long Beach, California listening to President Roosevelt announce that the United States had gone to war with Japan. I was twelve years old. My father had borrowed $100 in 1929 to create some electronic technology, which helped him build one of the largest neon sign companies in Long Beach. The dim-outs and brownouts mandated for coastal cities had already forced him to lay off employees and made it difficult to collect payments from those who were leasing neon signs.

That morning, Dad announced to the family that he would have to close down the company, since there were sure to be blackouts in Long Beach. Since the Pacific fleet had been so badly destroyed, he was convinced that Long Beach, with its shipyards, heavy concentration of naval vessels and the Douglas Aircraft plant, would be a target. He talked about enlisting, but worried about how he could support his family on a private's pay. He was a self-educated entrepreneur, who used to say that if he needed a college graduate, he would hire him!

That was the day I started to grow up. Six months later, after Dad had been forced into bankruptcy, I had a man-to-man chat with the all-powerful, most important mentor and influence in my life. I had taken the *Long Beach Blue Book of Business Leaders* to school to show Dad's picture and biographical sketch to my friends. Other business leaders, when describing their hobbies, indicated golf, tennis, hiking, etc. Dad listed only one hobby—his family.

Dad and I talked in the recreation room built behind our home near the ocean. It had been built for the children and we hosted dances for all the kids in the neighborhood. There was a small office in there for Dad to concentrate on important work that could not be done at his factory. This room, full of happy memories, was where we sat in June 1942, when I was told that I would have to be the man of the family for the next few weeks. Dad had to go inland to find a company that would hire him. Because his expertise was restricted to the neon sign business, he said there was no employment for him in Long Beach.

I learned many years later that Dad did not even want to look for a job in Long Beach because of the shame he felt after declaring bankruptcy. He had been the former president of the Long Beach Exchange Club and was considered a brilliant business leader. He had built his company from scratch, when he was twenty-two, and at age thirty-four had owned a substantial company.

Four years earlier, when I was eight years old, Dad told me that I had to learn to make money on my own, to develop some independence. I had to pay for half the cost of my clothes and anything else I might want to buy, and Dad would match this money. At age ten, Dad said that I should start paying my own way, so I had to earn money by cutting lawns to pay a small room and board fee. It did not bother me that my family was well-to-do—I was just a kid. My father used to tell me stories about Alexander the Great becoming a great military leader in his teens and how he, himself, had been on his own and responsible for his own part of family expenses when he was growing up in Montana. He had been a ranch hand and a prizefighter in the bars near their ranch.

I grew up believing that I could handle adversity, because Dad made me feel good about my ability to hold my own when faced with an intimidating situation. Before he left to find work, Dad also gave me a few cardinal rules: "Don't steal to get money—even for food. Don't lie or cheat. And don't take charity." He meant even from our relatives, many of whom were affluent. He said we were independent and we did not do anything that later would not make us proud.

Dad left a few dollars for food with Mom and headed east, where he ultimately found a job as a journeyman electrician at a Las Vegas defense plant. I went up and down my street asking for yard work and odd jobs and earned a few dollars over the next few days at 25¢ per hour. At that point, my mother asked me to go to the store with her and to bring my little red wagon. I was curious about her request, as we had a corner grocery store just a block away. My walk to a super-market with Mom was three to four miles, but I was delighted to see Mom fill the shopping cart with food—Dad must have left more money than Mom had indicated. However, when the checkout clerk held up a welfare check for $10 and told Mom she would have to return some groceries, because she had exceeded that amount, a big fat woman standing behind me remarked, in a loud voice, "What are welfare people doing in Belmont Shore?" The insensitive remark caused Mom to burst out crying with shame and I got mad! I told the fat woman to shut up, glared at everyone in line, daring anyone to say anything and told the clerk to take the excess food back herself. I then loaded the bags of food in my wagon and pulled the wagon back home while giving my beautiful thirty-one-year-old mother a lecture on *Pride:* she should never take a *handout* from anyone—even the county.

Mom said she would try to get by on what I could earn; she was under strict instructions from Dad to not accept help from his or her family. My anger was focused on my own inability to support our family. I was mad, which created a desire to grow up, be a man—and do it fast! At that point, a second mentor helped me by encouraging me to go into direct sales. A retired dentist, he had lost his leg due to a circulatory disease that I later discovered was a result of heavy cigarette smoking. The dentist had a woodworking shop and suggested that I get a magazine route. He said he would help me sell with a unique approach.

The movie, *Pinocchio*, had just been released, in the winter of 1942, and the dentist made a wooden *Pinocchio* costume for me. The contraption had hinges and straps so that I could walk down the street and go door-to-door to sell *Life*, *Look* and *Liberty* magazines. Housewives would open the door, be shocked and then amused when I, in my wooden costume would say in a squeaky voice, "Pinocchio wants you to have the *Liberty* to *Look* at *Life*. Which magazine would you like to buy?" Then I would try to sell all three!

I got 20 percent of each 10¢ sale to augment my gardening jobs. I also had a night job in downtown Long Beach, standing at an intersection, yelling "*LA Times, Herald, Examiner*." I would earn 20 percent on each 5¢ sale. When these earnings were added to the gardening and babysitting income, I earned enough money on very long days for my Mom to buy groceries the next day. We had to give up the phone, but the next-door neighbor let us use their phone for a call every week from Dad.

This routine continued for well over a month, while my uncles were told that everything was fine and we did not need money. Mom did not have to ask for another welfare check, and I was no longer a boy. I had become a *young man* in those few weeks. When Dad found a job and came back to take the family to Las Vegas, I was a little disappointed because I was relegated to being a kid again. However, I now had to earn all of my own spending money, buy my own clothes and contribute to the rent. Dad was only making $1.50 per hour, quite a reduction from the big income he had had as owner of his own business.

After about a year and through additional part-time jobs, Dad saved up enough money to go back to Long Beach and open up a small neon sign company, located in the rec room behind the house. He did his selling in southeast Southern California because neon signs could still be turned on in that remote area. Dad decided I should become an electrician, so at fourteen years of age I started an apprenticeship under Dad's supervision and eventually became a licensed journeyman electrician at age sixteen. In the meantime, Dad rebuilt his neon company and opened up a small factory in Long Beach. The war in the Pacific was being won and neon signs could again be turned on. I went on sales trips with Dad for two years and learned how to mentally add, subtract, multiply and divide quickly, while Dad showed me how to use shortcuts to calculate the cost of a job and profit margins. This ability to mentally calculate numbers was to prove indispensable to me in future years.

I had to take over again as the man of the family after Dad had an accident. He had been leaning back in a wooden chair in his new shop with his feet on his desk, when the chair collapsed and he fell on his back rupturing four spinal vertebral disks. His head hit the concrete and he was blinded and paralyzed. At age thirty-nine, his life became a living hell of pain, darkness and worry about how he could support his family. He hired a manager from another company, and within a few months, the manager had run the company into the ground and the landlord padlocked the factory.

I was a sophomore in high school. Being poor in a rich neighborhood was not fun, so I sat down at Dad's bedside and said, "Teach me how to sell neon service work." I then quit school and, with Dad's counsel, started to rebuild the company. I would take my fourteen-year-old sister on a drive around the streets of Long Beach at night and I would tell her to write down the names of the companies where signs seemed to be out of order. The next morning, I would call these companies from home and say, "One of our people [my sister] reported that your sign was out last night. May we send a serviceman [me] around to give you a quote to fix it?" Then, I would use the one remaining asset of Dad's business, a Model-A truck, to drive to stores and give quotes on repairing their neon signs.

I would then take the broken tubing, bad transformers, flashers or animators to a neon plant in downtown Los Angeles, where they would fix the tubing, replace the equipment and give me *one-day* credit to pay the bill. I would then go back to the store customer, repair the sign, collect the money immediately, then drive back to LA to pay the previous day's bill and get new work done.

By the time I was eighteen, I had built up a thriving neon sales and service business. I had reopened our small factory, hired a glassblower, several electricians, sign hangers, painters and salespeople. Buxton Neon Signs and Displays was again a thriving business and I was the owner, with guidance from Dad over the phone.

Then, in 1947, the Navy decided to move most of its ships from Long Beach to San Diego and our city became a depressed area. I spent a year paying off all the costs from liquidating my company by working two jobs. I was an electrician during the day and a neon salesman at night. I spent some time with another neighbor who became a mentor to me, a police officer with the Long Beach Police Department, Bill Heplar. He became a role model and helped me develop an alternative plan for my life: join the Army, pass GED tests for high school equivalency, get the GI bill, work my way through college as a police officer, then get a law degree and become independent. Nobody wanted jailer duty, except those cops going to school during the day so they could study all night. I decided that was to be my plan; I joined the Army in June 1948 and got a family allotment for my mother, four brothers and sisters. My Dad had been committed to an institution for treatment of his alcoholism. He eventually died after years of a living hell of pain and addiction when I was forty-two.

During basic training at Fort Ord, I met another mentor, a private who had a bunk right next to mine. We became inseparable and explored the quaint little town of Carmel, spent evenings at the Soldiers' Club, and hitchhiked to Long Beach over weekends so that my friend could enjoy some *family* and Mom's cooking. My friend's family in Connecticut had wanted him to go right into college when he graduated from high school, but he wanted to get a little experience in life, so he joined the Army.

He was deeply religious and talked to me about how *spiritual qualities* would help a person ultimately find happiness. My grandmother, a Christian Scientist, who had been a big influence in my life, had exposed me to this type of spirituality as a young boy. Mom had that same faith and the serene confidence that things would work out, because I would make it happen for me and for our family. She taught me, through example, what good Christian Scientists and people of many other faiths practice: the *power of positive thinking*.

I was in the service for four years when I met another mentor during a tour in the Arctic Circle, the Adjutant of the First Arctic Task Detachment, a man who loved to play bridge. I had learned how to play bridge from a few friends in the barracks who, in order to relieve boredom, formed a bridge group. One of them, a corporal who had been busted for failing to properly supervise people in the Army finance unit (some money was misappropriated) was the bridge teacher. This corporal was not at all bitter about being reduced in rank from lieutenant colonel, as the alternative would have been Leavenworth Prison, which is where those who committed the crime ended up. The corporal felt lucky to get off with a reduction in rank and the ability to stay in the army until he retired. He was a mathematician and a great bridge teacher, who taught me how to count cards! The Adjutant, his wife and I spent many an evening in the Arctic Circle in the Adjutant's quarters playing three-person bridge with a rotating dummy.

That year in the Arctic Circle was a turning point in my life. My early life experience had matured me so that I could be given responsibility at the young age of nineteen and assist in the administration of a Detachment. An important mentor had adopted me, and, for recreation, I had been a part-time radio announcer. The station manager, a British Major, who ran the Fort Churchill radio station, helped me sharpen my verbal communications skills. The year of Arctic duty eventually helped me get promoted to a position normally held by longtime veterans.

When I was assigned to Camp Roberts, California in late 1950, on orders for Korea, I bumped into the Adjutant, now a *Master Sergeant*. He had been reduced in rank after thousands of reserve officers were given the choice of staying in the service as non-commissioned officers, or hitting the streets in 1950 in the middle of a recession. My former Adjutant decided to serve out his time in the army and was Sergeant Major of the 7th Armored Division. He asked me to be his assistant, as an alternative to shipping out to Korea, which I immediately accepted. Six months later, the Sergeant Major was assigned overseas and I was promoted, becoming the youngest Sergeant Major in the army. The *information retrieval system* that I had developed as Assistant Sergeant Major made me indispensable to the Division Adjutant General. The trust and confidence the former Adjutant had in me, plus my reasonably good memory and communications skills, had resulted in great responsibility and authority at an early age.

When I was released from active duty in December 1951, I became a civil service officer and served as Assistant Adjutant General. Then, after I left Camp Roberts, I used the GI bill to acquire the knowledge for a new career, which was not *dependent* upon employees, the economy and capital. I passed entrance exams for Long Beach City College, received my commission as a Patrolman on the Long Beach Police Department and was to report to the Police Academy on June 5, 1952.

However, on June 2, 1952 I met a man, W. J. Hawkins, in a barbershop who, in a short visit while we were waiting for a barber, convinced me that I should examine alternatives. After four years in the service, he said, I should consider a way to take advantage of my sales, business and administrative experience. He had an opening in his financial planning firm for a person like me. We spent the afternoon discussing how Dad should not have expanded so rapidly in the 1930s. If he had built cash reserves to live through changes in the economy and technological advances, he could have changed the mission of his business to that of subcontractor to the Douglas Aircraft plant. The technicians, who could design, build, wire, paint, and hang a neon sign, could be trained to perform other tasks. Dad should have had an objective business consultant; he had lost his business because of his narrow focus on *his* passion—neon signs!

My new mentor, W. J. Hawkins, had been a top marketing executive in the oil business and was a frequent speaker at marketing seminars hosted by colleges in Southern California. He was marketing a unique plan for business people to create company reserves and insure the income of business owners, if they were disabled or died.

I thought about how, if Dad had adopted such a plan, he could have immediately closed his new company when he had his accident, instead of trusting another person to run it. My mom, brothers and sisters would have had a better life, and I would have already graduated from college at twenty-three, instead of *starting* college at that age.

W. J. Hawkins convinced me that I could attain an even more effective education by joining his firm. Then I broadened my educational objectives to include needed expertise in law, accounting, corporate finance, economics, investment management and many other subjects that eventually prepared me for my present occupation: Senior Advisor to CEO's of Private Capital Corporation's client companies.

After a full weekend of study and contemplation, I resigned my police commission and joined Hawkins. In four years, I had my first college diploma and was starting on my second.

I had built a solid client base of several hundred clients, had married the girl I met during the weekend of *my defining event* and had my own small unit of business financial planners.

I also met an important *spiritual mentor* who took me on my first retreat. My wife, Betty, recently wrote the following letter to our grandnephew:

Dear Collin:

Dick made his first Jesuit Retreat at Manresa in Southern California in the summer of 1952. He attended it with the man who became his "surrogate father" and mentor. Dick came back literally "floating" and filled with spirituality. So much weight had been taken off his mind with the realization that we are all God's children. My high school years at St. Mary's Academy attending many retreats had a profound effect on me also. His retreat at Manresa drew both of us closer as he learned more about the faith that guided me in my early years. Because his retreat was such an important event in his life, marking a new beginning, we are both delighted that you are going to have an unforgettable experience that will stay with you all your life.

Collin, you are one of the most exceptional young men we know. Your thoughtfulness, wit and loving nature are unique. We are certain you will never change. This event will add a new dimension to your comprehension of the spirit that allows young men and women to enhance their understanding of life, its challenges and joys.

With all our love,
Aunt Betty and Uncle Dick

Over the years, I continued as a part-time student until I was forty, then again went back to school for four more years starting at age sixty. I had discovered, at age twenty-six, a unique *open* college, The American College at Bryn Mawr, which offered a *cafeteria* selection of college-level courses in all of the fields in which I had an interest: law, economics, corporate finance, industrial psychology and many other subjects.

One college that sponsored The American College courses was the USC Graduate School of Business. One of my professors stimulated my interest in economics in 1958 and became another mentor. This man ultimately became Vice Chairman of the Federal Reserve Board. He and I remain friends and are both now helping to promote the partial privatization of Social Security.

I also adopted a number of other mentors along the way, who helped me channel my energies and continue to develop independence. One of these mentors suggested I accept an executive marketing position with a national financial institution to help other young people build financial service organizations. I spent the next twenty years with them before I again started my own independent business, bringing partners in with me who had the background and experience to advise senior executives of larger organizations.

I am very appreciative of the mentors who took an interest in my life. I make it a point to help talented people who want to better themselves, by sharing my philosophy and becoming one of *their* advisors. I listen to them describe their concerns regarding the direction they are going in life. I then ask them some important questions, which would cause people without a good *life plan*, to think deeply about their own situations, and then take action based upon *their own conclusions*.

Today, I envy no man. I am blessed with a great family, which has become my primary hobby, but golf is a close second. I have some great friends, outstanding partner/associates and a fifty-year solid relationship with my *life* partner and mother of four of my children. My fifth child, by an early and short marriage, has a deep Christian faith and I have two grandchildren and one great grandchild because of her union with her former husband.

I recently spent time with one of my early mentors, who had retired from the police force to become a private detective. As young men, Bill Heplar and Marian Morrison (who adopted the screen name John Wayne) had been lifeguards in Long Beach. Wayne introduced Bill to his close friend, Richard Burton. Bill became Burton's friend and bodyguard for many years. Today Bill is the unofficial *Mayor* of Belmont Shore at eighty-six years young! Most of my other early mentors have passed away, but are not forgotten by their families or by *ME!* Bill Heplar wrote me a note after our visit:

Dear Friend Dickson:

Your visit to me was a total surprise and enjoyment. I want to thank you for taking the time out of your busy life to stop by and bring me up to date on "what's happening" with you and the Buxton clan! I wish also to thank you for the book you sent me and the late lunch we had at Hof's Marina Restaurant! I have to admire you for what you have done with your life but also think what fun we could have had if you had kept your badge and we could have worked Motors, Vice and uniformed patrol together!

But lucky for you God intercepted your mind and persuaded you to do what you did. However, the pay for the LBPD was $260 per month when I went in and is now at $42,500 per year for beginning patrolmen.

Commanders retire at half pay in twenty-five years of $75,000 per year; $80,000, if you stay for thirty years. So, you can judge for yourself if you made any mistakes or not by leaving. Happy Holidays and Best Wishes for the New Year!

Bill

During many *defining events* in my life, those who have taken more than just a casual interest in me helped me resolve a number of critical issues and come to my own conclusions about actions I needed to take to resolve them. I get a lot of satisfaction from helping others, and I know that they learn best, as I did, from thinking through the situation and coming to *their own conclusions*.

Chapter 29

Afterward: The Mentoring Chain

Lives of great men all remind us,
We can make our lives sublime,
And, departing, leave behind us,
Footprints on the sands of time.

Henry Wadsworth Longfellow

Fiction can be used to help us learn important lessons by getting and holding our attention through telling a story. Therefore, I created a fictional lost soul, Ken Wilson, who is faced with his first real adversity as a thirty-six-year-old mid-level executive. The shock of having to adjust to reality, after living in an illusory world of dependence upon others for his security, results in the destabilization of his family and a period of disappointment so deep that he becomes discouraged.

His trauma is very much like what is currently being felt by hundreds of thousands of executives. They find they are not needed by companies that merge or downsize or when venture capitalists and banks pull the plug on companies that were formed to travel the Internet road to easy money.

Most of these Internet startups are now history and old economy companies are hiring former new economy entrepreneurs who have technical skills, but lack solid management and leadership experience.

Our character, Ken Wilson, starts out economically illiterate. He has not bought anything he or his family cannot eat, wear, drive or live in. He then becomes a slave to his emotions when his lifeline, his job, is in jeopardy. Logic is but a speck on the sea of emotions and Charlie Rowe, with the aid of the *Wise Men*, helps Ken analyze his life, his strengths and weaknesses, his attributes and contributions, so he can start to think logically again and eventually find his *own way* in life.

It takes some kind of external trigger to help us realize what we know intuitively because common *practice*, which is deeply ingrained, may be covering up common *sense*. We have to peel away the layers of habit to get to the kernel of truth…and we must do this ourselves.

Questions we must answer, after deep thought, can change our behavior. A lecture can stimulate us a bit, either positively or negatively, but does not change behavior. Nor does constructive criticism when it hits below the belt. Some people never forgive another for pointing out how stupid they have been. They perceive it as an attack or as patronizing behavior and reject the criticism. Therefore, to fully understand a situation we must first understand the order of things that intrinsically already exist.

Ken Wilson's life is fiction, but is based upon factual situations involving people I have known. I have blended a number of actual life experiences into a story that illustrates how a person, with help from a mentor, can come to grips with reality and refocus his or her life.

The immediacy of information provided through television has changed our lives over the last thirty to forty years. The Internet has also *radically* affected the lives and fortunes of

many millions of people, and tens of thousands of companies. In a positive way, the Internet can also facilitate a support structure for those who will be honest enough about
him or herself to *let it all hang out* and answer some critical
questions posed by a mentor. Our fictional subject is faced
with major challenges, then is lucky enough to have a mentor enter his life to help gain perspective. This mentor intro-
duces other mentors, with significant experience in dealing
with life challenges, to help our subject reach his own conclusions by asking him a series of questions to stimulate his
thinking.

People respond *best* to *their own* conclusions when resolving
critical issues.

Bob McKinnon's interview was the first in connection with
this book. I was so impressed with what I learned that I initially considered co-authoring a book with Bob to express
some of the very successful concepts he has developed in his
four decades of business and leadership experience.
However, as I replayed his interview with me, I was
reminded of other business leaders with whom I have been
involved in *private company* investment banking over the
years and who have become friends. I then decided to invite
a few of them to participate in this book and share the impact
that their mentors had on their careers.

The eleven *Wise Men* took a partnering approach over a long
period of time to create their management and employee
teams and to build significant organizations. These men were
influenced and motivated by mentors when they were very
young, as they were developing their habit patterns and attitudes concerning people in their families and those for
whom they worked. The people who worked for or with
them in the creation of their business organizations also
eventually adopted these positive attitudes.

My first book, *You've Built a Successful Business—Now What?* described the most important *issues* to consider in deciding whether to perpetuate a company or develop a viable exit strategy for the shareholders. Since that book was published, the American Family Business Survey was completed with information from 4,000 family-owned businesses with more than $1 million in revenues. The initial report dispelled myths and uncovered some important findings:

• One in four CEO's plans to retire within five years and 23 percent plan semi-retirement, but only 40 percent of the companies have named a successor.

• While 51 percent of family businesses engage in strategic planning, 38 percent of owners fail to share these plans with managers.

Lessons in Leadership and Life illustrates how to transition from *dependence* on a corporation and/or others to *independence*. It also describes the necessary attributes for *CEO competency*, the most important prerequisite to building a company that can be perpetuated or sold at a profit for the shareholders.

There has been much written by and about *Fortune 500* CEO's, their lifestyles, net worth, income and career shifts. Many are mercenaries who move from one large corporation to another as hired guns. These executives in many cases cause layoffs and plant shutdowns to create fortunes for a few investors and executives. They leave people on welfare or in the streets. Their example motivates a few people, but angers most and frequently results in anti-business attitudes. Those who are turned off by this type of greedy CEO behavior tend to support politicians who either feel the same way or pander to this anti-business bias.

For almost five decades, I have had advisory relationships with many hundreds of CEO's of mid-market companies.

Most of these leaders are a different breed from the sharks just described. The best of them build strong bonds with a small cadre of dedicated management *partners*, who in turn build bonds with *their* partners. A *partnering culture* develops in their companies, which is necessary for the long-term perpetuation of any business enterprise.

I have been interested throughout my professional career in how *Leader Mentoring* develops. Therefore, my interviews with these leaders focused on *their* personal mentors and the bonds created when they cared enough to listen to and follow the advice of their lifetime mentors. Some of these mentors also provided *personal guidance*, which led to a change in habits and behavior in their associates, and eventually resulted in the effective leadership model that people admire. The protégés of mentors, in time, adopt *their own* promising protégés, and the leadership chain is continued.

Isaac Newton, when asked about the reasons for his success, said, "If I can see further it is because I have stood on the shoulders of giants." People of vision have, in almost every case, been inspired by a number of mentors. Teddy Roosevelt's father, who was called "Great Heart" because of his caring nature and significant philanthropy, had a great influence on his son's life. Winston Churchill was in awe of his brilliant father, even though his father died as a failure. The *young* Churchill persevered against overwhelming odds to become an *uncommon man*.

In 1976, Roy Steinbeck (cousin of John Steinbeck) interviewed me as part of an oral history program for the American College. I was asked to describe the attributes of my most important teachers and mentors. Starting with my father, I described the attributes of a number of people who had taken an interest in me—and in my professional development. When preparing for this book, I used the same oral history process to get to know more about the lives of the eleven friends who agreed to participate. There are many other Leader/Mentors I have known over the years that I could have included, but I wanted some diversity in the careers of those I interviewed. I also wanted to interview those Leader/Mentors who had a long experience with shared ownership, the field I have specialized in for thirty years.

A major common denominator of mentoring leaders emerged after in-depth interviews with these successful CEO's—of both corporate and not-for-profit organizations. All had been in different fields and are from different parts of the country. I discovered that these eleven Leader/Mentors all made their associates feel good about themselves. In other words, they are *not* the self-centered, greedy, win-at-any-cost, hard charging type-A executives. They value mutual loyalty, trust, integrity and character in their associates. A very astute mentor once advised me, "If you run deep enough inside, then people trust you. Details don't matter." These leaders enjoy what they do, and when necessary help others, who view their job as hard work rather than a fun thing to do, find a different career or employment.

Good people are attracted to and stay with senior managers who genuinely care about them as people. Obviously, pay and benefits are important and must be competitive. The willingness to share ownership is appropriate for many companies, but not for all. It depends upon the type of employee and company.

A recent Watson-Wyatt worldwide study showed that replacing an employee costs roughly one and one half times a year's pay. Nearly all employee commitment studies show that, in addition to fair pay, satisfaction with day-to-day activities and career prospects helps retain people. However, care, concern, trust and respect for the employee associate rank much higher than most senior executives might think.

One of my valued associates, who has become like one of my family, feels that the most important attribute in senior executives is their caring for the associate as a person and showing that concern.

One of our *Wise Men*, Curt Ford, and I had a mutual friend, John O. Todd, who passed away a few years ago. Curt was in a study group with John for years and learned some of his concepts, along with the succinct and persuasive way to communicate them. John was one of our important mentors; he had a unique way of making each person with whom he had any contact feel that *they were special.*

The mind, stretched by a new idea, never returns to its orig-inal shape! Todd stretched minds for most of his long and highly successful career. I first met him in 1961 when, as President of the Portland Society of Financial Service Professionals, I attended a meeting at Bryn Mawr to discuss ways in which the American College could raise money. It was the first of many meetings over the next fifteen to twenty years, and a small group of us raised over $20 million. Prior to that John had spoken at several industry meetings and I had read his book, *Ceiling Unlimited.* Many people speak and write about what they would like to do. John is unique, though, because his achievements are more significant than the way he relates them.

Some of his original thinking regarding the way to do business left an indelible impression upon me after reading his first book. For example: "Men respond best to their own conclusions." He does not attempt a sale on the first meeting, telling his client, "Let *me* think this over on my own time"— a unique approach for a salesperson. I am still impressed with the way he did business.

In 1959, a close friend of our family, who was a Cargill executive at the time, described his personal visit with John, who flew from Chicago to Vancouver to explain the Cargill split-dollar plan to several executives. John's bearing and thoughtfulness left an impression upon my friend as it did with thousands of others with whom he came into contact during his active career.

We installed an ESOP for one of John's clients in 1985 when John was in his mid-eighties. He chaired the initial and subsequent meetings, provided liaison, and supplied impressive coordination for the project. A few years later, John and I met with the board of directors of this company at the Chicago airport. He took a group picture, then sent all of us a copy with a short note. He was always very careful with his relationships and took no one for granted.

When I devised the idea of having an ESOP assume estate taxes attributable to private company stock in an estate (that later became IRS Section 2210), John lent his support, which was critical in getting the bill passed. John's endorsement of the ESOP concept was a major factor in my career change when I decided to specialize in what, at that time, was a very new field. He had a fine technical grasp of advanced subjects and developed concepts that have produced many billions of insurance in force for thousands of agents. He also had a profound influence in the way financial planners built their careers.

When he wrote his second autobiography, *A Lifetime of Opportunities*, published by the American College in 1996, I was one of his editorial advisors. It is now essential reading for anyone in the field of financial planning. I was honored to have my endorsement included in the book, just after the comments by the man who approved the first major corporation Supplemental Executive Retirement Plan and preceding the comments by the President of the American College.

I marvel at the clarity of thought, ease of expression, and remarkable recall of a man who will be 92 on this forthcoming November 12.

> Reginald H. Jones
> Retired Chairman, General Electric

His continual thirst for knowledge and creativity in making money through interaction with *people* made this business enjoyable to him, all the way from the start. Anyone contemplating this career should have drives comparable to those which he so graphically describes.

The comments of the captains of industry regarding competent financial planning and the insurance contract will be thoughtfully considered by other business leaders and their advisors.

A Lifetime of Opportunities combines *inspiration* and *specific techniques* for building a financial planning practice in a book that you won't put down once you start reading; that you will read again and again, to pry the nuggets of wisdom out of each well-written chapter. Words are the handles by which you can direct conversation. John is not only one of our greatest innovators—he is a real wordsmith.

> Dickson C. Buxton, Managing Director,
> Private Capital Corporation

John O. Todd has told his story in a compelling and interesting way that keeps the reader continually curious as to what's on the next page.

There are numerous paragraphs that I particularly like and they are all related to acquiring knowledge and/or recognizing an ethical standard of conduct.

Of course, I was pleased with his references to Dr. Huebner and the Society of Financial Service Professionals' designation and the importance of continued study to improve one's capacity to serve.

Perhaps one of the most important insights in this book involves how life insurance is constructively used in the corporate world. Far too few people understand the career opportunities for those working in the corporate world who will properly prepare themselves.

> Dr. Samuel H. Weese, President,
> The American College

Several years ago, before John's book was published, I sent him a Christmas card, and included a note about how much I enjoyed reading the draft of his new book. I kept John's response and read it when I want to remind myself of the importance of having empathy and being a kind and gentle person with everyone, which was John's style. He wrote:

The note on your Christmas card is so incredibly kind that it just put a lump in my throat when I read it—first to myself and later to Katie.

As to the book, there has been a much longer delay than I had intended, but that seems to be a common characteristic when any amateur is trying to be an author. However, we are making real progress. The fact is, I thought we _were_ at the point where we would have had a manuscript ready for you and the other kind people who have volunteered to act as readers.

On what we thought was our final review, I had my assistant in the project read it aloud to me. We came to the chapters dealing with my decision to go back into personal production and terminate my responsibilities for the agency.

As I listened to what I had written, it was obvious to me that it sounded as if I were making excuses by blaming someone else, when actually my move was a very positive one. Therefore, it has taken us about a month (with all the other things that come along to interfere—such as celebrating a 90th birthday) to rewrite that part. I want to be very positive in indicating that for those who prefer it, management is one of the factors in a life insurance career that can be most rewarding.

So much for that, Dick. We're targeting now to be ready for our readers within the next 30-60 days. On another subject, I have read with interest the memorandum of 12/1/92 for MBR Capital Corp. I'm glad to see that you have found another company to acquire that has considerable promise. Keep up the good work! So much for now, and I'll try to be in touch with you soon.

Best regards,
John O. Todd

This giant of an industry leader took the trouble to respond to my card *and make me feel better about myself.* The little touch, caring about another person *and then letting them know about it*, is something we overlook in the day-to-day hectic life most of us lead.

When I left agency management in 1975 to devote full time to my present business, I had John's career in mind. He was a mentor for me, again, to make the transition.

John passed away a few years ago, but he had a significant impact on my career and, indirectly, upon the careers of many of my associates and all of my clients. The former Chairman of Mass Mutual once said, "We stay so busy doing the urgent, that we neglect to do the important."

Take time to let the people you admire know your feelings. It will make you feel good, and make them feel even better!

The idea for *Lessons in Leadership and Life* originated after a visit with an exceptional Leader/Mentor, Bob McKinnon, in 1997. He described reasons for leaving a secure position in a large company to join a much smaller, family-owned company, because of the way he had been adopted as a protégé by the family patriarch, a world-class North Carolina leader.

In December of 1997, Robert McKinnon flew out to San Francisco to be interviewed and start the oral history process, which led to this book. I had met him in August of 1997 during a Member-Guest Tournament at Sedgefield Country Club. My oldest son, Brian, was my partner and we had five, nine-hole games with other partner teams. So, even in golf, *partnering* works if one partner complements the other, as you must in *best ball* tournaments.

Bob was, at that time, CEO of a client company in Hickory, North Carolina. We met again the following month and during our leisurely lunch Bob described the impact that Harley Shuford, the founder of Shuford Mills, had had on his life, and how he felt about his very competent management partners, his stockholder partners and his employee partners. Our company and our ESOP Services affiliate had advised CV Industries in installing the largest private company ESOP in the United States in 1996.

Bob and I have since become good friends and, during a trip to Hawaii in 1999, he became acquainted with a number of my Island friends, two of whom were interviewed for this book—Robert Midkiff and Joseph Dacey. Bob is now co-chair of our Advisory Board with Bob Midkiff. One of his favorite expressions about the differences between *leaders* and those who do not make the cut is "They aren't *players*, they're *pretenders*." This book is for *players*.

I am hopeful the novella and short biographies will help you discover, as I have, the common traits of successful Leader/Mentors who, through their accumulated knowledge and experience, have acquired the necessary wisdom to mentor younger business leaders. It takes both raw knowledge and experience to develop wisdom in any field. One without the other will not work, no matter how high the Intelligent Quotient (IQ). All of those interviewed for this book have an IQ far above exceptional, but they also have a very high People Quotient (PQ) and Emotional Intelligence Quotient (EQ).

There is nothing more contagious than enthusiasm—except the lack of it. I was a speaker in the 1960s at a conference on Management Development. The keynote speaker was one of the greatest agency builders in America, whose organization covered several states. They managed hundreds of millions of assets (it would be billions in today's dollars). I remember one of his remarks: "I'd rather have a case of small pox in my organization than a negative attitude." He added, "You may have butterflies in your stomach, but you must make them fly in formation."

Another great agency builder in the 1950s and 1960s, who built one of the largest trucking companies in Ohio, while at the same time building the largest agency for a major life insurance company, was another one of my early mentors. He had a few basic rules. One of them was to stop trying to manage people. He asked me if I liked being managed. My friends know my answer. He then said, "Then don't manage others! Teach them, challenge them, then get out of their way." Also, "The first time you think about helping one of your associates find another career—do it! Trust your instincts." Every time I violated those rules it cost me money.

The idea of the crusaders, cruisers and losers in any organization reminded me of a basic rule: "You cannot make a silk purse out of a sow's ear." Crusaders are on a mission to achieve their goals; cruisers, without mentoring, will not attempt to improve their performance, they are satisfied with the status quo; and losers usually blame others for all problems that arise.

I worked on this book during the spring of 1999, while in France and Italy on a business trip to decide whether to export our pioneering ESOP and *Comprehensive Perpetuation Planning* (CPP©) proprietary concepts, systems and experience to build a European subsidiary. The objective would be to tap the biggest potential market for broadened ownership in the world—the almost 400 million citizens of the countries of the common market. The tax laws favoring employee ownership in many of these countries now help shareholders and companies increase personal and corporate liquidity and help management enhance productivity without forcing a mid-market company to deal with the problems of going public.

People come from all over the world to view the art treasures in Rome and Florence. As I was reviewing the transcripts of the oral history interviews, I was again reminded that management is not merely a *science*, it is also an *art*.

We spent some time admiring one of the most beautiful churches in the world, the Duomo, in Florence, Italy. The craftsmen who worked on this church many centuries ago had to serve an apprenticeship for years before they were allowed to supervise the activities of other apprentices. The results of this master/apprentice system have endured through the centuries.

A mentor is much like the early masters; the protégé could be compared to apprentices. All behavioral change is the result of one person having an impact on another person. Yet, many CEO's tend to consider people as part of *groups* and the result can be a lack of communication and alienation between those who must sell, produce, and administer a business, and those who are responsible for bottom-line results. The leaders I interviewed all learned, early on, the importance of a *one-on-one* relationship with their more gifted associates, thereby continuing the mentoring chain of which they were a part.

If you scratch the eggshell veneer of every person you meet, you will find the seven or eight year old child they will always be. Therefore, the character developed through that age is vital, and I found many common characteristics in the early lives of these *Wise Men*. They also share many common beliefs, one of which is that the *individual* is the new unit of business. We are seeing the emergence of the *Virtual Corporation* where *outsourcing* almost everything is much more prevalent and, in time, may become the norm rather than the exception. There are now over twenty million people working out of *their own* home offices. Employees and managers are now more willing to operate in a world where *no one else* is to blame.

Given the current desire for the *independence* that so many young people have developed, how does the CEO attract and retain a *team* of independent-minded and talented people? Most gifted CEO's make sure that they constantly screen their work force to identify those people with exceptional intelligence, who are a quick study, apply themselves effectively and do not take themselves too seriously. Then, over time, these future leaders are assessed by the trusted protégés of the *mentoring CEO* for the virtues that are expected to be constant. These virtue include integrity, dependability, positive mental attitude, loyalty to their peers, to subordinates and to those who have the ultimate responsibility for the success of their business unit company, and a *passion* for whatever they tackle. The objective for the CEO is to *adopt* people of solid character with these virtues as protégés. Initially they assign a *big brother* or *sister* mentor, to help the protégé develop a sense of direction and eventually, for the truly gifted, this person becomes a personal protégé of the CEO.

In order to concentrate my mind and focus on properly describing the evolution of a *mentoring CEO* who can build a *partnership organization*, I decided to categorize some of the concepts I believe are important in becoming a leader. One of my early mentors, who built a number of fine companies said, "There are only two kinds of people: leaders and followers!" We now have *Chiefs* and *Indians*, in addition to *Players* and *Pretenders*, and *Crusaders*, *Cruisers* and *Losers*.

So, how does a person become a *Crusader, Player* or a *Chief*? I believe it starts with a *Plan*...and the ability to think outside the box. A former Secretary of the Treasury once said, "You *live* life looking forward; you *understand* life looking backward." George Santanya, the philosopher, wrote: "Those who do not consider the lessons of history are condemned to relive the past!"

However, our *own experience* may be a liability in planning. A very creative North Vietnamese general built bridges every night that were blown up the next day. However, each night his soldiers were able to march across the river on *other bridges* that were built six inches *below* the water!

After deciding what has to be accomplished with a carefully considered *Plan*, the CEO has to assure that everything is *organized* to actually follow that plan. Delegation to other trusted people who *understand* the plan is essential. If they have had input into developing the plan, they will be able to creatively *organize* the necessary resources: the trained and motivated people, capital, appropriate technology and equipment. After everything is coordinated, *action* should be taken and a *control* system implemented to determine whether the plan is being followed in a timely fashion.

The most important part of the above process is the *people* factor—their knowledge, attitude, skills and habits to create a climate in which good people can grow. Leaders must first *understand* each person who is part of their team, then *prepare* the team members for what must be done by helping to open their minds to consider their *active* involvement. Leaders must carefully *explain* the individual's role, and how that interfaces with the roles of others on the team. They need to *show* them, graphically if necessary, what must be done, then *observe* the actions being taken in order to properly supervise the project—just like the architect supervises the contractor to be sure the building is going up according to plan.

The golfer who masters the use of each of the different clubs in the bag will have a good chance of shooting scratch golf. Most of us, however, are duffers because we do not take frequent lessons from an objective pro, practice enough or walk a new course before playing it. A golfer's stance and grip are also important. Bob McKinnon used sports metaphors to graphically describe his strongly held concepts, which create word pictures in the minds of those with whom he is communicating. His sincere humility and gentle method for getting his message across is refreshing. He truly believes in the partnership approach, but carefully communicates to his management associates and employee owner partners that he is the Senior Partner. Bob has two gloves: one for golf, that helps him play a very competitive game; the other, a well worn velvet glove that helps him keep a solid grip on his numerous leadership activities in various fields. One of his favorite expressions is, "Show me a good loser, and I'll show you a loser."

The mentoring CEO must be master of all of the critical functions of a leader and must also be articulate and able to communicate in word pictures. Most people understand pictures. Which is the more potent line: "I don't believe in killing innocent animals" or "I've never seen a deer like Bambi wear a bulletproof vest"?

Which is a more graphic statement: "Joe is resourceful" or "Joe reminds me of the person who, if his pistol misfires, he strikes you down with the butt of it"? Or Bob McKinnon's description of a person who talks before he thinks, "He pulled the trigger before his gun was out of the holster."

When I remember to do it, I question a person who is becoming a bit negative by asking, "Is this thought worth the amount of life it will cost you?"

One of the greatest leaders of this century, Winston Churchill, was gifted in all of the leadership skills. His official biographer, Martin Gilbert, thoroughly researched his life, especially the part he played in the failure of The Dardanelles campaign, which resulted in the loss of many ships and 60,000 soldiers. Two admirals and a field marshal undermined Churchill's leadership. There was divided responsibility, yet Churchill was held accountable.

Gilbert described his research method in his book, *In Search of Churchill, A Historian's Journey*:

> I explained what he was trying to do, why he wanted to do it, how he set about it, and the way in which he confronted the various obstacles, whether of nature, or of individuals, that were found along the way. I wanted to be able to establish the chain of events and

circumstances within which he worked; the essential context that would show to what extent he was alone, part of a particular line of thought, ahead of his time, or (as was often the case) beset by critics who would not hesitate to resort to smears and innuendoes in order to try to discredit him.

Churchill had to resign as First Lord of the Admiralty over the consequences of divided authority. When he returned to positions of great responsibility, he made sure that, if he was going to be responsible, he had to have sole authority—an important principal of war: *unity of command*. Jerry Stone describes hell on earth as "responsibility without authority."

Therefore, the planning process of a company should start at the most basic level by assigning authority and responsibility down to the smallest unit possible. Then, that unit must be integrated with others that are in some way connected to create Strategic Business Units (SBU's).

Plans for these SBU's should be properly organized, actuated and controlled by knowledgeable, visionary, compassionate, but people-savvy leaders. They must have positive attitudes, finely honed skills and deeply ingrained good habits, which will assure proper preparation, explanation and demonstration of a mission. If a leader's protégés are properly observed and supervised—without micromanaging—the objective will be attained and the CEO will be successful.

I am a *courier of knowledge*. Niale W.A. Fitzgerald, Chairman, Unilever, PLC, coined this phrase in *Wisdom of the CEO*, co-authored by Grady Means, the son-in-law of two of my long-time friends, Bob and Mary Rose Brown. Grady is managing partner of Strategic Consulting for Coopers & Lybrand. Because of my association with the American College, I have been able to continue my education and gain cutting-edge information on corporate finance and other indispensable topics for my field.

In 1970, this quest for knowledge led to my discovery of how an ESOP could help facilitate the perpetuation or exit strategy desires of almost every successful CEO with a genuine affection for his employee group. It also led to the creation, over time, of PCC's unique and proprietary system of *Comprehensive Perpetuation Planning©*.

While writing this book and reflecting on the defining events of my eleven *Wise Men,* I tried to determine the *defining event* which caused me to leave the solid financial security of a senior management position in a field that has created sizable estates for many of my friends. I eventually decided that it occurred in 1973, during a ride on an Army bus coming back from East Berlin. I was on the first European travel mission, which another friend and I organized, to help San Francisco cope with an energy crisis that had increased airfares and resulted in many canceled conventions.

I was Vice President of the Convention Bureau at that time. Another friend of mine, Harry Orchard, one of the senior IBM executives in the Bay Area, was on the trip. Harry later resigned to work with us to form the National Association of ESOP Companies (now the ESOP Association of America) as the first Executive Director. Our convention bureau staff produced tri-media presentations in English, French and German to sell San Francisco as a tourist destination to over a thousand of the leading European travel wholesalers.

We flew our Bay Area wines, cracked crab and French bread in for these receptions. The United States Travel Service provided funding and the Chief Administrative Officer of San Francisco joined our group of San Francisco hotel, restaurant and financial people to host receptions at our embassies in Paris and London, and major hotels in West Berlin and

Amsterdam. As a result San Francisco attracted hundreds of thousands of European visitors over the following years.

The day before our sit-down dinner at the Berlin Hilton for 300 of the leading German Travel wholesalers, the US Army commander in West Berlin arranged for us to go through checkpoint Charlie to visit East Berlin and see what life was like behind the iron curtain.

We went through the checkpoint and had to negotiate the tank barriers designed to keep a bus from crashing out. We saw the barbed wire on the Berlin Wall, with the freshly raked sand dividers on the East Berlin side, which provided evidence for a guard's court-martial if footprints were left during the night. We then spent a few hours with the inmates of a system that punished entrepreneurial drive.

The deadness in the eyes of the people we met was like those of prisoners I had seen in 1952 when touring a jail, as I considered a career with the Long Beach Police Department. Their expression said, "No hope!" I had been in West Berlin for a few days before that trip and enjoyed the bright lights, laughter, warmth, and great spirit of the people. *East Berliners were the same nationality, but what a difference in attitude and spirit.*

Then I thought of the employees I had met at so many of our client companies. They were not as demoralized as the East Berliners, but did not have the same spirit of the employees of the ESOP company which I had joined as a director.

When I returned to San Francisco, the ESOP concept was studied even more carefully. Then we developed financial control and human resource systems to avoid the difficulties with which our first ESOP client firm had been faced. Over the next two years we installed a number of plans properly and, in 1975, I decided to focus all of our activities to help companies develop broadened ownership plans to provide economic opportunity for the people that helped them build the enterprise.

The lessons I learned while trying to deal with a badly designed ESOP, together with the passion and commitment for the concept created by that 1973 trip to East Berlin, led to the building of Private Capital Corporation (PCC), an entirely different type of investment banking organization.

My former partner, Joseph Schuchert, Esq., became an important mentor in 1975 by helping me fully understand the legal and financial issues involved with private company investment banking. Joe, John Menke, my friend and current partner in an investment partnership, and I were pioneers in a new field of corporate finance. We also provided guidance and initial funding for the creation of the organization that is now the ESOP Association.

In 1991, one my most recent mentors, Jere Smith, helped me combine all the PCC systems we have developed along with our experience with over one thousand client projects into a carefully designed method of operation, which has attracted a very talented group of associates and advisory board members.

I recently met a broadened ownership advocate, Sam Ginn, one of the most successful business leaders in the world. He was founder of Airtouch Cellular and, after he merged his company with Vodafone in April 2000, they were the seventh most valuable company in the world. Sam is now a venture capitalist, and will only recommend that his partners consider investment in a *real company*—one that makes a profit and you can own for ten or fifteen years, not one that is built to be sold or go public. What a refreshing idea in this day and age of *company spins*!

Thousands of Sam's employees' 401(k) accounts rapidly increased in value as the company grew. His executive team also had additional stock and options, which kept them focused. He described the way he talked to employees who were reluctant to participate in their 401(k) Plan, which included Airtouch stock. "Listen to me, this is your father talking—tighten your belt if necessary, but you need to save for the future...and you need to participate in owning part of the company *we* are building."

After Sam resigned from one of the top executive jobs in the country as CEO of Pacific Telesis, he and his associates built a great company, spinning out a small division, then building the world's premier cell phone company. He said the pleasure he got from seeing his fellow employees rewarded properly gave him even greater satisfaction than his own financial rewards—a true Leader/Mentor!

It is great to feel that your work has made a difference. Blessed are those who are lost in a cause bigger than themselves. Our associates have passion, enthusiasm and commitment for a cause...and I envy no person in the career choice I made twenty-eight years ago in an army bus on a tour of East Berlin.

Chapter 30

Planning & Control

One of the common denominators and *secrets to the success* of the very experienced business leaders interviewed involves the ability to separate wheat from chaff in their daily activities. They do not stay so busy doing the urgent that they neglect to do the important. The challenge any business leader faces is to focus their attention every day, hour and minute of their business time so their *ideas* can be transformed into an *effective execution* of plans.

Most leaders are creative, and, unfortunately, most great ideas by creative people are not fully developed, because the person gets sidetracked with whims of fancy that on further reflection, turn out to be impractical. Thus, many *great* ideas get lost in the *clutter*. A few are picked up and adopted by those who have the disciplined follow-through to convert an *idea* into a complete *concept*, and then into an *action* plan. Then, well-organized executives can assure the implementation of that plan through interaction with other members of a competent project team.

Recently, a talented executive sent me the biography of Vince Lombardi, *When Pride Still Mattered*. He included a very thoughtful note, "Somehow, it reminded me of you." *That* aroused my curiosity.

Lombardi's life and impact on his athletes, assistant coaches, the press, business community and public is a fascinating biography. One anecdote described an interview by a well-known sports reporter friend of Lombardi during a visit to Green Bay. It was very difficult for this fellow to get anything out of Lombardi about his past and he finally confronted the great coach and said, "You have no audio or visual memory of the past."

He eventually determined that Lombardi had developed the habit of discarding, almost completely, any thought that was not connected with winning football games. Lombardi was so single minded that he had erased the memory of almost any kind of activity other than recruiting, training, motivating ballplayers and developing plays that could be easily communicated (and remembered) by his well-trained protégés. Therefore, Lombardi's biographer had to learn about his subject through significant research, which included reading many books and articles about this great coach, and personal interviews with those who knew him well.

Lombardi's personality and behavior was shaped by exposure to a number of well-known leaders, and he developed many of their stronger traits. But the trait he most admired and developed was his conviction that he must be *proud of his every action*. Pride is considered a *spiritual* sin. However, a person can have *justifiable pride* in the accomplishments of those they have mentored. They also can be proud of the creation of a meaningful concept, product or service.

A couple of years ago I commented, early one morning in a discussion with a friend, about how many of our great ideas over the years went nowhere due to too many *other ideas* crowding out a *very good idea*. That very good idea was put on the shelf and later picked up by others who capitalized on the idea by *focusing* on an *action plan* to guarantee implementation. Ideas are a dime a dozen, but people with the ability to make them work are rare. This conversation caused me to reflect on some of *my own* lost opportunities.

That same evening, one of my associates commented about my numerous *adventure capital*—more gamble than investment—projects that he thought could become distractions to the continuing development of our *Comprehensive Perpetuation Planning©* process, which has been so successful.

I had started my day discussing lost opportunities because I did not separate some very *important* ideas from just the *interesting* ones. I concluded in a discussion that reminded me that some of the future activities, which I feel are going to eventually bear fruit, might not be as important as continuing my *focus* on the activity where we have very little competition. If we get distracted and do not stay focused, others who become exposed to our concepts and systems might run down the road with them.

Therefore, I returned to my *roots* of **Planning & Control**, which were planted by two McKinsey & Company senior consultants when I was a regional manager for a major financial institution in the mid 1960s. McKinsey had been retained to develop a **Planning & Control** system for that company to help them get better organized to recruit, train and supervise what has become one of the most powerful financial services organizations in the country. I spent one year working with McKinsey, then two more years implementing the system in my own organization and helping the other senior managers of my company understand and adopt the same system.

I was asked to work on the McKinsey & Co. project by the CEO of this company, who is one of the finest executives I have ever known. He was one of my most important mentors and one of his basic rules was "do it now; do it right; do it right now; do the hardest thing *right now*."

Every time I forget that four-part rule, I am penalized in some way. Either I procrastinate taking action and the situation is worse when I finally do what I sensed had to be done when confronted with the issue, or I decide to let time take care of the problem, thinking it will go away. It seldom does, and I crowd out other creative thoughts by worrying about a *molehill* that eventually becomes a *mountain* in my mind. Problems are like thistles. Touch them and they will hurt you, crumble them firmly in your hand and, if it is *callused with experience*, no pain!

The McKinsey experience helped me build a successful organization for the company over the next few years, then find independent financial backing to build my own financial services organization very rapidly. My **Planning & Control** system helped me make a paradigm shift in the way that I was able to focus, then achieve better than average results, when I was a financial services manager, before we expanded our activities into private company investment banking in 1975.

Planning & Control is only possible if we develop a *daily* habit of recording the amount of time we spend in our very important areas of activity. A system was developed to record the hours I invested and an acronym was created: ROPED.

<u>Recruiting</u> (R) 40 percent of my time was allocated to my most important activity: **recruiting** associates. We were in the upscale financial service markets that are now being targeted by the private banking groups of major banks, which normally recruit people who are public relations oriented. My associates, however, had to find their own prospects, then determine the most appropriate way to approach them to *personally* discuss the problems of living too long, dying too soon, losing their income due to disability or being caught

without reserves in the event of a business or personal emergency.

I built my first two field organizations for a major financial services company utilizing their *campus-training* program, which I had helped to create while a marketing executive in their home office. We recruited many campus agents who served an internship with us. Some of the top producers in the nation started out as interns with this company. They stopped using interns because of the deferred results. Unfortunately, so did I. We then started to recruit people who had already been trained in sales and tried to teach them our very complex financial planning processes. We had to teach old dogs new tricks.

Eventually we started using industrial psychologists to help us recruit candidates who would be able to acquire the legal, accounting and financial knowledge to properly *counsel* our clients, while also developing their *selling* skills. After they had *educated* a target client, they had to get a *decision*.

One of my very talented associates has a background comparable to mine and has coached a number of highly successful producers for another major financial services company. He has taken up boxing as a sport and has a graphic description of the differences between those who only briefly discuss the critical issues that must be resolved, and those who can get a *commitment* to resolve them! He said, "Some people can dance around the ring, but they can't punch." In other words, most people *dance* around many of the *brute issues* that must be resolved by those who would like to perpetuate a company or an estate, instead of graphically describing those issues. Then they must have the executive skills to be able to get a decision, by helping the client understand that procrastination might be fatal.

I became personally involved in the selection process for new associates, because I was responsible for any financing losses on these new people, who could not validate our financing plan. While in their home office, I helped the financial institution I represented develop a very creative method for financing new agents, which was validated with *written reports of activity*, rather than earned commission income. For two years, we—I shared in the losses and profits from the production of an agent—would finance the *development* of a person, not just the *creation of new business.*

I also discovered that retention of my new associates increased dramatically if they got to know me well during the recruiting and orientation process. However, taking the one-on-one time to meet with each person was a real problem as we were recruiting fifteen to twenty people each year. Therefore, to give our recruits a better opportunity to know more about me, I dictated a two-hour audiocassette tape, with breaks every twenty minutes for my candidates to take notes with questions for me later. I covered my background, experience, education, and deeply-held beliefs, then invited them to create an outline so that we could get to know *them* better. The tape also outlined our selection process, pre-contract training, financing, expectations of activity and compensation. No one could claim later that they had not been told the price they would have to pay to be successful in our field!

The McKinsey experience had convinced the company, and me, that we should invest in the *intellectual capital* of a new producer and not merely their ability to make us money fast. The persistency of the business produced by agents who were selected, trained and financed with that method assured the long-term success of a large number of today's very prosperous financial planners. The continuous quality of their business also assured long-term profitability for the company.

Therefore, rather than letting people guess *who* I was and *how* I might react in certain situations, my cassette tape gave the person concrete answers and a sense of comfort in sharing his or her life story. Through this information we could determine whether he or she had the deep-seated desire to achieve the significant financial rewards available to those who are successful in the financial planning world. This desire would keep them *focused* and willing to pay the price of success by investing long hours, and having the dogged tenacity to achieve daily and weekly results. We also looked for their competitive spirit to want to be "number one" in achievement.

Other (O) Other types of activity time would be recorded after time spent helping to build **Comprehensive Equity Corporation, Development** of my associates and **Personal Production**. (Details on these activities are covered later.) If **other** time consumed more than 20 percent of my total time, then I had a *defensive* day versus an *offensive* one. A winning football team usually has more time-of-possession than the losing team—they are on offense more than on defense. But a good strong *defense* is necessary too. Any activity that did not fit the four essential *offense* actions would be lumped into the **other** category.

At the end of each week, if it appeared that time spent in **other** activities was increasing, I would make a correction and get back to the 80 percent of my time on offense, 20 percent on defense, which was my perpetual goal.

One of my mentors, Frank Sullivan, was an assistant to Frank Leahy, a great coach for Notre Dame during the time that Vince Lombardi was building his reputation. Sullivan built a solid financial services practice in South Bend, Indiana. He also became a trustee of Notre Dame and was then elected as the first president of a major life insurance company to come from the field. Most life insurance company CEO's have actuarial, financial or legal backgrounds.

He helped me raise the goals of my associates when I was building my third financial services organization in San Francisco. He was also one of the earliest ESOP pioneers and advised me not to train *agents* for this type of business planning, as ESOP programs were and still are complex and take a lot of time to complete. Most top producers relying on commission income would not stay with this type of case for very long.

Frank was right, and I eventually sold my agency back to the company to get the capital to form a fee-based consulting and investment-banking firm dedicated to the creation of perpetuation plans which might involve ESOP's.

Frank believed that the difference between mediocrity and success for a producer was that the successful person would spend the majority of their time on *offense*: prospecting, approaching, communicating and designing financial plans for prospects and clients. A small amount of time would be on *defense*: essential detail work and public relations activities.

He believed that marginal producers were those who ultimately failed because they spent most of their time in *busy work*, avoiding the uncomfortable initial contact with a person who does not know them, but who might need their service. Or they shunned the very important, but time-consuming work of mastering the technical issues involved in creating a viable success plan for an estate or business.

Personal Production (P) I worked my way through college by marketing various types of financial service contracts to owners of small businesses. I then spent over twenty years in financial services sales and marketing management before phasing into our present field. However, I always maintained a small, but select, group of clients, with staff assistance from one of my colleagues. I allocated 10 percent of my time for **Personal Production**, which also helped me to relate to my associates, who spent all or most of their time acquiring or servicing their clients.

Up until 1975, I specialized in estate and tax planning for senior executives of public companies and successful entrepreneurs. Because a large number of my agents and brokers negotiated group insurance contracts, I also negotiated these contracts for a few clients, including the San Francisco Convention and Business Bureau. Since I was a director, I devoted a lot of time to increasing local support for the biggest business in San Francisco—tourism.

Because I only allocated a small part of my time for personal client building, I had to again try to communicate more effectively than *one-on-one* for all meetings. Therefore, thirty years ago I created a videotape presentation to be shown to the Senior Directors of the San Francisco Bureau, since I would be on one of my trips to the East Coast on the presentation date. One of my assistants invited the Executive Committee to our conference room, and he hosted a TV luncheon in my absence. At the conclusion of my televised presentation, we were appointed to handle the retirement and group insurance program for the employees of one of the biggest Convention Bureaus in the country. This success encouraged me to prepare and use videotapes in recruiting and training my associates.

Today, my colleagues also use very carefully prepared videotapes, CD-ROMs and our Web site to introduce our services to our clients, and then to assure an *in depth* due diligence and fact-finding phase of our initial client relationship.

When I was a home office marketing executive in the late 1950s, we introduced audiovisual presentations for our new agents, which I narrated, and which were used to guarantee uniform communication of our presentations to thousands of prospective clients, all over the nation. I recently met the chairman of the board of a mid-sized financial institution at an American College function, who surprised me by reciting the organized presentation I helped create when this man was a new financial planner.

I have continued to maintain a personal working relationship with a number of clients, and it still gives me great pleasure to stay involved as a financial advisor to some very smart people. I have increased my involvement in this activity so that about one-third of my time is now in some form of client activity, but I always have a colleague work with me to make sure that we follow through on all of our commitments.

A number of our client engagements involve *conflict resolution* between shareholders and officers in our client companies. My experience in building financial services organizations consisting of independent-minded, intelligent producers taught me that *eagles don't flock*. Helping to resolve conflicts between these associates led to accepting client engagements in which we have developed some very creative resolutions to serious conflicts between stockholders and/or creditors of our client companies. Because of the unique background of our senior consultants and analysts, we now have significant experience in identifying sources of conflict so that solutions that are attractive to all parties can be developed.

We normally deal with larger mid-market companies, so our solutions also have to be approved by the advisors of our client *and* the advisors to those who are in conflict with our client. Successful resolution requires coordination between many different professionals on both sides of the conflict for a *fair* solution to the conflict. Peaceful and inexpensive *conflict resolution* is very unusual, because traditionally, several law firms representing all parties normally handle the resolution between the parties. More often than not, such a confrontational approach involves significant expense and, in some cases, can cause the sale of the company, or bankruptcy.

A businessperson will *listen* and respond to someone with practical experience. They will tend to avoid a lawsuit if there is a *common sense* solution to the problem. If the consultant can *listen* to all sides of the issues and shuttle between the parties, they can ease the tensions that have developed. Solutions *can* be reached without formal legal action (complaint, cross complaint, discovery, depositions, hearings, etc.) and all too often a Chapter 11, which usually becomes a Chapter 7.

Many business conflicts occur because of the *structure* of a deal or loan. There would not be as many conflicts after a deal or loan has been made, if proper investment banking practices had been observed in the beginning. Control issues and reasonable covenants should be decided upon in advance; voting trusts designed where appropriate; loan payment schedules should provide for *minimum fixed* earn out payments rather than *high fixed* payments.

However, some business people do business with little more than a handshake, rather than a formalized agreement. Eventually, family members, partners, or other shareholders might start to complain about inequities, which can result when those who have been successful in building the business become adversaries in a serious conflict. A peaceful coordinated resolution to these conflicts is less expensive and more satisfying than having teams of attorneys and accountants doing battle with each other while their clients foot the bill!

As Assistant Adjutant General of the 7th Armored Division, I received my earliest training for conflict resolution counseling. I observed how the Adjutant General (AG) was able to resolve conflicts between the heads of the various G sections (G-1, 2, 3, and 4) who would sometimes be at each other's throats. The AG was a distinguished lawyer who had been recalled for active duty when the Korean War broke out. He became one of my most important mentors and gave me great responsibility, when he appointed me as the Sergeant Major of the Division at age twenty-one—promoted over a lot of capable World War II veterans.

While I was the assistant Sergeant Major, I established an information retrieval system at division headquarters so that the AG could have immediate access to information on any issue that might require his attention. The Sergeant Major was transferred overseas and the AG interviewed all of the regimental and battalion sergeant majors, but did not find anyone who could respond as quickly as I could in locating a pertinent regulation or change thereto. That was my first experience with "knowledge is power."

I used the AG's example of resolving conflicts between strong-minded bird colonels to help me build three very successful financial services organizations of intelligent, creative agents, all of whom thought they were smarter than anyone else—especially their coach!

Today, we have an *advisor* relationship with our clients and we represent them to resolve disputes with those who might, if they dealt directly with them, trigger even further conflict. A relationship of trust with both parties to the conflict becomes a necessity. Even though the other party knows we have a higher degree of accountability to our client, both sides understand that a confidence will not be betrayed. *Shuttle diplomacy* in conflict resolution is the most satisfying part of our client relationships.

In one situation, the co-founders of one of the largest privately owned supermarket chains in the country had been at odds with each other for twenty years and still addressed each other as Mr. X and Mr. Y. After we resolved their conflict with the creation of a very unique voting trust, one of the senior executives of that company told me that at a birthday party for the vice-chairman, the chairman and his *partner* the vice-chairman embraced each other to the applause of all in attendance.

This client firm paid us a reasonable fee for our work and we funded estate plans for both founders, while working with one of our associates. The real contribution we made, however, was that the company remained independent after the divorce of one of the founders and his subsequent permanent disability, then the death of the other founder. We had resolved the conflict and then developed the structure that would assure perpetuation of the enterprise. The protégé of one founder and longtime close friend of the other founder are now the co-trustees of this voting trust and over 7,000 employees continue to enjoy partial ownership of a solid company. The heirs of the founders continue to own stock in the company, and the CEO has equity participation through the voting trust.

Comprehensive Equity Corporation (E) was formed by two of my friends and me to market preventative health care and employee communications. I invested 10 percent of my time in this endeavor. One of our founders was a director of what was to become the seventh ESOP company in the nation. He recommended me as a director when he had to resign due to other activities. The other founder was Major General Carroll "Red" McColpin, who had just retired as Commanding General of the Fourth Air Force.

Red had a deep interest in preventive health care and the other founder was a communications pro. We ran a field test in San Francisco before a CEC franchise program was developed to help franchises sell our system to a corporation to get more bang out of their employee benefit buck by valuing, then communicating the full extent of all their benefits. To reduce the cost of health insurance, we had a contract with an organization that had developed a preventive health care system that did not interfere with the doctor/patient relationship.

Our client inspired Lou Kelso on his path to national recognition for a unique concept. He had been trying for fifteen years to get ESOP's recognized, and the publicity given this ESOP resulted in *Wall Street Journal* and *Business Week* articles that helped Lou create his company, which we later acquired.

I spent far too much time on the CEC activity in the late 1960s and early 1970s, but the ultimate payoff was significant for most of the people who worked on that ESOP project. Sidney Allen, Business Editor of the *San Francisco Chronicle*, wrote an article about this ESOP on December 1, 1971 entitled "Employees Buy Control." That article helped Lou Kelso become famous as people called from all over the country wanting to know how employees could buy a company without using any of their own money.

The article also caused the 15 percent shareholder and CEO of our client company great grief. His 100 plus employees wanted to know why they could not control the company, even though he had to personally guarantee about $2 million of debt incurred for the ESOP to buy his partner's 85 percent interest. These communications issues caused a lot of employees to resign in order to withdraw the equity from their ESOP account. Our nation was heading into a recession and profit sharing trust assets had been used, together with a bank loan, to acquire the partner's shares, along with another business. This early pioneer ESOP company had become highly leveraged and had a very unhappy employee group.

Over two-thirds of their employees left within the first couple of years because their big-eight accounting firm, their chief financial officer and the plan administrator had *all* misinterpreted the provisions of the plan. The company was buying back, for cash, shares from the ESOP accounts of those who resigned, without giving them the right to hold the shares; a fact that the trust officer did not know was not allowed. The IRS eventually disqualified the plan. Since one of my associates had introduced Lou Kelso to our client, guess who was on the hot seat!

I went on the board of this client company and helped them develop an employee communications program so that their employees would know both the *risks* and the *rewards* of ESOP participation. We then changed the distribution policy and helped employees understand that the ESOP was a *retirement* plan and that they could not have a call on all the company's assets by merely quitting.

We also changed trustees, administrators and accountants. I studied every single provision of that plan with advice from the attorney who had drafted the plan, Roland Attenborough, a former Kelso lawyer and partner in another ESOP consulting firm headed by a man who would later become my partner. Roland and I became good friends and he has been of counsel to Private Capital (and the Kelso Company when I was chairman) for over twenty-five years. We worked with our client's new accounting firm to get the IRS to reverse their disqualification and got a private letter ruling (PLR) to permit a *call provision* if certain stipulations were included in the plan and bylaws of the company. Our PLR later became part of an ESOP legislative improvement.

This initial ESOP trauma forced me to learn more than I had ever imagined I would want to know about a most complex legal and financial transaction. I still have the five page overview of all of the documents that were part of the plan used to help another friend understand how he could use an ESOP to take his company—the fifth largest trucking company in California— *public, internally*, without complications.

When I met Roland's partner, Joe Schuchert, in 1975, this brilliant securities lawyer was surprised to meet a business consultant who was familiar with all of the legal aspects of a concept and plan that so few *law firms* understood. We went into business together and formed Private Capital in 1976. Therefore, the time I spent in research and development to find a way to market our Comprehensive Equity Corporation concepts eventually resulted in a total change of my career, the formation of a new company and eventual acquisition of Kelso & Company in 1978.

My longtime friend and colleague, Ron Gilbert, who left a very secure management position in the financial services industry to join Kelso & Company as a vice president, feels the ESOP concept would have had a serious setback if we had not found a way to successfully market ESOP's. Ron is very generous in giving us the credit, and also in the dedication of his book on ESOP's to Joe, Lou and me.

Ron co-authored what is now considered one of the most complete ESOP resource books in the country. He also is indirectly responsible for this book, as he negotiated the ESOP transaction with CV Industries, backed up by my son Jeffrey's analytical skills, so that he could install the largest ESOP in the nation four years ago. That transaction resulted in my close friendship with Bob McKinnon, who was the first of the *Wise Men* I interviewed. Bob also referred his former colleague, Joe Wisniewski, to us to become our PCC Managing Director of Strategic Planning. Ron has made a great contribution to the growth of our company and the ESOP concept.

Development (D) The most important activity in building my organization was the *Self-Development* of my associates. All development is self-development. However, when a person is motivated (has fire in his belly, according to Vince Lombardi), he or she needs a guide. One of my great mentors, Ralph Walker, who initiated the creation of a very effective marketing program for Pacific Life, was one of the greatest business leaders I have ever known. During a visit, while talking about the subject of management, he said, "Lead firmly, but with a gentle hand." He was also one of the most important mentors to an old friend of mine, Harry Bubb, who retired a few years ago as Chairman and CEO of one of the largest financial institutions in the world.

The life insurance industry, during the time the major companies were building career agencies, invested heavily in recruiting and training their field management. These were the field coaches who were responsible for recruiting, training and managing the career agents. These career agents built the initial base of assets, which provided one of the largest sources of long-term capital in America. *Agents* are responsible for creating a long-term loyal client base that generated billions in annual premiums and, ultimately, trillions of assets managed by their respective companies.

Trusting in the integrity of their life insurance agent, most people sign contracts that ultimately provide the great bulk of the estates that they leave for their families and liquid reserves they create for themselves.

Recruiting people, who will dedicate themselves to four or five years of intensive study before becoming trusted advisors to sophisticated business and professional people, was a real challenge. Over a period of twenty plus years, I recruited a large number of agents and helped many of them emerge as professionals after they had been carefully selected, trained and helped to develop into an entrepreneur and professional advisor.

Some of these talented people determined, after a year or two, that the communications skills they had learned would help them to build a different type of career, which would give them greater satisfaction. I still hear from many of them. One is a highly successful senior vice president of a major real estate organization; another built a chain of art galleries in the Bay Area; another owns a number of vineyards. Most of them are still in the financial services field. These successful people got their basic training in time-control, while learning how to fail successfully and many other lessons. At our *Buxton Associates Boot Camp*, they received a two-year training program with daily supervision, until their achievements and financial success made them independent of our financing and overhead support.

The secret to the success of any plan is to *control* the plan. I accomplished that by keeping track of every fifteen minutes of time spent during the day. Then, at day's end, I added up the time spent in each activity. The objective was to spend four hours in *Recruiting* (R); two hours in associate *Development* (D); one hour in *Personal* client services (P); one hour building *CEC*, the company which led to the creation of Private Capital Corporation (E); and two hours in all *Other* activities (O).

Obviously, a *daily* time-control plan is not necessarily effective in a complex activity. However, a *trend* can be detected if, at the end of a particular day, I recorded *no* time in R, D, P and concentrated on E and O. The next day, I focused more of my time on the essentials to keep my *present* business functioning: **Recruiting** and **Development**! If I rated my activities in order of their importance it would have been RDPEO, but this acronym was hard to remember, so I changed the order, but not the importance of each function, to ROPED, as I wanted to be *tied* to the attainment of my *own* objectives.

If at week's end the activities were not in balance, there would be a change in concentration the next week. Each month and at year-end I would review, if the planned sixty-hour week (3000 hours per year) was exceeded, the least important of activities was reduced. If necessary—and this was the toughest job—we would cut someone from the team if he or she did not return *value* commensurate with the time and money invested by their supervisor, staff support people and me.

We had a great outplacement system that assured loyal associates got positions where their talents could be better utilized. Bill Dauer, who built some of the finest Chamber organizations in the nation, had the same concept. Many of the people Bill and I helped find other careers for remain good friends of ours to this day.

Each of my management and agent associates learned the same **Planning & Control** (P&C) systems, and we compared our goals and achievements with each other on a regular basis. In other words, we mentored each other in a P&C system that we had jointly developed.

Successful builders lead by personal example. Therefore, I have to try to do the same. I have gone back to basics and have now developed an easily remembered acronym (like ROPED which I used *daily* when I was building three agencies) to safeguard my focus. I can still make a weekly, monthly and annual review of *time* invested to guarantee that I control the written **plan**, which has been carefully developed. The new acronym is CABO and was created during a retreat at Cabo San Lucas:

C - Client Activity
A - Associate Development
B - Book – finishing this book
O – Other

I set time objectives for each of these four functions. Now, I have to *work my plan!*

These basic *planning & control* ideas can be used by anyone in a career setting or in life. Set goals, make a plan, implement your plan and keep a written record of your time invested. Periodically reevaluate your goal, your plan, etc. and keep your eye on the final achievement. Find a mentor or two whom you admire. Hitch your wagon to someone who is going where you want to go or has already arrived in an honorable way. Ask questions, listen to their suggestions, follow their lead and you, too, will succeed.

ACKNOWLEDGEMENTS

Thanks to all of the people who helped me create this book.

Steve Love, who said, "Tell a story"; Dick Toomey, who said, "Tell a few stories"; Don Curran, who helped clarify our message and taught me an important lesson as a young man: "Prior planning prevents poor performance." Ralph Christie, who came up with the title, "Lessons in Leadership and Life," and Phil Broyles, who suggested the subtitle, "Secrets of Eleven Wise Men." My gifted Senior Editor, Sarah Raymond, who provided a unique perspective on the true life situations I have described, as well as sharing her knowledge of the English language. Richard Toomey, Jr., Gary McDonald, Dan Wilson, David Nickell, Frank Roberts and John Thomas, who were also critical initial readers. John also gave me some very astute observations about my *Wise Men* after he read my oral histories and the second interviews by my eight editorial advisors.

Tom Tierney for his inspiring remarks at a recent Hawaii Executive Conference and Hal Johnson, whom I observed creating a partnering culture in one of our client companies. Jeffory Morshead, whom I met through his cousin Larry Brackett, for sending me the note on the four-letter word *Love* that is missing in most organizations.

Joe Rafferty, who has been my partner for over ten years and has mentored many hundreds of successful army officers in his long and successful career. He gave me great insights into *military mentoring*. Ron Gilbert, who has been a valued colleague for twenty-three years, as he evolved into a Leader/Mentor.

Jere Smith, who has been a mentor to me for the last ten years. Those who know him see him tending toward leadership wherever he goes. He also has the magic *presence of leadership* of the *Wise Men* I interviewed. People sense he is a leader, but you never see him leaning on anyone. He also never gets ahead of his headlights.

My talented assistants, Nancy Koch and Marina Strauch, who translated my verbal and written thoughts and words into a coherent message about how a person can transition from dependence to independence.

Lastly, I want to thank the most important mentor in my life—mother of us all—Betty Buxton! She also happens to be the major love of my life and has been for the five decades since I met her when I was just out of the service at age twenty-two. I was ready to adapt to civilian life, get an education and find the right kind of career—which I did *for me!*

It is with a profound sense of loss and with a heart filled with a father's love for his children that I dedicate this book to my son, Jeffrey Scott Buxton.

Just as September 11, 2001 shocked the nation and refocused the American people on our values and freedom, November 2, 2001 shocked our family and close friends. Jeff's death has made me more aware of the supreme importance of relationships with my family and close friends. It is with a renewed sense of love and determination that I embrace, nurture and am nurtured by, enjoy and protect these special gifts and relationships.

Three days after Jeff died, I wrote the following eulogy:

Jeffrey Scott Buxton
Everyone's Best Friend

Our lives changed forever when we learned about Jeff's death on November 2, 2001. Betty and I then began the long process of coming to grips with the most profound grief that parents can experience, the death of a child.

We spent time with family and friends and received calls from many other friends. Most had known Jeff. Ron Gilbert said, "He's everyone's best friend." I did not grasp the significance of his comment until early Sunday morning as I tried to get back to sleep, to regain balance in my thinking. My every waking hour, since Friday afternoon, had been full of him, his beautiful mind, disposition, puckish spirit and tenacity of purpose.

Betty and I had raised a *gentle genius*, who was not encumbered with the eccentricities, quirkiness and ego of this kind of gifted person. I had heard many thoughtful and loving comments from those who knew Jeff, including Joe Wisniewski, who said, "He died on All Souls Day, just after All Saints Day." I said, "He *was* a saint." Joe corrected me: "He *is* a saint." His brother Brian said, "He is my soul brother."

I then reflected on Paul and MaryAnn Gallagher's experience. They lost their beautiful Liz eleven years ago when she was thirty-three. They celebrate her birthday every year and visit her final resting-place every Sunday. They don't *want* to forget; they cherish their thoughts about this very special girl and keep her in their mind and spirit.

My best friend, and personal saint, Jeffrey Scott Buxton, will occupy my mind and spirit for the rest of my days. Hopefully, I'll become a better person. He was kind to everyone, in every way, never too busy to help and encourage. Betty, his wife Jane, brothers, sisters, relatives and closest friends will carry his memory in the same way and with the same result. The people who knew him will have a richer life as they remember who and what he was...and is!

The mind is its own place and in itself can make a heaven of hell, a hell of heaven. Jeff will *stay* in my mind to help keep my thoughts focused on living as he did: enjoying every day, in every way, looking for the best in others and giving the best that he has.

Three weeks later, on November 25, 2001, just after a difficult Thanksgiving, I was finally able to begin focusing my mind to continue my life. A life made complete by a loving wife who stands by me, wonderful children who are a source of joy and pride, an abundance of close friends who have enriched my life, and business activities and associations that have challenged and sustained me.

With Jeffrey's death, my foundation has shifted.

Spirit is that which differentiates us from one another, determines the depth and quality of our thinking and behavior and gives us the inner strength to shield us in sudden misfortune, such as the loss of one who has so deeply touched our hearts and minds. Jeffrey's life is now a marvelous memory and inspiration to many others whose lives he touched and to me.

Jeff's spirit is now one with mine.

Twenty years ago, he felt the same need as I did to do more than just make money using his fine education, personality and creative talents. He eventually became the senior financial architect of many hundreds of plans that created independence and security for many thousands of people who participated in Employee Ownership Programs.

His grasp of the intricacies of numerous legal and financial issues, together with his expertise in computer programming, resulted in the graphic exhibits he prepared for transaction memorandums. These resulted in positive decisions by sophisticated senior executives and shareholders to share ownership of their companies with those who helped build them.

He also generated a glow of warmth, enthusiasm and humility which helped attract our clients, associates and affiliates.

His quick wit, gentle impish humor and deep interest in everyone with whom he became involved caused me to think about a quotation from *The Celtic Twilight* by W. B. Yeats:

> *We can make our minds so like still water that beings gather about us that they may see, it may be, their own images, and so live for a moment with a clearer, perhaps even with a fiercer life because of our quiet.*

If I had gone before Jeff, he would have mourned my passing and been very sad for a time. Then, my spirit would have joined his spirit and he would have become stronger and wiser as he grew older. However, he always had an old *soul*.

My challenge now is to do what my personal saint would have done. To paraphrase the AA creed for recovering alcoholics concerning their sobriety, I resolve that "today" I will be happy because of the forty-five years I had with my beautiful boy and that I will carry his spirit in my heart.

EPILOGUE

I have tried to describe a practical method for taking advantage of life's defining events, rather than being disadvantaged by them. The sword is best sharpened by something it cannot cut. The short stories of eleven outstanding men demonstrate that they have all learned how to *fail forward*. They were all lucky enough to be surrounded, early on, by examples of this type of leadership.

Napoleon was asked what he would do if he found his army surrounded on all three sides and with the ocean at his back. His response was "my genius is that I would have never allowed myself to be there in the first place."

An ounce of prevention is worth a pound of cure. The hospitals and nursing homes are full of hundreds of thousands of people dying from emphysema, cancer or heart disease because of an early addiction to cigarettes. Yet, very intelligent people continue to smoke, intending to quit someday. That *someday* becomes months, then years until a defining event: a life threatening illness. For the most part, that person is surrounded on all three sides by forces they cannot fight their way out of, the ocean at their back is full of sharks and they have no boat.

There are many other addictions that are not good for us. For example, a diet heavy in fat; aversion to regular exercise; and two-faced gossip, which leaves the person who hears that gossip wondering what you say about *them*. The biggest problem, though, is financial illiteracy—keeping up with the Joneses by living over your head until adversity pulls the rug out from under you and you are on your rear. Then, loss of face occurs, which causes those who are not extremely strong to retreat and resort to the various local, state, and federal programs for helping the have-nots or end up on the streets as beggars.

You cannot help those who will not help themselves. Yet, we all need to be inspired. Some find that inspiration in religion; many find it in mentors. The fact that you have read this book, which would be boring to the average person, indicates that you have the capacity to be a role model for others.

My first book, *You've Built A Successful Business—Now What?* deals with the reasons for only 1.5 percent of all companies surviving into the third generation as independent entities. A corporation is not like income property that can be purchased, maintained just enough to satisfy local codes, and then generate income until the owner becomes a slumlord. It does not sit on land that is scarce to become more valuable over time.

The first book started out as a manual to help my associates and affiliates become better advisors to their clients. It was also written to anticipate the problems involved in perpetuation of the enterprise, rather than wait until it is too late and the company has to be sold at forced sale or liquidated. However, after a number of our clients and friends reviewed the manuscript, it became a non-fiction resource book.

One of our advisory board members recently asked that I send that book to a friend of his, who had built one of the largest companies in his state. That person read the book then invited me to tour his company. When I first met him, he said, "I think you wrote your book especially for me." This CEO developed a perpetuation plan, with the help of our creative associates, which allowed him to turn over the CEO responsibilities to a gifted CEO we helped him find. Broadened ownership has been created for the key management group of this company.

Therefore, my first literary effort resulted in a book that was very helpful to our associates and clients, as a number of clients retained us. It was technical, but for those who were trained to resolve very complex issues, somewhat helpful.

The book you just read started out to be our contribution to the communications program of one of our best client companies by sharing their reasons for adopting a broadened ownership plan to perpetuate their company. However, as I interviewed the talented CEO who orchestrated this plan, I realized that I knew a few other people who had the same kind of core values as he did. I decided to find some *common denominators* among these Leader/Mentors, and thus was born the oral history interview process, which resulted in the short stories.

One of my good friends, Steve Love, who joined my editorial advisory board, convinced me that I could get the message across more effectively by telling a story. After grappling with how I could demonstrate the qualities of my eleven *Wise Men*, I came up with the Ken Wilson character.

I spent over twenty years recruiting, training and supervising the initial activities of hundreds of rookie financial planners. Some of them evolved into very talented professionals, others have gone into different fields but have excelled. Unfortunately, many of them washed out because of their inability to master their own emotions; they became discouraged in a very tough field to master. There is a fine line between disappointment and discouragement. But when you pass that line, it is almost impossible to get back up again.

Ken Wilson had reactions and reponses comparable to a number of my associates, who rose above disappointment to fight back and, ultimately, tame the demons within them that would have them quit a difficult job before it was done.

Several of my oral history subjects and editorial advisory board members have suggested that we create a *how to* book, as a sequel to this one. Therefore, the complete oral history interviews for each of the eleven *Wise Men* will be included in the next book or on a dedicated website. We will also describe the specific way in which an action plan can be designed to help someone who has not had specific *Planning & Control* training.

My own experience, working with two McKinsey and Company senior consultants, was a turning point for me in my career and it took me some time to realize that *Planning & Control* is a science, not an art, and can be learned if studied carefully.